RAISING A CHILD WITH SOUL

Wishing you blessing and Joy

as you raise children

with Joy.

RAISING A CHILD with SOUL

HOW TIME-TESTED
JEWISH WISDOM CAN SHAPE
YOUR CHILD'S CHARACTER

Slovie Jungreis-Wolff

ST. MARTIN'S GRIFFIN
NEW YORK

RAISING A CHILD WITH SOUL. Copyright © 2008 by Slovie Jungreis-Wolff.
All rights reserved. Printed in the United States of America. For information, address
St. Martin's Press, 175 Fifth Avenue, New York, N.Y. 10010.

www.stmartins.com

Book design by Mary Wirth

LIBRARY OF CONGRESS CATALOGING-IN-PUBLICATION DATA

Jungreis-Wolff, Slovie.
  Raising a child with soul : how time-tested Jewish wisdom can shape your child's
character / Slovie Jungreis-Wolff.—1st ed.
      p.   cm.
  ISBN-13: 978-0-312-54196-5
  ISBN-10: 0-312-54196-1
  1. Child rearing—Religious aspects—Judaism.   2. Parenting—Religious aspects—
Judaism.   3. Jewish ethics.   4. Conduct of life.   I. Title.

HQ769.3 .J86 2009
296.7'4—dc22
                                                                            2008030153

FIRST EDITION: JANUARY 2009

10 9 8 7 6 5 4 3 2 1

To my father,
Rabbi Meshulem HaLevi Jungreis zt'l,
"Abba Zaydah":
May his memory be for a blessing.

Not a day goes by that I do not hear your voice,
see your smile,
or feel your presence at my side.

I miss you with all my heart
but
know that you remain within
my soul.

CONTENTS

FOREWORD

It is with a sense of profound gratitude to the Almighty G-d that I write this foreword. It is not every day that a mother is privileged to introduce a book that her daughter has written. My gratitude is intensified by the fact that I am a survivor of the Holocaust. My grandparents, my uncles, and my aunts all perished in the gas chambers of Auschwitz. The very fact that G-d granted me the gift of rebuilding our rabbinic family is in and of itself awesome, but that this family should continue the legacy of our forefathers is truly cause for joy, and my daughter Slovie, who carries the name of my saintly grandmother, does so with honor and distinction.

Very often, I have been asked, "How did you retain your faith at Bergen Belsen? How did you transcend the sheer cruelty and inhumanity of your environment?" The answer is simple, and it goes back thousands of years. It is that which enabled Joseph, a young lad, to triumph over the decadence and corruption of Egypt—it is that which enabled our forefathers in every generation to raise their children with love, faith, and timeless values. And it is that which enabled my beloved husband and me to raise our children with "soul" despite an environment in which virtually no one lived by those values. Instead of succumbing to the influence of their peers, Slovie and her siblings remained steadfast and inspired others to commitment.

What, you might ask, is the key to this special way of raising children?

The Torah sums it up in three words: *deyukno shel aviv,* the image of a father. Embedded in the heart of Joseph was the image of his parent. In his mind's eye, he not only saw his father, but he heard his voice, his teachings, and it was that which kept him anchored.

But that which was so readily available to past generations is no longer accessible today. Our children no longer see the image of their parents—their voices no longer speak to them.

To be sure, there are many contributing factors to this, not the least of which is the sad reality that the parents themselves have been raised in a spiritual vacuum and have precious little to impart. Additionally, raising children with values, with "soul," has become increasingly challenging. There was a time in the not-too-distant past when parents could feel reasonably secure in the knowledge that their children were at home, safely ensconced in their rooms. Today, that confidence has been shattered. Today, they can be in their rooms, but with the click of a mouse they enter chat rooms, view x-rated films, and are exposed to many other ills of our society. Moreover, as a result of economic stress, in most families, both parents are in the workplace, leaving children to fend for themselves or in the care of hired help. But even those who are stay-at-home moms are on the run and have lost the art of parenting. That which was innate to past generations remains hidden. Alas, today's parents are also victims and in need of guidance in raising their children.

To fill this vacuum, our Hineni organization established parenting classes so that that eternal wisdom might once again illuminate our path. Slovie is the perfect teacher—she "walks the walk" and she "talks the talk." She has raised a most magnificent family. Her children are true role models—spectacular validation of her teachings. I have resided just a short distance from her home since being widowed over thirteen years ago and have witnessed firsthand her gentle but powerful manner and her firm but loving discipline. Today, she is a grandmother and has the joy of seeing her own children transmitting that wisdom to yet another generation. Slovie's impact has been far-reaching: Her parenting seminars have mushroomed; young couples flock to her classes and thirstily drink in her every word. The fruits of her labor are many. A new generation of children raised with soul are making a difference in their families and their communities.

Recently, the need for a book on parenting has become obvious. "You must commit this wisdom to writing," Slovie was urged. How to impart kindness, wisdom, sacrifice, commitment, gratitude, respect, and honor is the magic with which this book is woven. In every chapter and on every page, you will discover the treasure that will forever change the dynamics of your family, not only for one generation, but for many generations to come.

—*Slovie's mother,*
Rebbetzin Esther Jungreis

Raising a Child with Soul

INTRODUCTION

Roots

I was born into this world upon the ashes of the Holocaust. My father's mother, brothers, sisters, nieces, and nephews all left this world in the fiery flames of that awful time (my paternal grandfather passed away right before the deportation). Besides my father, only one brother remained. My mother miraculously survived the horror of Bergen-Belsen, together with her parents and two brothers. Tragically, her grandparents, aunts, uncles, and cousins all met their end in the concentration camps.

My mother arrived to this country as a young girl of twelve. Though she was young, her mission in life quickly became apparent. *"Tikkun olam,"* she was told by her parents. *Healing the world.* "We will bring healing and blessing back into this world. Whomever you meet, wherever you go, you will bring goodness and G-dliness into their lives."

From that moment on, my mother, Rebbetzin Esther Jungreis, touched the lives of all those that she came in contact with. I hesitate to call her a survivor. She did so much more than survive the abysmal darkness of hell. Rather, with the help of G-d, my mother triumphed over evil. Together with my father, Rabbi Meshulem HaLevi Jungreis (may his memory be for a blessing), they established a beautiful family.

They had four children, each one of us named for a family member who perished in the flames: Chaya Sarah, Yisroel, Slova Channah, Asher Anschel—strange names for American kids. Yet, it is through these names that we are each reminded of our mission in life. We are the children who carry the names of our holy grandparents and great-grandparents. We bear their torch; their flame burns brightly within us. Though they gave their lives, their light has not been extinguished. They continue on through us, through our words and deeds.

Ever since I can remember, the words *tikkun olam* beat in our hearts. Our legacy was clear even while we were young children. We would live and bring goodness into a world that has been witness to so much evil. We would raise families anew, drawing upon our beautiful heritage and Torah wisdom. We would not just study Jewish traditions and values but would impart these ancient truths to our children. And finally, we would reach out to others with love and compassion.

My parents established a synagogue in North Woodmere, Long Island. Our home was constantly open, filled with a myriad of people from many diverse walks of life. Some came looking for solace and comfort. Others came seeking solutions to life's numerous problems. Many came touched by the light of Torah that illuminated our home. My parents had constant patience and boundless energy. We learned invaluable lessons growing up—precious lessons of life that remain emblazoned in our hearts and souls even today. I realize, though, that the greatest and most valuable lesson of all was the love and respect that my parents shared with each other and with us. Their relationship, coupled with a love of G-d, is the driving force behind this book.

Armed with my father's blessing, my mother took her vision of *tikkun olam* to even greater heights. In 1973, she founded Hineni, one of the first organizations dedicated to Jewish outreach. *Hineni* means "here I am"; the phrase was the response of Abraham, Isaac, Jacob, and Moses when called upon by G-d. Thousands upon thousands of lives have been transformed through my mother's dynamic Torah classes and her amazing insights on the vicissitudes of life. We, her children, have each tried to follow in her colossal footsteps. Each of us, in our own way, has carried on the legacy of our parents and grandparents. We continue to teach our timeless Torah through Hineni and bring a measure of healing and blessing to this world.

I have had the great honor and privilege of teaching "Hineni Young Couples" for the past twelve years. Together we explore the intricacies of relationships and family life through the eyes of the Torah and our venerable sages. We study in Manhattan homes, infusing each family with new-found wisdom and understanding. After one such class, a group of young women approached me. These women had studied with my mother as singles and now, newly married, have continued their path of study with me.

"Let us ask you a question," they began. "Now that we are starting families of our own, does the Torah have anything to say about raising children? Are there any glimmers of knowledge that you can share with us on creating homes that can withstand the pressures of our difficult world?"

I was moved by their questions. The many hours we had spent studying together were now taking on a new life. The next generation was ready to say, "*Hineni*. Here I am." A brand-new link in our chain back to Sinai was being formed, right here in Manhattan. "Of course," I said excitedly. "The Torah offers us a wealth of wisdom and knowledge when it comes to raising families. G-d is our partner in our creation of life. He has given us direction on everything from discipline and sibling rivalry to raising children who appreciate all of life's precious gifts."

We began to study. Word spread about our parenting classes. More mothers joined and additional classes were formed in new communities, each filled with unique women dedicated to creating wonderful families. This book is a window into our classes, where I have had tremendous joy watching families flourish through Torah's universal wisdom. I have witnessed precious little souls grow into young people filled with awareness of G-d and a sense of moral clarity. The journey of *tikkun olam* continues even in these littlest of beings.

All of my work would not be possible without the constant support of my incredible husband, Mendy. G-d has blessed me with a partner in life who is my *bashert,* my true soul mate. I am forever grateful to have you, Mendy, at my side. You have filled our home with your love of Torah and your great zest for life. You have encouraged me and shared my dreams. Together, we have been privileged to build a home filled with joy and blessing.

G-d has also blessed us with the most incredible gifts of all, our children. Dear reader, allow me a personal moment with my most precious children.

There are no words to describe the awe of setting your eyes upon your child for the very first time. This soul that had been inside of you, whose heartbeat was yours, is now in your hands. How can I adequately thank G-d for the sheer joy that these souls have brought into our lives? Each day brings a new prayer to my lips, asking G-d to watch over my little *neshamahs,* my little souls; a new prayer for wisdom to help us guide our children so that they may grow in character and goodness. You, my children, have brought heart, soul, spirit, joy, consolation, and great light into my life.

I pray that G-d always surrounds you with His presence. It is with the greatest of joy that I watch you, the next generation, begin your journey of *tikkun olam*.

Finally, my precious mother, Rebbetzin Esther Jungreis, has given our family the strength and courage to carry on since our father's death. You, Ema, have shown us the tremendous potential that lies dormant within. Your profound perspectives on life and your unconditional love are legendary. Throughout the years, we have heaped our daily worries upon your narrow shoulders, yet no burden has been too great for you to bear. Instead, you gently wipe away our tears and infuse us with your infinite energy. No matter how grueling your day, regardless of how many countless people you have counseled, we have always been your greatest priority.

It is my privilege to be known as the daughter of Rebbetzin Jungreis. It is my fervent prayer that I give you true *nachas*, or parental joy, as I try to share your life's lessons.

ONE

Raising Spiritual Children

Igave birth to my son Eli on the holy day of Shabbos. Mendy and I couldn't wait to share the excitement with our family. As soon as the Sabbath was over, my parents drove our children to the hospital to see their new baby brother. We marched to the nursery, looking anxiously through the glass window. Bassinets were lined up in even rows, filled with little blankets of pink and blue. The distinct cries of newborns permeated the air. Finally, we spotted our baby. His soft brown eyes were wide-open. My father's face was aglow with joy. He turned to me and whispered, "This little soul has just arrived from heaven. Our sages teach us that in the heavens above he was learning Torah from the mouths of angels. He came into this world the purest of the pure. Watch over him, Slova Channahlah, and teach him well."

We are given these precious souls, and they are indeed a gift from Above. Parenting is not a simple road. There are many detours and challenges along the way. How do we know which direction to take? How do we know that the path we are leading them on is the best route available? What happens when we lose our way?

I have always been amazed at the amount of planning parents put into the minutest details of their babies' lives. Months before the baby is even born, the baby nurse, nursery colors, the brand of stroller, and even the preschool have all been discussed. As the child grows, so, too, does the List. Swim, karate, ballet, art, French, chess, and tennis lessons from the time they're tots—all ingredients that spell overload for both parents and children. We strive to give our children the best that we possibly can. We worry that they receive proper nutrition, cultural experiences, and an excellent education. What is most painful to me is the fact that rarely have I heard parents discussing their plan to develop their child's soul.

We have become so consumed with thoughts of our child being in the right place, with the right crowd, in the right clothing, but what have we done to help this child become a spiritual being—a person of substance and character? The problem becomes even more acute as our world becomes more obsessed with the pursuit of materialism. When was the last time you heard parents discussing their hopes for their child's moral development? I am afraid that more time is spent researching the type of car we buy than the type of child we hope to raise. We must ask ourselves which qualities we desire for our children. What kind of character traits do we wish to imbue in them?

Each week women are given the unique opportunity to pray for their children. As Jewish women all over the world kindle their Shabbos lights, they utter a plea that has been passed down from mother to daughter for thousands of years. Growing up, I watched my mother encircle the flames with her hands, cover her eyes, and whisper her prayer through her tears. Today, my children observe me each Friday night as I do the same.

I believe that this Sabbath prayer gives us the direction we need when raising our children. We ask G-d: "privilege me to raise children and grandchildren who are wise and understanding, who love G-d, children of truth, holy offspring . . . who illuminate the world with Torah and good deeds."

I kindle my Sabbath lights and beseech G-d to help me raise children who will contribute goodness to mankind, children who are blessed with kindness, honesty, compassion, love of G-d, and spirituality. I ask that my children discover courage and inner strength in a world that has been overwhelmed with fear and terror. I want so much more than merely polite children—manners is not a complicated subject. I pray for children who will possess a moral compass pointing them in the right path no matter how difficult the situation. In Yiddish, we call such an individual a *mensch*.

It is true that there are numerous books written by psychologists and psychiatrists on the subject of child-rearing. The problem is just that— an overabundance of books! Every few years new theories and ideas are introduced. We are told to discard the old techniques and try the latest new-and-improved approach. What is a parent to do? The beauty behind the Torah path to raising children is the fact that Torah is immutable. It is a constant, neverchanging, eternal truth.

The holy Torah was given to the Jewish people by G-d thousands of years ago. We study that very same Torah today. If you open your heart to its wisdom, you will find solutions for every situation you encounter, a way to approach and live your life. Since family is the center of Jewish life, the Torah is a virtual storehouse of information and knowledge concerning the creation of our home.

Decorating an apartment or renovating a house is easy. It is a far more arduous task to transform that house into a home, a haven of spiritual comfort and serenity. I have visited some incredibly beautiful homes. There were magnificent marble floors, lavish powder rooms, endless arrays of bedrooms, and toys enough for an entire kindergarten. As soon as I entered, though, I felt something was missing. A vital ingredient was absent. I realized that it was a sense of peace acquired by living with a spiritual connection that was absent. We try to provide physical and emotional security, but what about our children's spiritual security?

BRINGING SPIRITUALITY HOME

In Judaism we are taught that the key to our survival is the strength of our home. The Torah commands us: *Veasu li mikdash veshachanti besocham.* "They shall make a Sanctuary for Me so that I may dwell among them." Our sages teach us that these words include the understanding that if we build a home enveloped in sanctity, then G-d promises His presence within. We call this unique home a *mikdash me'at*—a sanctuary in miniature.

Understand that this is not about creating a physical place of worship. You don't need to build a temple or set up an ark in your living room to discover holiness within your life. It is, instead, a spiritual outlook that encompasses your home and that you take with you wherever you go. The Torah is giving us a personal invitation to embrace holiness in our daily moments of living. It is the way you speak, the way you conduct yourself, the way you relate to your spouse and children as you build your life together. Your entire perception is transformed as sanctity accompanies you throughout your days. It remains embedded deep within your soul.

Children who grow up in a home where the presence of G-d is consistently acknowledged are spiritual children. These families experience genuine warmth and blessing. They develop an awareness of G-d that provides comfort and fortitude even in the face of life's travails and difficulties. There is no life that is completely shielded from problems and pain. Yet, a child raised in a *mikdash me'at* sees all of life's challenges through a spiritual eye.

My family suffered a tremendous blow when my father was diagnosed with cancer. I vividly recall the moment when I heard the news. I had just finished teaching a class at the Hineni Center. As I was walking down the hall, I met my mother climbing up the stairwell. A single tear was rolling down her cheek. Her face was ashen. "What, Ema, what is it?" I asked, my heart pounding. When she told me of the doctors' diagnosis, I felt as if I would crumble. My father was ill? Impossible! Throughout his entire life, I had seen him only full of life and laughter. His six-foot-two frame and broad shoulders easily carried the weight of the world. There was no burden too heavy for him to bear. Whether it was his family or his congregation, his strong yet kindly presence was a constant reminder of his personal faith and courage. After taking leave of my father, you left the room filled with hope and gladness. His positive spirit was contagious. I can still hear his voice, as he would smile and say, "*Shayfelah*, my sweet little dear, don't worry. Everything will be all right." He had an extraordinary ability to allay my fears and apprehensions, and I always felt so much better after talking with him.

Now it was my father who had to face worry and fear. He was admitted to Memorial Sloan-Kettering Cancer Center in New York, enduring excruciating treatments and extraordinary pain. Through it all, neither he nor my mother ever lost their faith. I watched, in awe and amazement, as my father transformed his gray hospital room into a place that exuded sanctity. He requested that his holy books be brought from home and transformed the windowsills into bookcases.

My mother never left my father's side. She was a constant companion to him, both day and night. My siblings and I spent every moment we could in the hospital, cherishing each precious second. One afternoon, my father and I had a few moments alone. He motioned to me to come closer. "Please bring me a *Chumash,* one of the five books of the Torah, and sit beside me," he said. "There is something that I want to tell you, *shayfelah.*"

I brought him the *Chumash* and he asked that I open it to the portion of *Vayechi,* in the Book of Genesis. He went on to say: "I want you to read the portion where Jacob is ill. He is ready to leave this world, but before he does, he gives a blessing to his children. Read this out loud, Slova Channahlah."

My heart felt as if it was breaking, shattering into a million pieces. I turned to the verse my father pointed to and read aloud as he had requested. My voice trembled, yet I summoned the strength to read.

> And it came to pass after these things that someone said to Joseph, behold your father is ill. So he took his two sons, Menashe and Ephraim with him. . . . So Israel exerted himself and sat up on the bed. . . . He blessed Joseph and he said, G-d before Whom my forefathers Abraham and Isaac walked . . . G-d who shepherds me from my inception until this day, may the angel who redeems me from all evil bless the children and may my name be declared upon them, and the names of my forefathers Abraham and Isaac.
>
> GENESIS 48:1–16

There was silence in the room. "Listen to me," my father began. "When I came to this country so many years ago, I was all alone. I had lost everyone I loved, everyone. I walked through the Valley of the Shadow of Death. Where should I go? What should I do? I was all alone. I didn't even know a word of English, but Hashem, G-d, surrounded me with angels. Do you know how I know? Because I met your *ema,* your *zaydah,* and your *mama.* Hashem gave us beautiful children. We started a family and I saw life again. I never thought that I'd see life again."

I began to sob loudly and buried my face in the soft crevice of my father's neck. "But I had the angels of Jacob with me," he continued. Tears rolled down his cheeks slowly. "And now I know that my time has come to leave you. So what could I possibly give you, my child? I was thinking, what would have a lasting meaning? A piece of jewelry? Some money? Of course not." He took my face in his hands and said, "I leave you with my blessing, the blessing of our father Jacob. I leave you with the blessing of the angels. May they always surround you and watch over you and your children and your children's children."

. . .

I will never forget that day. My father's voice remains in my memory, engraved in the depths of my heart. I know that he gave me and my children his most precious gift; he gave me his final blessing.

Parents who create a *mikdash me'at,* a small sanctuary, can bring light and peace even into a dark and dismal hospital room. They can infuse their children with unique fortitude and strength. I will always be my father's daughter, replete with his blessing to face the challenges of life with faith and resolve. As a parent, you have the awesome opportunity to offer the same precious gift to your child. *Mikdash me'at* is the key. Let us now unlock our hearts.

CREATING A *MIKDASH ME'AT*

One Sunday morning, Mendy and I took a trip into Manhattan with our children. We decided to spend the day at Chelsea Piers, an enormous sports complex on the Hudson River. Once inside, the kids decided to attempt the rock-climbing wall. My then four-year-old son, Akiva, insisted on joining his older siblings as they began their ascent. I watched him, harnessed in ropes, as his little figure grew smaller with each step. My heart beat just a little quicker until he finally made it down. I ran over and hugged him hard. "Akiva, weren't you scared?" I asked. "You were so high, so far away!"

He looked at me for a second and then replied simply: "No, Mommy. Of course I wasn't afraid. Why should I be? I was connected!"

It dawned on me that this small child had just uncovered a significant truth. You can go through an array of life experiences, some quite difficult to bear; however, if you feel connected to a higher source, you never have to be afraid.

. . .

There is no question that today's world can be awfully frightening. We are the generation of 9/11. Newspapers are glutted with painful images of war and human suffering. Our children's vocabulary is vastly unlike our own when we were growing up.

Terrorists, suicide missions, roadside bombs, and high school massacres are now common terms in our vernacular. We need only enter the island of Manhattan to see soldiers with machine guns checking out suspicious vans and trucks. Our televisions and the Internet vividly bring the world's disasters into our living rooms. Portraits of grief and terror can shake our children to their very core. Sadly, our children are subjected to this, all before we even attempt to deal with the many difficult childhood struggles that life brings our way.

Enter the world of *mikdash me'at*. No matter how burdensome a child's day has been he returns to his haven unafraid. Here walls are fortified with more than expensive hardware. A powerful, spiritual bond allows him to rise above life's challenges with renewed strength.

A life imbued with moments of personal sanctity help us create meaning and purpose as we transmit this wisdom to our children.

We, as parents, can enable our children to forge a unique connection with G-d. We have the ability to harness them with pure faith as they scale the various mountains of life. Though there will surely be deep crevices along the way, this spiritual bond allows each child to go forth, motivated and empowered. The challenge we parents face is: how do we construct this *mikdash me'at*? How do we build this metaphysical sanctuary so that the essence of G-d becomes a constant presence within its walls?

It is not an easy task for families today to prevail. One out of every two marriages ends in divorce. Those marriages that do survive are often riddled with strife and miscommunication. Financial pressures may consume the serenity that was once found within the walls of our homes. Many parents work all day and are exhausted upon returning home at night. When dad (and often mom), finally walk through the door, the children are too busy on their computers, PlayStations, or cell phones to notice. Some families don't even talk together anymore; instead they text message each other to keep in touch. Instead of growing closer, our children end up growing apart from one another and from us. We have become like two ships just passing in the night. Tragically, our *mikdash me'at* is crumbling. The fabric of our homes is unraveling and fraying at the edges.

In creating our haven, our first priority is to develop a personal relationship with G-d. Most people believe that there are two partners in creation; father and mother. We are taught by our sages that this thought is erroneous. There are really three partners in creation; father, mother, and G-d Himself. From the moment a couple discovers that they are to become parents, this personal relationship begins. There is so much to pray for, so many hopes and dreams for which we yearn.

The Creator of the Universe has chosen this specific soul to be

brought into this world through you. Raising this child with soul becomes your life mission. What an awesome and holy task! Take time each
day for a few private moments with G-d. Ask that this new life be blessed
with good health, a love of G-d and family, joy, inner peace, wisdom,
compassion, courage, and the strength to endure life's challenges. Pray
for insight and an understanding heart so that you may parent wisely.
These are the precious gifts that no amount of money could ever buy.
These are the precious blessings that we ask G-d to bequeath to us and
our children.

· · ·

Once we decide to bring G-d into our lives, it is with great ease that we
are able to transmit this spiritual bond to our children. Children who observe parents committed to faith and spiritual pursuits become individuals who are familiar with G-d. They grow up with a profound awareness
of the sanctity that lies within each and every one of us. They grow up
with soul.

Children are like sponges. They absorb our every action, our every
word. We are their greatest role models. A child who watches as his mother
kindles her Sabbath lights knows that these flames will forever illuminate
his path. A child who observes his father's dedication to mitzvahs, such as
charity and Torah study, comprehends that there is more to life than merg-
ers and acquisitions. (Mitzvahs are G-d's commandments given to us in the
Torah. Many commandments involve kindness and doing good for others.
Today, when one does a good deed, we call it "doing a mitzvah.")

Parents who teach their children to become cognizant of G-d convey
a deeper meaning and purpose to their days. They live committed lives.
Sadly, an entire generation is being raised devoid of any real spiritual
presence. And even those who do grow up with knowledge and traditions are often left with their hearts wanting.

My brother still speaks about his memories as a young boy when he
would spend the High Holidays with our grandparents. He would sit beside my grandfather on the bimah, the platform where the Torah's ark is
kept. My grandfather would hold his prayer book in his hands, contemplating each word, while quietly sobbing. My brother would ask, "Zaydah, why are you crying?"

"Ah," my *zaydah* would sigh deeply. "I am remembering my *zaydah*.
How he would cry for us as he prayed! Though he perished, I believe that

it was his holy prayers that allowed us, his children, to survive that terrible darkness. Now it is my turn to pray for you." Zaydah's heartfelt prayers ignited a spark in my brother. As a young child, he watched his grandfather's faith come alive. Prayers didn't remain meaningless words, sitting lifeless on a page. Instead, they were a link to the past, a hope for the future. My brother was able to feel more easily connected to G-d. His observations created an indelible imprint on his soul.

Today, my brother leads our Hineni Rosh HaShannah and Yom Kippur services. His sons sit on the bimah beside him as their father once did. Now it is their turn to forge a spiritual bond as they observe their father immersed in sincere prayer. Zaydah's spark never died.

If we take our responsibility seriously, then our *mikdash me'at* begins to take form and flourish. Prayer, a love for traditions, and respect for G-d's creations allow children to realize a loftier purpose. Parents can create a vibrant spiritual identity as they form roots for the next generation to grasp on to.

More than twenty years ago, Mendy and I embarked on our own mission to create a *mikdash me'at*. The excitement we felt upon learning about our first pregnancy was unfathomable. I could barely contain my overflowing joy as I dialed my parents' home to share the exhilarating news with them. To celebrate the occasion, I asked my mother to accompany me to my first doctor visit.

We sat in the doctor's office, thrilled with our delicious secret. The checkup was perfect with just a few details to review. I was asked if I had any concerns.

"Well, as a matter of fact, I just have one small question," I replied. "There is this little bump on the side of my neck, it feels like a tiny pea. I thought I'd mention it, though I'm sure it's nothing."

The doctor rose from his chair and examined my neck. A deep frown formed on his forehead. I glanced at my mother worriedly.

"I don't know," he said slowly. "This really needs looking at. I'm going to send you over to Dr. ———. He's an oncologist and I want you to see him ASAP. In fact, I'll make one phone call and I want you over there right now."

I thought I'd collapse. The excitement, the joy of the day had just dissipated in an instant. I was left with deep dread. What now? My mother gathered me in her arms as if to shield me from the pain. Together we drove from the OB-GYN to the oncologist.

I was immediately brought into the examining room. The oncologist-surgeon entered, his white coat splattered with blood. My chest began to pound. Once again my neck was examined. Rather matter-of-factly, he told us that I would need immediate surgery. This was most probably a tumor that required removal at once.

"What about the baby?" I whispered.

"I didn't hear you, what did you say?" he responded.

My mouth was dry. I tried to get the words out but they felt like lead.

"What about the baby?" I asked slowly. "This is my first baby. How can we do surgery?"

"Listen, there's nothing to talk about. You need surgery now. Schedule it immediately and then we'll see what to do."

I looked at my mother. Her beautiful eyes were filled with my pain. I knew she felt my anguish as only a mother could. We took care of the paperwork and scheduled the surgery for the day after next. There were blood tests to be done and Mendy had to fly in from an overseas business trip.

My mother took my hand as we walked to the car. "Shayfelah, everything is going to be all right. Don't worry. Let's go now to Mama and Zaydah. We're going to get their *bracha*, their blessing."

My *zaydah* and *mama* were always our source of comfort. They were our link back to a world that had been nearly extinguished. When you looked at my *zaydah*, you felt as if you were gazing at an angel. His face radiated holiness. The moment you met Zaydah you were taken with his sheer goodness. His saintly eyes, ever moist, reflected his pure soul. His flowing white beard felt soft to the touch. I never heard Zaydah raise his voice. All his words were said in the most tranquil of tones. After all the suffering he had witnessed, this was most remarkable.

Mama was a tiny woman, exploding with energy and wit to match. She had deep wrinkles that reflected her profound wisdom and life experience. Mama's sparkling eyes mirrored her enthusiasm for life.

You would enter Mama's remarkably small living room and find huge piles of clothing. People would drop off garbage bags filled with all types of garments that they didn't need anymore. Mama would patiently sift through the many pants, tops, dresses, and shoes.

She would make piles for needy families, knowing exactly which sizes they required. When they would arrive to pick up their bags, Mama and Zaydah would greet them as if they were long-lost family. No one would leave without a plate filled with Mama's delicious delicacies and Zaydah's kind words. Of course, Mama's sharp advice was given freely along with all the home-baked goodies. Mama and Zaydah's lives were imbued with compassion for others. A blessing from them was an extraordinary experience.

We walked into their tiny apartment burdened with the events of the day. I had always felt a special bond with my *zaydah* as I had been named for his mother, the Rebbetzin Slovah Channah. Whenever Zaydah would see me, his face would light up. He would lift his hands toward me and sing in Yiddish, "Slovah Channah, come here my sweet princess." I would run into his arms and feel at peace under his flowing beard. This time I didn't wait for Zaydah's greeting. As my mother told our story, I found myself sobbing on Zaydah's shoulders.

My grandfather slowly placed his hands on my head to bless me. His hot tears mingled with mine. Our pain was palpable. He cried aloud, "*Yevarechecha Hashem veyashmerecha.* . . . May G-d bless you and safeguard you, may G-d illuminate His countenance for you and be gracious to you. May the angels of mercy accompany you, my precious child."

I wanted to remain beneath my grandfather's shelter forever. Mama approached me and enveloped me in her warmth. She, too, placed her hands upon my head and gave me her blessing. "May G-d grant that you be like Sarah, Rebecca, Rachel, and Leah, may G-d bless you . . . and establish peace for you."

She whispered softly in my ear. "You will see, my child, you will have a most beautiful little one. I know it."

Her eyes filled as she gazed at me. I embraced the moment and felt renewed. Though the events of the day had been dizzying, hope was born within me. We spent the night at home, ensconced in prayer. Though I felt anxious and afraid, my grandparents' blessings definitely kept me going.

The next afternoon our phone rang. The oncologist asked to speak to me and my mother. He cleared his throat as I gripped the receiver.

"Well," he began, "You're not going to believe this. Your blood tests just came back from the lab. You don't have a tumor after all. You have mono. That lump in your neck is really a huge swollen gland."

I thought I was dreaming. The room began to spin around me. No tumor? No surgery? I looked at my mother and we both began to cry.

"There is one more thing," he added. "You must see a hematologist. This is the first trimester and you do have a virus."

I knew that our prayers of these past two days had just begun. All nine months of my pregnancy were filled with mixed emotions. The hematologist did not want to take any responsibility if I continued to carry the life within me. He warned us that he was removing himself from our case.

Mendy and I spent countless hours trying to calm each other's fears. Whenever I became overwhelmed I asked my parents for strength. Each morning began with a call to Zaydah, Mama, and my parents; I needed to hear their blessings.

"Please, G-d, please help my baby be healthy." I woke up with these words; I fell asleep with these words running through my mind. My thoughts were consumed with a deep desire for my baby's well-being.

King Solomon teaches us that a rope bound with three cords is much stronger than one bound with merely two. It is able to withstand intense blows. The three cords symbolize the union of both parents and G-d. I held on to that rope and braced myself with it throughout my entire pregnancy. The emotional turmoil of those months revealed a part of my inner self that I had, heretofore, never known. I had dug deep within the recesses of my soul.

One morning I was sitting on the couch in my parents' living room reflecting on the tumultuous events of the past few months. I thought about the awful fear that my parents and their families experienced as they had tried to survive the agony of war. They had overcome insurmountable obstacles with great courage and faith. How could I not do the same as I went through my own personal trial?

Of course there are no guarantees in life. I would not know if this baby would be born healthy until I held him in my arms. At the very least, I could confront this challenge strengthened through my deep belief in G-d. My parents had taught me that no prayer is ever lost. No plea to G-d is for naught. Perhaps we don't always understand G-d's answer. Maybe the response is not the one that we had hoped for. Nevertheless, our sages teach us that G-d listens to our every word, channeling our petitions as He sees fit. One thing was for sure; my child would come into this world soaring on the wings of countless heartfelt prayers. This thought brought me much comfort and solace. We would endure.

On a bright and sunny September morning our beloved baby arrived. I gingerly grasped his tiny fingers as they curled around mine. I traced his delicate features and stroked his soft black hair. Our hearts wanted to sing out loud, thanking G-d for this most precious miracle. He looked at me, his dark eyes slowly fluttering open. As I held him, I began to whisper to him his very first prayer here on earth. Modeh Ani is our initial prayer as we wake up in the morning, grateful for having been given the gift of life once again.

"*Modeh ani*," I hummed in his tiny ear. "Thank you G-d for giving us this life. Thank you for restoring my soul with compassion." Could I ever adequately say "thank you" for this little one?

This little soul was about to begin his spiritual journey in life. I was privileged to be a part of this magical moment. We named our son Moshe Nosson Aharon. Moshe Nosson was my father's brother; Nosson Aharon was my father-in-law's brother. Both men had been known as extremely righteous individuals. Both had been brutally murdered in the Holocaust simply because they were Jews.

This child would live, with G-d's help, for those who could not. We would begin the sojourn of *tikkun olam,* repairing the world, together. Light in a world of darkness, blessing in a universe permeated with pain; our mission had begun. We would try to bring healing into this wounded world of ours. We would live our days with this desire in mind.

As your child grows, so, too, do your hopes and fears. Despite all your greatest efforts to guide your child, you still need G-d's direction. How many times does a parent silently murmur, Please let him be healthy, please help her find good friends, please help him get rid of all the anger and find inner joy, please help him be safe . . . do we ever really have complete peace of mind?

Let us begin by opening our hearts and minds. Find time each day to pray. Prayer is our daily opportunity to converse with G-d. Realize, too, that perhaps you've been on this path of prayer without even knowing it. Each whispered plea that is emitted from your heart really is a silent prayer. Rediscover your roots. Children today have no sense of history. They grow up arrogant, believing that they "know it all and better" than their parents. It is only when children realize the greatness of previous generations that they acquire humility. When we know where we've come from we gain the insight to know where we're going.

Allow your child to observe your spiritual connection. Communicate your desire to live a life filled with meaning. You will find yourself transformed as you inspire your children. Perhaps the results will not always be immediately apparent. Realize, however, that just as soft droplets of rain nourish the earth you are constantly nurturing your child's soul. You are creating a magnificent *mikdash me'at*. The flame of genuine faith has been kindled. You are raising a spiritual child; a child who will be morally anchored. The legacy that you build is forever.

A child was once walking down the street. The Kotzker Rebbe, known for his sharp wit, passed by and motioned for him to stop.

"Let me ask you a question, little boy," said the Kotzker Rebbe. "Where is G-d?" The youngster smiled. "Oh, that's easy," he replied. "G-d is everywhere." The Kotzker Rebbe looked at the boy for a moment. "No, my son," he answered gently. "G-d is only where you allow Him to enter."

If we allow G-d to enter our lives then we can establish our spiritual haven. Children who observe a life reflective of faith, flourish within the warmth and glow of a *mikdash me'at*. They will never have to travel through life feeling alone or abandoned.

Your legacy is a treasure not to be taken for granted. A commitment to a home established on a bedrock of faith allows you the infinite potential to transform a good family into a great one. The qualities of a great family are found within the parameters of your home. Constructing the foundation of our *mikdash me'at* is our next challenge.

TWO

The Foundation: Gratitude

APPRECIATING THE GIFT OF LIFE

We decided to give our daughter Shaindy a crafts party when she turned six. As the last child left, we began to pack up our belongings. I noticed a bunch of jackets hanging on the coat hooks.

"I'm sorry," I said to the store owner. "I'm afraid we'll have to wait here until the parents return for their kids' coats."

"Don't worry," he answered, with a wave of his arm. "No one is coming back. This happens all the time. I just take them all down to the basement and send them to Goodwill at the end of the year."

He was right. Not one parent returned. I was really surprised. It was then that I realized that we parents have failed to teach our children to value all that they have. Instead of training our children to take care of their possessions we just buy them new ones. How can they possibly come to an appreciation for all that they have been given?

"You lost your jacket, your Game Boy broke, you can't find your CD player? It's okay, we'll just buy another one."

Everything is replaced so easily. We live in a throwaway culture. Disposable cameras and dishes join broken toaster ovens and DVD players in the trash. Who bothers to fix things anymore? Just throw it away and we'll buy a new one.

Growing up in a disposable society, our children have lost the ability to cherish what they have. After a while, even their friendships are easily discarded. I have overheard parents tell their children, "Sweetie, don't worry about her, you'll find a new friend. She'll be even better, you'll see." Instead of trying to mend that which is broken, we encourage our children to dispose of all that inconveniences them. Even the people in their lives. As they grow, it becomes easier to ditch belongings, friends, values, and even marriages.

The "Supersize Me" Generation

We have also created a world of excess for our children. Ours is the "supersize me" generation. We watch giant home theater flat screen TVs, drive huge SUVs, and order overstuffed sandwiches with jumbo-sized burgers and Cokes on the side. My local coffee shop has fifteen different flavors to choose from and that's before you even consider decaf. Cable television offers us a dizzying array of channels, movies, and sports stations.

Regular seems so, well, boring. We need bigger, better, new and improved. Excess has become the accepted norm. We live in a land of plenty and don't realize what we have become.

I've been in homes with playrooms that look like Toys R Us. The kids don't even know what they have. Game rooms set up in the basement with Ping-Pong and pool tables, foosball, arcade games, and huge entertainment centers. And still the children complain. We're bored. We have nothing to do.

We find closets filled with multiple shoes in a rainbow of assorted colors; all for a two-year-old. One grandmother proudly showed me photos of her newborn granddaughter. Half the pictures were of the baby's jampacked closets. Hanging neatly in rows were countless pink outfits that will surely never be worn.

Children tear the wrappers off their birthday presents as they yell, "But I have this already!"

"Again we're going out to Chinese?"

"Do we have to do Disney again? I'm so bored of it!"

"Only one DVD? We always take out two or three."

After a parenting lecture on gratitude, a mother approached me. She relayed that my description of children who lack appreciation hit home hard. Her two teenage sons constantly rolled their eyes, mocking both her and her husband. Even her homemade dinners did not escape their cynicism.

"This is supper? Mom, your food is pathetic."

A group of women standing nearby nodded in agreement. No matter the ages of their children, each had similar experiences to relate. "Forget about gratitude," one mother added, "I'm just grateful if my kids don't complain."

A Virtual Thankless World

Added to all this is the virtual world that we've created on the Internet. Take a moment and think about it. Your son comes home from school. He wants to race cars. In a second, he's on the computer and there he goes. After a few rounds, he gets bored. He wants to play Pac-Man. Touch a button and it appears. Millsberry then brings him an instant family with dollars to boot. (I quote: "Millsberry is a virtual city where kids rule and there's always something new to do!")

Now he decides that he needs a new hockey stick. Click the mouse and voilà. Whatever his heart desires is before him in an instant. There's no effort involved, no longing, no anticipating. He searches, he views, he compares. There is no one to ask, "Excuse me, can you help me, please?" No lines. No turns to wait. He never even needs to say thank you. A world devoid of gratitude and appreciation.

To whom should he feel grateful? Yahoo? The Net?

Gratitude is out of the picture.

Parents who carpool know that most kids just get out of the car without a backward glance. A mumbled thanks is the most you can hope for. Hold a door open and watch kids just walk through. It's as if it's expected. Of course you'll drive me, of course you'll hold the door open for me. What's the big deal?

And really, what is the big deal? Is a thank-you so crucial to a child's character? Isn't it just a pleasant formality and a display of good manners? Is there any connection between expressing gratitude and appreciating the gifts of life?

Keeping Humble

We wake up in the morning and the first words out of our lips is the prayer of Modeh Ani. We are grateful to have been given another day.

In *lashon kodesh*, the holy tongue, *modeh ani* means "I thank you." It also means "I admit." You see, the two are related. If I thank you then I must admit that I owe you. And for most people, this is quite difficult. No one likes to think that they owe anyone anything.

Judaism teaches us that saying thank you is much more than just a show of good manners. Expressing gratitude is character-building. It keeps us humble. If I voice my appreciation and recognize what I've received from you, I cannot possibly become arrogant. I owe you. I realize that I need you. I acknowledge that I cannot do it all alone. You've helped me and now I am indebted to you. Conceit is replaced with humility.

Children who grow up lacking appreciation and gratitude become selfish and demanding. Feeling a sense of entitlement, they speak with arrogance. They walk around with "attitude." Nothing is ever good enough. "Thank you" is not part of their vocabulary. Appreciation is not often felt and seldom expressed.

The Root of Gratitude

Leah, the wife of our patriarch Jacob, bore three sons. When she gave birth to her fourth son she was overwhelmed with gratitude. She was especially grateful knowing that she had been granted more sons than she could have possibly hoped for. She combined the letters of G-d's name together with the root word that means *thankfulness*. She then called her child Judah.

Judah would become the father of the future kings of Israel. The majestic dynasty of David and Solomon traced their kingly roots back to Judah.

Monarchs who live in royal palaces, whose wishes become commands, can quickly grow conceited. Excess destroys one's soul as layers of arrogance shroud the heart. Leah wanted to provide "character insurance" for her future generations. She conveyed a message to her royal offspring.

Kings, remember your roots. Remember your forefather, Judah. As you speak his name, embrace its definition. Always remain humble and true to yourselves. Always be grateful for all that you have been given. Never lose sight of your blessings.

We, too, can embody the lessons of Leah.

It is time for us to teach our children the most important foundation for living: gratitude. To be grateful for all that we have. We must teach our children that not only do we value our possessions, but we also value our friends, our siblings, our parents and grandparents. We value time. We cherish each day and every breath we take. We treasure life itself. In Hebrew, we call this concept *hakoras hatov*—recognizing the good. We thank G-d for all that we have been given. A home built on the foundation of gratitude is a home filled with appreciation and respect.

Appreciating the Gift of Life

We begin with ourselves. We begin with our own appreciation of life itself—and even in our ability to bring life into this world.

How often do we take a moment and reflect upon the gift of our days? How often do we savor the sweet joy that family brings? Ordinary life becomes plain and unappreciated in our eyes. It's almost as if we live our days in a blur of black and white . . . the color has gone missing.

We wake up in the morning and take our time here for granted. We have our children and quickly forget the anticipation, the enthusiasm, the passion we once held for life. The thrill of parenting slips away as we rush through each stage, barely noticing time go by.

The foundation of gratitude starts with us, the parents. Appreciation is born when finally, one day, we get it. At last we understand and delight in being here, being part of all the moments large and small.

How can we not wonder at this opportunity we have been given? How can we not be incredibly grateful for having been blessed with the ability to live each day, to create and inspire, to parent with soul?

• • •

I attended a *bris,* a ritual circumcision, not too long ago. A dear friend of mine became a grandmother for the very first time. Her daughter, the brand-new mom, stood beside her mother. Their hands intertwined as the baby's wails filled the air. From the front of the synagogue we heard the blessings as the baby was named. "And may his name be called in Israel, Rephael."

Cries of "Mazel tov!"—good luck or congratulations—embraces, and joy surrounded me. For a moment I was taken back to a time of painfully different cries. Just three years before, this new mom had been a vibrant young teenager. One day she was suddenly given the agonizing diagnosis of cancer.

My friend's life became excruciatingly difficult. The pressure and stress of dealing with the burden of her daughter's hospital stays and chemo treatments, while attempting to maintain a relatively normal family life, placed a tremendous weight on her shoulders. Amazingly, through all the pain, her faith and trust in G-d never wavered. She was sorely tested, asked to dig deep within the crevices of her soul. Each week brought new challenges for the entire family. Multitudes of people were immersed in fervent and heart-felt prayers. I watched from a short distance. I hoped. I held my breath.

Slowly, the thick fog began to lift. My friend's child came home. "*Chasdei Hashem,*" my friend whispered, over and over again. "G-d is so very compassionate."

I noticed a gradual change that year in my friend's demeanor. It seemed as if she had lifted herself up from the arduous challenges that she faced and began to live her life on a higher level. Her deep belief in G-d's compassion served as a conduit of hope to all who surrounded her. Our eyes were opened to *chasdei Hashem,* as if we were witness to a stunning sunrise for the very first time.

Each joyous moment was transformed into another brilliant ray of light. My friend's daughter became engaged to a wonderful young man. Words could never describe the sheer joy one felt at that wedding. Exhil-arated, we danced around the bride for hours. Everyone was eager to be a part of this awesome story. Our world was painted with bright hues of hope, healing, and gratitude.

And now, thanks to G-d's infinite kindness, a beautiful baby boy has arrived!

The night before a bris we have a time-honored tradition. In Yiddish it is called a *Vach Nacht.* It is a time when little children gather around the baby's crib and pray for his good health and strength. The prayers of these little precious souls are considered most pure and innocent. As we stood around the bassinet, the children sang the ancient Hebrew prayer of the Shema. Their sweet and melodious voices enveloped the room.

And then, the children began the prayer of the angels, "*Beshem Hashem* . . . may the angels surround you . . . may the angel Michael be on my right, may the angel Gavriel be on my left, may the angel Uriel before me and the angel Rephael behind me and above me is the presence of G-d." Each angel has a name that is symbolic of his mission in this world. That evening, we beseeched the *malachim,* the angels, to watch over this baby and shield him from harm. As we bid each other good night, we knew in our hearts that the morning's bris would yet hold an-other radiant color for all of us to behold.

As the bris ceremony came to a close, friends and family intoned the final prayer: "Just as he has entered the covenant so may he enter into the Torah, the marriage canopy, and good deeds."

The guests streamed into an adjacent room that had been prepared with colorful fruit platters, assorted bagels, hot steaming coffee, and mini-chocolate rugelach. The baby's father rose to say a few words.

After thanking his wife and their families, he dwelled upon the meaning of his child's name. He said, "You all know that today we named our child, Rephael. The angel Rephael, whose presence is said to be behind each individual, is charged with the mission of healing. Rephael's position is behind us because when something is behind you, you easily take it for granted. It's as if it were on the back burner of your mind. In life, many people take their health for granted. Others take pregnancy and children for granted. I make a promise to all of you today. I promise that we will hopefully take neither for granted . . . ever. And our little baby, Rephael, will ensure that."

I looked around and saw that there was not a dry eye in the room. My friend's steadfast whisper of "*Chasdei Hashem*" rang loud and clear.

This story, however, would not yet be over.

Following the bris I ran some local errands. As I strolled along our main street of Central Avenue, my cell phone rang. I noticed that an unfamiliar number was coming up on the caller ID.

"Hello?" I said. I did not recognize the voice on the other end.

"Slovie?" a woman's voice asked softly.

"Yes, that's me," I replied.

"I don't know if you remember me. My name is Jenny K. I met you when you gave a series of lectures in my community a few years ago. You had been traveling with your family and were kind enough to take the time to speak in our synagogue. Somehow we stayed in touch for a while. . . . Do you know who I am?"

It took a moment, but I remembered Jenny without much effort. Tall, beautiful, with a sparkling smile, she was difficult to forget.

"Of course, I remember you," I replied. "Tell me, what's going on?"

She began with much hesitance. "It's like this. I have two little girls. They are eleven and nine. They're great kids, though believe me, we've had our ups and downs like all families. My husband is a really nice guy but sometimes we've hit some rocky terrain. Things are finally settling into place and . . ." Her voice grew low.

"What is it, Jenny?" I asked.

"I'm pregnant. This baby was never planned. It's a huge mistake. We don't want this baby." She began to cry. "I'm not the mothering type. I always hated being pregnant. I can't stand the noise and the dirty diapers. I can't stand always running to the pediatrician. My career is finally taking off. Dave and I love to travel and we've reached the stage that we can get away without a hassle. The girls are now independent. My life is in a good groove and now this. . . . Dave thinks that our marriage can't survive the stress of another baby and I think he may be right . . . I don't know. Anyway, I'm scheduled to have an abortion at 9:00 A.M. tomorrow morning."

Her voice was now filled with anguish as she whispered, "Slovie, it's a boy. The baby is a boy. What do I do? What do I do?"

I felt as though the wind had been knocked out of me. Frantically, I looked around for a chair and sat down. People passed before me, but it was all a blur.

Considering the conflicted values of today, I knew that this would be a hard decision for her to make, but I also knew that I'd try to guide her with the eternal wisdom of the Torah. I took a deep breath and asked Hashem to give me the proper words.

"Listen to me, Jenny," I began. "There are no such things as accidents in life. We believe that every moment, every encounter, every soul is *bashert,* meant to be. It's Divine. This baby is no accident. This baby is heaven-sent. You don't know what the future holds. No one knows, including your husband and myself. Only G-d knows.

"This little boy is being sent to you because he belongs in your family. He is no mistake, but rather, he is your magnificent blessing. Maybe the day will come that your daughters will be needing a brother. Or perhaps this little boy will bring you incredible joy that has remained untapped and he'll allow you all to bond and do things together as a family as you grow older. Who knows? There is only one thing that we can be one hundred percent sure of. This child is your son. He's a gift from Above and part of your family."

The fresh memories of the morning's bris came rushing back. A picture of baby Rephael flashed through my mind. Every nuance was clear; his tiny little fingers, his innocent eyes, his newborn wail.

I went on to tell Jenny about the bris that I had attended earlier that day. I relayed to her the entire story from the moment of diagnosis to the *mazel tov* cries at the bris. I recounted the young father's pledge, to never take life for granted.

"Jenny, you're worried about your marriage surviving a baby, but I'm even more worried about your marriage not being able to survive this termination. Sleep, travel, and your career are things that you can always catch up on. What I fear is that when tomorrow comes you will never forgive yourself or each other. You'll always be haunted with the thought of what-if. . . . The child you are carrying is your son, and for some reason you are being given this most precious and priceless gift. I beg you, Jenny, please don't take this gift for granted."

There was a muffled cry on the other end of the line. "Jenny, there comes a time in each person's life that defines one's character. This is your moment. Who are you?"

There was a second of silence. "I know you're right but . . . I need to speak to Dave. I'm so scared."

"Listen," I added, "I'd be happy to speak with Dave, I'll do anything to help you."

"Okay, I'll call you back later with Dave on the line," Jenny said. "Thank you so much."

The day passed but my phone didn't ring. The moments seemed like hours. By ten o'clock that evening I decided to call Jenny myself. I can't say that I wasn't nervous, but I felt responsible for this little child's *neshamah*.

I dialed the number and waited. After several rings, I realized that no one would be picking up. That night I could not sleep. Thoughts of the birth of one child juxtaposed with the loss of another gave me no peace.

I summoned up the courage and called once again early the next morning. The shrill ring sounded in my ear. Over and over again it sounded. Sadly, I put down the receiver. I sat and cried for a short while. I knew that I had made a concerted effort, yet there was no response from Jenny and Dave.

Friday morning, I began my usual Shabbos preparations. The luscious aroma of chicken soup and potato kugel wafted through my kitchen. My cell phone rang.

"Slovie, is that you?" asked the voice on the other end.

"Jenny?" I held my breath to hear her response.

"Slovie, I would like to invite you to a bris."

I gasped.

Jenny blurted out, "I didn't do it. I couldn't do it. I can't take this life for granted."

"Oh, Jenny," I shouted excitedly. "I'm so very happy for you! You will see that this little boy will bring you great joy and blessing. He will tickle your heart, and you will love him to pieces. You'll see!"

Jenny laughed into the phone. "So, I'm having a son. Thank you for everything. I'm running to meet Dave for lunch. Good Shabbos, and I'll keep in touch."

Chasdei Hashem—G-d is good. I thought of my friend's words and smiled.

Recently, I received a letter from Jenny. Attached was a photo of her beautiful son, Daniel. He has the same sparkling smile as his mom. Jenny wrote:

> I cannot imagine life without our Daniel. I have come to believe that there really is a Master Plan for each and every soul. My girls have become more loving and have a special place in their hearts for their baby brother. We are not the same family that we once were. Thank you.

Each child is an entire world unto himself. Each soul on this earth brings with it a myriad of possibilities, infinite potential, and future generations. Unfortunately, we have come to take this exciting and unique world for granted. Instead of savoring each day, we find ourselves complaining about the multitude of responsibilities we face as parents.

We resent the infringement on our time. We whine about homework, crying infants, and carpool schedules. We feel entitled to an easier, stress-free life.

We grapple with our days instead of relishing the deliciousness of youth. We have forgotten how to appreciate our blessings. It is time to cherish and truly value the beautiful souls that have been entrusted to us. Not only must we teach our children to be grateful, but we ourselves must become living and breathing role models of heartfelt gratitude and appreciation. Above all, we must appreciate the gift of life, the legacy of being able to raise a child.

PRACTICAL PARENTING

Once we parents come to the understanding that gratitude is vital to our children's character, we remain with crucial questions to address.

How do we begin to teach this belief to our children? Can we open our children's eyes so that they value all their blessings, despite our society of "supersize me" excess? How can our kids come to feel gratitude if their virtual world requires no thankfulness? Is it possible to overcome the selfish society that our children are growing up in and replace arrogance with humility? Where do we begin?

Learning to Appreciate Time

I recall that as a little girl we would often have family get-togethers in my parents' home. There was always a lot of noise and excitement when all the cousins would meet. At one point, the activities would come to a standstill and the small children would be hushed.

My grandfather would sit at the head of a long table, his face beaming at the sight of his beloved family. He spoke softly in Yiddish as he glanced at each one of us. "I would like to make a blessing tonight," he would say. *"Baruch atah . . . shehecheyanu vekeymanu vehegeyanu lazman hazeh."* Blessed are You, our G-d . . . Who has kept us alive and sustained us and brought us to this time.

On each occasion, Zaydah would recite the same blessing as his voice cracked with emotion. I would observe my *zaydah* in wonder. I couldn't really comprehend why my grandfather was so moved by this blessing. After all, it was just a small family gathering. Why all the emotion?

It was not until I became a parent myself that I began to feel the same sentimental stirrings within. My children sit around our table laughing out loud with one another as I snap a photo in my mind. I drink in their lovely faces, taking in each of their movements. As life pulls them in different directions, our time together as a family becomes more special and precious. The clock is ticking. The moments are fleeting and I want so very much to hold on to each second. *"Shehecheyanu."* My grandfather's blessing echoes in my mind.

Each milestone brings awareness of this blessing home. Our son's bar mitzvah brought us incredible joy, yet my father's chair was glaringly empty. I had never imagined celebrating our first bar mitzvah without him. What we wouldn't have given to have my father dance just one more time with his grandson! One more hug, one more smile, one more blessing, one more precious kiss.

My *zaydah* said it so beautifully. He understood how miraculous a gift each moment was. Time together cannot be taken for granted. Now I, too, recite the same blessing with great intent and wonder.

We must teach our children to appreciate the preciousness of time. Parents who allow their children to sit in front of a TV or play their Game Boy for hours give the message that time is for wasting. Kids left watching DVDs all Sunday long understand that it doesn't matter how you spend your time as long as you "stay out of your parents' hair." Parents are communicating that you can do what you want with your time as long as you don't bother me.

It may take planning and input, but parental involvement is needed to teach children from the time that they are young that our days are valuable. When your children have free time, don't allow them to just sit around mindlessly. Lounging for hours in front of a TV, even as a family, encourages kids to do and say nothing. We must help bring purpose to their days. I don't mean that every minute must be organized. Rather, it is important to allow children to rediscover the value of communication, friendship, free play, and carefree imagination.

Take a trip to the library, plan a day visiting cousins and grandparents, take up a cause and volunteer as a family, laugh while you run in the park, play a game together. Do something to help children appreciate their time.

And when your family does get together, be sure to gather everyone around and take a moment. Relay your personal feelings, even say a blessing. Show your children how to cherish their family and their days.

"Let's go kill some time." "I have fifteen minutes to waste before my appointment." These are such unfortunate expressions. Our time here is a gift to be used wisely. My daughter's high school principal once explained to me the reasoning behind the girls' class schedule. Classes begin and end precisely at an exact minute: 8:37, 11:52, 4:26. "What's this all about?" I once asked. She replied that students should know that every second counts.

Just the other day, my daughter relayed to me that this wisdom has impacted her for life. Though she has graduated and moved on, she is still left with a feeling that every second counts and time must be used wisely. She tries to make the most of each moment.

Begin Your Day with Gratitude

Try to begin each day with the Modeh Ani prayer: "Thank You, G-d, for giving me another day." When children wake up with a thank-you on their lips, they start their day in a grateful mode. This thoughtful blessing helps us all become more mindful of the gift of life.

Our world is filled with astounding beauty and magnificence. Children bring life into our days. It is human nature, though, to overlook life's simple pleasures. We race through our days, allowing the moments to pass us by.

We need to stop sometimes. Turn off our cell phones and BlackBerrys. Disconnect our iPods and really listen. Let's take a good look at our world, at our families, and be cognizant of all that we have been given.

Our children need to discover life's little wonders. They need time to inhale the brilliance and majesty of our universe. We can help children appreciate the colorful world they live in and fill their days with meaning as we savor our time together.

Parents should look within and ask: What type of picture have we painted for our children? Have we become overly negative, sarcastic, and pessimistic? Have we become hardened and uncaring? Have we tasted or depreciated the moments of life?

Learning to Appreciate Our Possessions

There is a seemingly perplexing mitzvah in the Torah. We are told that when we besiege a city in battle, we are not permitted to destroy and cut down the fruit trees (Deuteronomy 20:19–20). Is it possible that while fighting a war, we need to worry about a fruit tree? What's the point of something so seemingly insignificant?

We must understand that G-d is most concerned with the shaping and development of our inner essence. The Torah is our built-in GPS system, providing us with direction for life. As we follow its guidance, we gain values and character traits for life. This mitzvah, not to destroy a fruit tree while in battle, originates from the concern that we not become destructive human beings.

In war it is very easy to get swept away in purposeless destruction. How often do good, fine soldiers lose themselves in the heat of the moment? Destruction abounds. It is difficult not to get carried away when one's mission is to devastate.

G-d is instructing us that even while battle is being waged, we must care for our souls. We should always exert every effort to be a force of goodness in this world. We are being taught to respect the sanctity of life, in all its forms. In this case, it is the fruit tree that we must look out for, to see and understand its value and to treat it accordingly. If we are able to watch over and care for a fruit tree, think how sensitive we become toward human life.

The Torah is imparting to us the importance of not allowing ourselves to degenerate into destructive human beings under any circumstances. Value your world and all its treasures.

It is here that our sages teach us about the fundamental precept of *bal tashchis*—"do not destroy." Living in our society of plenty, it is easy to needlessly destroy and be wasteful. In Judaism, this is not only thought of as a deficient character trait, but it is considered a sin.

Our sages teach us that we are molded by our actions. If we easily stomp on the world around us, we ruin more than just a tree or a flower bed. It is not just a fence that we playfully knock down and destroy, we extinguish a force within that encourages us to be architects of this universe. We are obligated to share this teaching with our children.

For example, when you are waiting in a restaurant for your order to arrive, don't allow your children to open all the sugar packets and pour them on the table. Spilling food for no reason is transgressing *bal tashchis*.

I've watched kids place order after order as their parents silently looked on. At the end of the evening, they left their table with enough food on their plates to feed a family of four. Dishes of untouched portions are left sitting, waiting to be thrown away. *Bal tashchis*.

Telling children that "there are kids in Africa who are starving" is not the solution. Our children need to acquire an understanding that speaks more than superficial lines.

Once, on a family vacation, I was sitting on a hotel terrace that overlooked majestic mountains and beautiful fields of green. A toddler and his older brother sat themselves down besides some huge flowerpots and began pulling out the blossoms one by one. Colorful petals were strewn all over the brick patio.

"Look," someone called out to the children's father, "your kids are tearing up those flowers."

The father glanced up from his morning paper for a second.

"That's okay." He laughed. "At least I'm getting my money's worth here."

Kids who tear out grass and flowers "just because," who purposely tear holes in clothing and walls, who pour out bottles of glue for the fun of it, who throw bread at each other across the lunchroom table, have all thoughtlessly disregarded this lifetime principle of *bal tashchis*.

We can't just dismiss these behaviors as harmless, unaffecting our children's souls. These seemingly unimportant actions shape our children's ways. Habits that deface, waste, or ruin create children who do not spend much time and effort on conserving, preserving, and protecting our world.

One dark December night, a group of more than thirty teens and young adults trashed the historic farmhouse that had belonged to the poet Robert Frost. *The New York Times* describes the damage done by their "alcohol-induced mischief tinged with certain anger."

There were smashed windows, dishes, and antiques. Chairs had been broken and used for firewood. Fire extinguishers had been discharged, their contents sprayed everywhere. I was shocked to read how vomit, urine, beer, and phlegm covered the home's interior. The teens had spent the night drinking, vandalizing, and wrecking; then they left their awful mischief behind.

People wondered how this could have happened and "what ever happened to respect?"

A police sergeant commented that after photographing and finger printing more than two dozen youths, he especially could not get over the indifference of one teen who "asked whether he could use his mug shot on his Facebook page."

Living by the principle of *bal tashchis* means that we instill in our children an attitude of caring for our world from the time that they are young. It means that we impress upon them the understanding that they are here to build and never destroy. They are the keepers of our universe and all that lies within—from the fruit trees and the flowers to the very chairs they sit on.

Teaching the Value of "Things"

When my children were younger, they would love to visit my parents' home. Across the street was a serene little lake with flocks of geese honking and waddling around. One of my children's best memories was when they'd walk with my father to feed the geese. Holding tightly on to my father's hands, each child would clutch a small bag filled with my mother's leftover Sabbath challah bread.

Instead of throwing out the pieces of bread, my parents imparted a crucial lesson to their grandchildren. There are others—even geese— who would be happy with what you easily discarded.

My children would feed the birds and laugh gleefully as the geese flocked around them. As they honked loudly, my father would exclaim, "Listen to the geese, they're saying thank you."

We can also help our children learn gratitude as they outgrow their clothing. Tragically, we know that there are many children in this world who are without, and to whom these articles of clothing would be of great use. Instead of just packing up my children's gently used clothing myself, I have my kids help me sort through their garments. They then put them neatly in a bag.

I would tell my little ones that there is a little girl or boy who is cold. She stands outside the schoolyard shivering, wishing that she could have a nice warm jacket.

"Just imagine," I would tell them. "One day, she comes home and her mommy brings out a great surprise. A new, soft, beautiful coat waiting to be worn. A great smile appears on the little girl's face. She's thrilled and grateful as she skips outside to play.

"And you, my child," I would say, "you did a huge mitzvah. You finished wearing your coat and now you've given to another."

My child's eyes would open wide. Her little coat held enormous promise for goodness in this world. Instead of just discarding things without giving them a second thought, our children can learn to become a sensitive *baal chessed*, one who is filled with kindness. Instead of growing wasteful and destructive, our children can become builders and pillars of goodness. They can fulfill their mission of *tikkun olam*. Compassion and goodness emanate from children who appreciate and value life, who seek to preserve and sustain as they contribute to the furtherance of others.

Learning to Appreciate People

Gratitude begins with two words: "thank you." You may be wondering in astonishment right now: Do you mean to tell me that I actually need to sit down and teach my children to say thank you? Will it make such a difference in their lives?

Yes.

Take the time one day to observe kids on an airplane, in a restaurant, in school, or even with their parents at home. You will be dumbfounded as children are being served and catered to and they hardly give an appreciative word. The arrogance and sense of entitlement is astounding. How can we turn this around?

Gratitude begins with us parents. Children need to hear their parents give voice to the two simple words of "thank you" to each other. They need to witness appreciation and regard for another's efforts. We are our children's most powerful role models.

Each Friday evening before our Sabbath meal concludes, my husband gives me a most cherished gift. In front of our children and even guests, he voices his appreciation to me for "our magnificent, delicious Shabbos." For more than twenty years, with unabashed enthusiasm, my husband has expressed his gratitude to me. Our children's eyes have been opened to appreciate their mother's efforts. They have learned to follow in their father's way. They've come to understand that it's not all just coming to them; instead, love and hard work are acknowledged and recognized.

I, too, gladly reciprocate the appreciation to my husband in front of our children. When we are fortunate enough to take a family vacation, I make a point of thanking my husband for his hard work that made our time together possible. Our children follow suit and graciously thank their father for the special memories. Even purchases of shoes or holiday clothing are an opportunity to stop for a moment and say thank you to parents.

A seed has been planted. A paramount lesson has been taught and inculcated. Don't take your parents for granted. Don't just expect life's gifts to be handed to you; rather, acknowledge and value them.

When we were little and took a trip that required a bridge crossing, my father would always choose a manned lane over an automated toll. We would ask him why and he'd smile and say, "It's one more thank you in our day!"

The bus driver, the librarian, the bank teller, the shopkeeper, were all given cheerful smiles and thanks that still make an impression on me today.

Recently, I was asked to give a parenting workshop on gratitude in the month of December. Parents were concerned that amid all the gift-giving and treats, children would begin to take these special moments for granted. Watching their kids grow accustomed to receiving presents made gift-getting and excess a worrisome holiday norm.

"What can we do to help our kids feel gratitude and appreciation?" one mom asked.

"Well, besides the usual idea of giving a toy to a child who is ill or can't afford one himself, or limiting the amount of gifts, I would like to suggest something. Recently I spoke to preschool teachers and I asked them about all the times that they've baked with their students. Usually, the children just eat whatever it is that they've made. Why not bake for others? Why not show gratitude to the office staff, the bus drivers, and the crossing guards? Why must our kids always consume?

"Kids love to bake and to do arts and crafts. This holiday season, turn the tables around. Have your children give the gifts of their hands instead of just taking. Open their eyes to the people around them. Grandparents, teachers, doctors, the doormen, the firemen down the block—they all deserve a gift of thanks. Involve your kids. Have them draw thank-you cards and be a part of the giving instead of just taking more and more. Help them express their thanks to others."

The next day I received an e-mail: "I already started to incorporate your ideas from the class and I'm so excited to teach my children how to give during this holiday season."

The Education of Appreciation

The Torah teaches us an extraordinary lesson about gratitude. When Moses was an infant, his mother secured him in a basket and placed it on the Nile River. Moses grew older and returned to Egypt to bring on the ten plagues.

At the onset of the first plague, G-d did not allow Moses to strike the Nile River. Instead, Aaron was given the commandment. We are taught that the reason for this was *hakoras hatov*. Moses needed to acknowledge and appreciate the river that had kept him alive and displayed kindness to him.

Now, let me ask you: Does a river feel? Would the Nile even know the difference? Moses was carried to safety with the river's natural current. Why make such a big deal about it? Isn't a river supposed to flow anyway?

This wasn't about the river at all. G-d was shaping the character of Moses, the future leader of the Jewish nation. The issue was not about the sensitivity of the Nile, but rather the development of gratitude within Moses.

We who study Torah are most fortunate in our ability to gain insights for living through Torah's wisdom. Yes, the river is supposed to flow. Mommy is supposed to provide a splendid Sabbath meal. Daddy is supposed to support the family. The bus driver is supposed to take you to school. The waiter is supposed to serve you. The teacher is supposed to teach.

But that doesn't discount the fact that we are obligated to value their efforts and express gratitude for all that they do. Even if we think that they are just doing their job, we must take a moment to say thank you.

It is up to us, this education of appreciation.

As we model a life of gratitude we raise children who are thankful, not thankless. Children who live life with humility instead of posturing with insolence and arrogance appreciate life and all its blessings.

A mother approached me after a parenting class and said: "Last class you spoke about 'attitude.' I realized that things have been difficult for me lately. I dread my kids coming home from school. There's a bad feeling in the house. And then it hit me, it's their arrogant attitude that's wearing me down.

"It's just like you said. They walk through the door, throw their backpacks and jackets on the floor and the first thing they do is make a face if dinner isn't ready or to their liking.

"I followed your advice. I sat them down and said, 'I've waited for you all day. I'm home because I love you. I've worked hard on preparing food for you and making sure that I am here for you. Then you come home, don't say hello, throw things on the floor and complain.

" 'It hurts my feelings and makes me really sad. From now on, I'd like you to come in, hang up your stuff and ask me about my day using a nice voice. "Mommy, how are you, how was your day?" Those should be your first words to me, not your complaints and nasty eyes.'

"Well, I can't believe it, but this really worked. Now they come home, speak in a pleasant tone and have a completely different attitude. The other day I overheard my ten-year-old son say to my housekeeper, 'Lily, how was your day? How are you?' She had tears in her eyes and said to me that in all her years of working in different homes, no child has ever asked her how she was feeling or spoken to her with such respect. He has become a different child.

"I've noticed him speak to the people around him with a newfound consideration. The best part is that I feel happier and able to parent better. I just wanted to thank you because expressing gratitude is what it's all about."

MAMA'S EYES

When I first married, I moved with my husband to his hometown of São Paulo, Brazil. I was just twenty and sorely missed home. The culture was foreign and the language seemed so strange to me. Though everyone tried their best (especially my husband), I was happily married but living miserably in Brazil. I longed for familiar company. My grandmother,

Mama, decided to come and visit. For Mama, this kind of venture was no easy task. Here she was, a great-grandmother who had just recovered from a broken hip. She spoke a broken English and had never traveled anywhere alone. But she was a woman of great spirit. Flying solo with her trusted cane in her hand, she journeyed across the world.

I counted the moments until Mama arrived with great anticipation. I couldn't wait to share my misery with her. I was sure that Mama would be supersympathetic to my plight.

Finally, Mama arrived. After many excited hugs and kisses we entered our car. "Ah," I thought to myself, "now someone is here to feel my distress. Do you see this place, Mama?" I asked, expectantly. "Nay!" Mama said in Hungarian, which I realized was her expression of amazement. "Nay, look at the trees. I've never seen such trees in my whole life."

"The trees?" I asked, unbelievingly.

"Slova Channalah, you are so lucky! Hashem made such a big, beautiful world and you are able to see it. I have never seen such gorgeous trees and I'm almost eighty years old. Now I can die without feeling that I haven't seen Hashem's wonders. Oy, what a world we have!" Mama had a huge smile on her face. Her passion for life was never quenched.

I realized that I had better see life through Mama's eyes. I had been feeling sorry for myself, overcome with self-pity and melancholy. Tinges of sadness served no purpose. There was so much beauty to be had and I was missing it all. Mama had lived through the horrors of the Holocaust and many difficult hardships, yet she never lost her vision and appreciation for the splendors of life. The awesome trees, the giggle of a child, the sweet breaths of a newborn never ceased to bring sparkle to Mama's eyes. From now on, I would be fortunate to perceive the world through her perspective.

Parenting is much more than an opportunity; rather it is our responsibility. We are charged with the duty of raising children with an education of appreciation. It is crucial that we instill in our children the ability to cherish the bounty of life. Not only does that include their own personal possessions, but it also includes the individuals who, together, comprise the circle of life. The blessing of *shehecheyanu,* thanking G-d for granting us the privilege of existence reminds us to be grateful. Once a home is infused with this spirit of gratitude, we relate to each other as a family that appreciates one another. We become kinder and more loving. We observe the world through "Mama's eyes," and never forget to be grateful for life's blessings.

THREE

Happiness

Once upon a time, couples married, raised their children, worked together on their struggles, and lived "relatively happily ever after." Today, one can find numerous depressed people trying to raise happy families despite their unhappy state. Many families barely survive or, unfortunately, simply fall apart.

We find that it is not just parents, but children, too, who are on medication and in therapy. "I'm so depressed" is a common whine heard even among six-year-olds. Stand on line in Disneyland, which should be one of the happiest places on earth and watch all the unhappy faces. Look around. It is difficult to find individuals who live with a joy for life. What's going on? Why is it so difficult for people to be happy?

I first met Laurie when she was expecting her second child. Through the years she enthusiastically attended my parenting classes. Bronze-skinned with sparkling blue eyes, Laurie's effervescence matched her outer appearance. Her husband, a successful doctor, adored her and together they made an impressive couple.

After one summer break, I noticed a change in Laurie. Newly platinum blond, she wore glaring designer brands from head to toe. Laurie was now rail-thin and had undergone obvious Botox treatments. But despite all the changes she seemed to be extremely unhappy. Her smile wore thin and weary. Even her voice had become lackluster. As the year passed, her attendance became more sporadic. Puzzled, I called Laurie, but all she said was that her schedule had become too hectic to allow her to study.

Soon after, I received a call from Laurie's husband, Marc.

"Slovie, I have a question for you. How is it that my wife studies Torah, but has come to lack values? She's never home for the kids. Her credit card bills have gone through the roof. It seems as if she's always looking into another cosmetic procedure. She's been driving like a maniac, taking more and more antidepressants, and she sees a bunch of therapists. What's most hurtful of all is that she's become aloof and estranged from me. We hardly even talk anymore."

"Marc," I replied, "I don't know how to tell you this, but Laurie stopped attending my classes months ago."

"You're kidding!" Marc was shocked. "She never told me. She's always loved Torah study, I can't understand what happened to her."

"Well," I said, "Maybe you could tell me what's going on. Think back. Has anything changed recently? How did all this begin? This is not the Laurie that I've come to know and love."

There was a moment of silence on the line. Marc spoke hesitantly.

"I'm not sure," he began, "but I think it has to do with our good friends who visited us for an extended stay this summer. Laurie and I both noticed that their marriage seemed strained. They snapped a lot at each other and were unusually quiet. The wife confided to Laurie that their marriage was at the breaking point. She just wasn't happy. She didn't feel in love anymore. Her husband had become boring, life had become dull. She felt stressed out from her kids. I think those talks somehow stirred something within Laurie. I feel as if their stay was toxic for us. I was even wondering if divorce and unhappiness might be contagious."

"Look," I said, "our friends' impressions and conversations definitely impact our own thoughts and feelings. I'm going to call Laurie and see if she'd be open to meeting with me. Let's try to get to the bottom of this before the situation gets out of control."

As the conversation came to a close, Marc asked me to please keep in touch. His anguish was palpable and I promised to exert every effort to help.

Laurie agreed to meet with me the following week. Two hours out of New York, the trip to her home gave me much time to collect my thoughts. Finally, I pulled up to her estate. A winding driveway led me to a most beautiful country manor. A large fishpond, acres of luscious greenery, and exquisite landscaping took my breath away.

Laurie met me at the front door. I noticed that she had become even thinner. We sat down in the living room, surrounded by Laurie's impeccable taste.

"Laurie, what's going on?" I asked. "I look at you but I don't recognize you. What happened?"

Laurie's eyes began to fill.

"It's just a mess," she answered. "My life is just one big mess."

"What are you talking about?" I asked. I gestured toward the silver frames that filled the bookshelves and end tables. "Look around. I see photos of your beautiful girls and your husband who loves you. You've been happily married for ten years and you live a beautiful life. You're the envy of so many women. What's a mess?"

Laurie looked at me sadly and I noticed that her eyes had lost their light. "I realized this past summer that I'm just not happy. In fact, I realize now that I've never been happy. I just did what I was supposed to do. Get married. Have kids. Schedule everyone's life. Plan vacations, entertain, and live a certain lifestyle. But none of it's been for me. I've done it all for my husband and my girls. Don't get me wrong. I love my kids, but I've been swallowed up living my life for them. My husband's a great co-parent, but that's about it. The passion's gone. I realize that I don't really love him. I don't know who I am anymore, and I'm just not happy. It takes all my strength just to get up in the morning. My life's a mess and I'm tired of trying so hard." Laurie began to cry.

I took her hand in mine and spoke from my heart.

"Laurie, every marriage has its ups and downs. But we need to look at the whole picture. You have a husband who adores you. He's adored you for years and you've loved him back. I've watched you raise your children. You and Marc have always been on the same page. You've built a beautiful life together. Where did all that go?

"You can't tell me that it's all been a farce. There's no way you could think that you're happy and fulfilled through a decade of marriage and then suddenly wake up one morning and lose it all. Something must have changed. Please, talk to me, Laurie. Let's work this out together."

Laurie was silent. She looked down at her hands and played nervously with her wedding band. Finally, she took a deep breath and spoke.

"Okay, I had a good friend open my eyes this summer. I saw my life through hers. She shared her unhappiness with me and I realized that we're in the same boat. Sure, my husband's a nice guy, but that's about it. The passion is gone. He always counted on me to do it all. My kids are great but their needs have taken over my life. I've been going out with my friend, having fun, and finally doing things for me. Now it's my time. I'm going to tell Marc that I want a divorce."

"Well, that would be great," I said, "if at least you'd be happy from this newfound lifestyle. Take a look at yourself. Honestly. Do you really think that you're happier now than you've been for the past ten years? Laurie, I'm sorry to tell you this, but you look miserable. To me, you seem depressed. In fact, I've never seen you unhappier than now, when you're supposed to be discovering this whole new exciting life. I can't believe that you'd give up ten years of a great marriage and family life just like that.

"Do me a favor. I've never asked you for anything before. Let's meet, you, Marc, and me. Let's talk about the Torah's views on marriage and relationships. Let's try to put it back together if we can. At least, let's give it a shot. Otherwise, you'll never know if you gave it your all, and ten years down the road you'll be living with regrets. When your girls grow older and start asking questions about this time of your life, you'll be wondering yourself whether you made the right decision."

Laurie didn't respond.

"Just one time," I pleaded. "That's all I'm asking you. Let the three of us meet and see if we could find some way to start again."

"I'll think about it," Laurie answered. "I'll really think about it."

A week went by. I called Laurie and asked if she would take me up on my offer. On three occasions we scheduled to meet, but each time Laurie canceled at the last moment.

Marc called me in a panic. "I'm losing her, Slovie, and I don't know what to do. I've spoken to her doctor and her therapists. They just keep recommending more sessions and different medications. She's glued to her BlackBerry while we're at the dinner table and even while she's in the bath. I have no idea who she's talking to. I try to reach out to her but she just pulls away. My girls have begun to fight with each other and wet their beds . . . something they haven't done for years. She's destroying all of us and I don't understand why. You've got to help her," Marc pleaded.

I felt so sorry for this beautiful family that was about to be torn apart. Tragically, they would become another sad statistic of American society.

"I can only help her if she wants to be helped, Marc," I said. "If she refuses to meet and shuts me out, then it'll be impossible to get through to her. I'm going to call her again, but I can't promise you anything."

I dialed Laurie's number and after a few rings, I heard her strained voice on the line. "Well," she said, "I may as well tell you, Slovie. I've decided. I'm asking Marc to move out and I'm getting divorced."

"Why?" I asked.

"I'm not happy. I'm just not happy," Laurie kept repeating.

"And what about your kids?" I asked. "How do you think they will feel? They love you and Marc. They've grown up in such an incredible home. Have you stopped to think about their happiness?"

Laurie was quiet for a moment. "Well, my mother did the same thing to me, and I survived."

"You survived!" I exclaimed. "Is that all you want for your children in life, to survive? And then, when your children grow up, would you want them to just flick their kids off the moment that they feel unhappy? Is this your legacy? Your mom's misery and now you repeating the same story? Isn't there more to being a mother than giving birth and hoping that your kids survive your unhappiness? There is so much more for you to transmit to your beautiful girls! Come on, Laurie, how could you possibly find happiness while you destroy your own home?"

"Stop making me feel guilty," she snapped. "Don't you think that I've thought about all that? So, I've upped the girls' therapy sessions. They're in group therapy and now they each have their own private half hour. I'm even going to end each week with a psychiatrist who specializes in issues of children from divorced homes. Why are you making me feel so guilty?"

"Making you feel guilty?" I asked. I took a deep breath. "Listen, Laurie. If one of your girls was playing with matches, wouldn't you scream out? Wouldn't you shout, stop it! You're playing with fire and you could get burned! I'm just telling you that if your home collapses your children will never be the same. Their life as they know it will shatter. And for what? What's the point of all this? You're playing with fire, Laurie. I'm asking you to consider the price that everyone will pay for your so-called unhappiness and at least let's try to pick up the pieces before your family disintegrates."

"It's too late," Laurie said softly. She began to cry. We said our good-byes sadly and hung up the phone.

Reluctantly, I called Marc with the dismal news. He let out a heart-breaking cry over the phone. "Do you know what I feel most sorry about?" he asked. "We've spent years trying so hard to have fun, seeking out excitement and pleasure, but we neglected our souls. Our definition of happiness was warped, and now we're paying the price."

Marc was right. Our society's definition of happiness is distorted. We are given these incredible families, such precious children, but we make a grave mistake. We find ourselves constantly running, pursuing the newest and latest, believing that each new pleasure will rectify our unhappiness.

Somehow, though we still can't seem to find real happiness. We remain with a deep gnawing emptiness, never realizing that true happiness lies within.

We brew discontent by imagining that life would be better if only: "If only I had a better job, if only I had a bigger home, if only I could take better family vacations, if only I had her husband, his wife, their perfect kids, *then* I'd be happy."

We look at other people's lives and believe that if we'd live like them, we'd finally feel the joy. We even train our children to follow our lead as we pile into the family car and spend Sundays driving around, looking at other people's homes longingly. "Wow, did you see that one? Imagine living there!" We keep our eyes on everything but our very own blessings. We never seem to be content with what we have, assuming instead that we'd be happy if only our circumstances would be different.

Listen carefully as children mimic our example. "I promise, if you just get me that toy/iPhone/Wii just like my friends have, I'll never ask you for another thing. I'll be so happy."

When we spend our days chasing false dreams of happiness and thinking that each "quick fix" of pleasure will be the ultimate answer, we end up losing sight of our potential to experience daily joy. We forfeit the joy of family life.

We dream about tomorrow, never realizing that blissfulness can be found today—right on our very doorsteps.

Parenthood holds countless opportunities for day-to-day moments of joy. Beyond the miraculous wonder of infanthood, raising children can help you savor the delicious celebration called "life." Seeing the world through the eyes of your children helps you rediscover the magic of being.

Unfortunately, I have heard countless parents complain and whine about the burden that parenting brings into their lives. Raising children is taxing and demanding, cutting in, too often, on "my time." Simply put, parenting is seen as a restrictive, loaded obligation (sigh), minus the joy.

In fact, I've found that there are blogs dedicated to forums for griping moms to vent their anger and resentment. They describe their boredom, lack of pleasure, ambivalence, and self-pity.

One mother writes: "I truly don't foresee my marriage surviving children . . . the rage I feel is unreal." Another writes, "I have a cushy life with a housekeeper. . . . Still I'm so bored and my life is very lonely. I eat and go on the computer all the time. My husband works all the time, too."

On the road to living a joyful family life, how is it that we've taken a convoluted detour and lost our way? Why are so many people unhappy or blasé about their existence? Where did we go wrong?

"THE PURSUIT OF HAPPINESS"

Our Declaration of Independence boldly tells us that each individual has the "right to life, liberty, and the pursuit of happiness." We are raised to believe that we are entitled to life, entitled to liberty, and just as important, entitled to our pursuit of happiness. The three are of equal significance. And so, nothing can come between me and my happiness because it is, after all, my right. Happiness is my privilege, no matter the cost, no matter who gets hurt.

In stark contrast, Judaism teaches us that it is a mitzvah to be *b'simcha,* to be happy. As a mitzvah, happiness is not my right, but rather it becomes my obligation. Commandments require great effort and deep commitment—independent of my moods and emotions.

Knowing that my joy is my responsibility brings me to the realization that I am not *due* a life of happiness. No one owes me a life filled with pleasure. Not my parents, not my mother-in-law, not my husband, not my wife, not my children, my boss nor my friends—nobody in this world is charged with bringing me happiness but me. Ultimately, finding joy requires my own constant efforts. *I* am held accountable for my own happiness. *I* must answer for my life. *I* am forced to confront my continuous whining and lackluster attitude toward life. *I* am responsible. Period.

Fun Versus Joy

Another mistake we make in our quest for happiness is that we often confuse "fun" with "joy." Many of us have experienced pleasure but not real happiness. After the fun is gone we remain feeling void and empty. We set out and search for yet another new thrill, thinking that this will be the magic solution.

The Torah is written in *lashon hakodesh,* literally meaning the holy tongue, G-d's language. Incredibly, in the entire Torah the word *fun* is never found. The Torah speaks about joy, gladness, and happiness but never mentions fun because fun is fleeting. Joy, on the other hand, transcends the moment. Joy lives on. Going out one evening and seeing a Broadway musical hit is fun. Watching your baby take his very first step is joy. It is important for us to distinguish the difference. Once we comprehend the definition of real happiness and decide to set new standards for ourselves, then we can help our children obtain *simchas hachaim,* joy for life.

The Key to Finding Joy

In our Sabbath prayers, we say, *"Yismach Moshe . . ."* Moses rejoiced in the gift of his portion. What is it that brought joy to Moses? What exactly was his portion?

Moses transmitted the Torah to the Jewish nation. He taught us about the beauty and intricacies of Shabbos. The happiness that Moses felt is forever linked to the fact that he had a vital role in life. He clearly understood that he had a mission—to be the teacher and leader of the Jewish people. He was the messenger who helped kindle the light of Shabbos in the world. This sense of purpose brought him true *simchas hachaim,* true joy for living.

The Torah teaches us that happiness is not an end unto itself but, rather, a by-product of a meaningful life. When one lives life without any sense of purpose, life becomes dull. If one lacks a sense of accomplishment, days become tedious and boring. It becomes easy to feel monotonous and weary.

Our mission as parents must encompass more than just shopping for our kids, scheduling trips, and carpooling. If we wake up each morning with an understanding that our role as parents is essential to our child's body and soul, then our sense of purpose becomes renewed each day. Every interaction, every conversation, every exclamation is a teaching medium as we develop our child's inner essence. Creating a life and molding a soul can never be thought of as taxing and boring. It is, instead, the most wondrous mission one can accomplish!

· · ·

My mother would often tell me about a cousin who was on the quiet side. After many years of being childless, he was blessed with a baby. Suddenly, his personality began to take on a huge transformation. Every time he ate, he would enthusiastically say a blessing in a loud voice. "Why the change?" people would ask. "Ah," he would exclaim, "now the walls have ears. I have a child who is always listening." He was exuberant in his newfound mission.

When we come to the realization that we are living a legacy, our entire sense of being takes on a new dimension. We become cognizant of the fact that we have a vision to impart. As our revitalization takes place, we understand that it would be impossible to withdraw from our mission. This sense of purpose allows us to experience the kind of inner joy that sustains us through the various seasons of life.

My father was extremely close to my children. When my kids would hear his familiar knock at the door, they would drop whatever they were doing and run into his arms. His ebullient laughter would mingle with theirs. They would sit on the floor together, playing puzzles and building blocks. My toddler would climb onto my father's torso, as he'd read stories to the older children. One couldn't help but be touched by the incredible warmth and love in the room.

As my eldest son grew older, my father played a new role in our lives. He became my son's Rebbie, or Torah teacher. They would immerse in reviewing Torah studies together, connecting on a deeper level.

The day that I found out about my father's awful diagnosis, I had been teaching in the city. My father had no cell phone and he wasn't answering his home phone. Besides feeling extremely sad, I began to feel very anxious and worried. Where could my father be for all these hours? Why wasn't he responding? How is he dealing with the news of his illness? My mind began to race as I imagined the fear in my father's heart. Where could he be?

As I pulled up to my driveway all my questions were resolved. The light in my dining room was burning brightly. Seated at my table, I saw the shadow of a small boy with a large figure bent over him. I ran into my house and there sat my son, Moshe Nosson, with his *zaydah* beside him. My father and my son were studying Torah together. My father's face was serene as he concentrated on my son's every word.

His warm eyes held my son's gaze. It was as if this whole nightmare had just been a made-up dream. Had I imagined it all?

My father stood up to leave and we embraced.

"Abba," I said, hesitatingly. "I was so scared. I couldn't find you anywhere! Are you all right?"

My father's face lit up with his wide smile. "This is the best place in the world," he replied. "Learning Torah with Moshe Nosson brought me such *nachas*. Your *kinderlach* gave me incredible happiness tonight. There is no place I'd rather be than here. Don't be afraid, my *shayfelah*."

We hugged one more time as I accompanied my father to the door. As he walked down the driveway I took in his every movement. I didn't know what the future would hold for us. I had no idea of the difficult good-bye that was awaiting us, down the road. But I did learn a very powerful lesson that evening.

My father had a choice. He had received a terribly painful call from his physician. My father could have locked himself in a dark room and shouted for hours, "Why me?" He could have asked for some tranquilizers to drown out the pain. No one would really blame him. Instead he chose to seize the remaining opportunities of joy in his life. He transformed that dark night into a cherished memory of light.

My father understood his mission and refused to allow despair to bring him down. This sense of purpose remained with him throughout his entire illness. Each visitor left feeling more strengthened than when he had entered. My father's joy resonated even in a dismal hospital room because no matter how difficult the day, he was a constant source of giving. It was he who extended comfort to those who sought to bring him solace. It was he who provided courage to those whose hearts were breaking. Until his very last breath he continued to fulfill his lifetime mission.

Our sense of joy rests upon our ability to live a purposeful life. Beyond seeking the latest thrills and pleasures, looking past an "if only" existence, parenthood brings us to the highest and loftiest mission of all. The bequeathing of a legacy. As we mold our child's soul we transcend the dull and mundane. Discover your children's spirit. Permeate their days, their very essence, with character and vision. Discover joy.

PRACTICAL PARENTING: TEACHING OUR CHILDREN JOY

We're going through a hard time with our son, Charlie. He's being constantly bullied by other kids. We're working on solutions using different ideas that you've spoken about in class. . . . So far so good. We feel as if we're handling it okay. We are trying to understand something—why are these kids so mean? What's going on? Can we schedule a phone appointment with you?

I received that e-mail from Karen and Alex, a couple who had attended my parenting workshops over the summer. Charlie, a third grader, was overweight and shy. The children in his class chased him around the playground. They called him "contaminated" and excluded him from their games. The bus ride home was torture. Older children tossed Charlie's backpack from seat to seat. Kids refused to sit next to him. He had come home feeling dejected and sad. Charlie's parents were working hard trying to help him maintain his spirit. That night we spoke.

"I know these kids," Karen said. "I know their parents. Most of them come from good homes. I've seen these kids in the local shops. They're arrogant and loud. They never say thank you. They're rude to people around them. I don't understand. Why are they like this?"

"Charlie's not the only one they bully," added Alex. "They even bully their parents. Nothing's ever good enough for them. They never seem happy. What's with them?"

Karen and Alex did not have to explain further. I knew exactly what they meant.

Angry kids. Arms folded, contempt written all over their faces, they exude insolence. They seem restless. Aimless. Children who should be incredibly happy, who have so much going for them, and yet they walk around with a chip on their shoulders.

Parents learn to live with their angry sarcasm and one-word answers like "whatever."

Karen and Alex asked a question worth pondering: Why the anger? Why the need to bully? Their child was suffering, being excluded and hurt by kids who supposedly had everything. Shouldn't these kids feel happy and fulfilled? Doesn't contentedness bring forth kindness and joy? Why did they seem so miserably angry? What were these kids lacking?

I once had this very same discussion with my mother. I had observed some children display extreme meanness and I was perplexed.

"What's their problem?" I asked. "You'd think these kids would be the nicest, happiest kids around. What's missing here?"

"Think about it," my mother replied. "In order to feel happy, a person needs to feel fulfilled. It's written so beautifully in *Ethics of the Fathers*: 'Who is wealthy? He who is happy with his *chelek,* his share' . . . meaning his role. You could have everything in life but if you think that you have no purpose, you feel as if you're worthless.

"Let me ask you, what role do today's kids have? Which child feels that he contributes a vital share to his family, to his world? Parents today raise kids to take, to expect more and more from everyone around them. We are raising a generation of takers, and takers can never feel successful.

"If I never give, I am not productive. I have no real function. I don't know why I'm needed here, what my purpose is. I become selfish and unhappy. The more I take the more dependent I become on others and the less content I am with myself. I grow miserable and knock others down to feel good."

"That's so true!" I thought to myself. Now I clearly understood the problem.

These kids are unhappy with themselves because they lack a life that speaks of purpose and meaning. They are constantly catered to and coddled. They consume. They demand. They belittle. They expect. They do everything but contribute. As they grow, they become self-centered and selfish, caring little for those who seem vulnerable or weak.

Of course, they're angry and miserable inside. Without a meaningful role they've become unhappy. We furnish them with everything but purpose. These children lack vision and feel inadequate. They are spiritually deficient. So why are we surprised to find a generation plagued with boredom, selfishness, and unhappiness?

The Road to Happiness

Throughout this book you will find that I will often stress the importance of raising children with a "sense of mission." Children who believe that they have a "role in life" feel purposeful. They know that they are essential to their families and to their world. They feel vital. Their days have meaning and direction. Feeling valued, they come to feel cherished and loved.

Happiness, self-esteem, compassion, and self-respect are all bound to this concept of "mission." Children are transformed from takers into givers. Instead of demanding consumers, they grow to become more sensitive contributors.

Let us never underestimate the power of our children's potential and their innate ability to give. Let us not make the mistake of allowing our children to sit around and grow self-absorbed as we cater to their every whim. We worry about their happiness but not about their soul. The key to true happiness is discovering a sense of mission and purpose. Fullfillment is achieved with the nourishment of one's soul.

The Joy of Purpose

Now that we've established the link between "happiness" and "purpose," what can we do in our daily lives to help our children discover their role? How can they gain an understanding of "my mission"?

I have found that there are many little moments that we overlook that offer our children greater opportunities to feel purposeful.

For example, when my husband returns from an overseas business trip, my younger children plaster the door with colorful welcome home signs. Whenever we have guests, all the children are involved in the many preparations. The resulting smiles and appreciation teach them that they make a difference in our lives. They've become more sensitive to others with their ability to warmly welcome people (and family) into our home.

Shabbos brings a wealth of opportunity for children to contribute as they discover their role. Each child brings an individual ingredient that completes the day. Even the youngest toddler can help bake a cake, set the table, or prepare a favorite dish. As children grow they can contribute *divrei Torah,* the Torah wisdom, that they've learned and elevate table discussions. Beautiful voices add pleasure and harmony.

Ask yourself, What can my child's mission be? Watch your children's joy as others savor the fruit of their labor.

The Joy of Kindness

I know a child who, after each heavy snowfall, rises early the next morning. He gladly shovels the walkway of an elderly neighbor. His parents never asked him to perform this act of kindness. It was his own idea.

What's most amazing to observe is this child's great sense of accomplishment when he returns home. He may be exhausted, fingers frozen, cheeks scarlet-red from the cold, but you should see his ear-to-ear grin!

• • •

I was asked to speak to a room full of educators about "raising children with soul." At the end of the evening, a woman approached me, visibly moved.

"The session before yours we were asked to recall our happiest spiritual memory. I don't know why, I haven't thought about this for years, but an image popped into my mind. I remembered being a little girl and helping set up chairs for the High Holiday services in my synagogue. After you spoke I realized that my happiest memory was one of giving and helping. . . . And that memory took place in your parents' synagogue! Then it hit me—my kids will never have such memories. When was the last time my kids ever really extended themselves and felt the joy of giving?"

• • •

After my father passed away, my mother moved down the block from us. It was an emotional move that came after more than thirty years of living in the same home and community. The first Shabbos, and every Shabbos that followed, we had the privilege of having my mother's presence grace our Shabbos meals. As the day came to a close, my husband performed Havdalah, the traditional ceremony bidding farewell to the Shabbos. The sky was black and inside the Havdalah flame glowed. My son, Moshe Nosson, who was just thirteen at the time, took me aside to ask a question.

"Mommy, who is making Havdalah for Bubba?"

I was embarrassed to realize that I had not been as sensitive as my son.

"Moshe Nosson," I exclaimed. "I am so impressed with your thoughtfulness. You are the one who will be honored with the mitzvah of saying Havdalah for Bubba!"

A huge grin appeared on his face. On that night, when Shabbos was over, a tradition was established. Each week, my son would walk to my mother's house and proudly sing Havdalah for her. I observed that with his return home came a fresh sense of purpose. He had a mission. He had made a huge difference in his *bubba*'s life. We counted on him and he was thrilled with his new responsibility. He most definitely had created a treasured *chelek* for himself.

When Moshe Nosson went off to study in Israel, his younger brother assumed his role. That first week that my older son was overseas, his younger brother, Akiva Chaim, happily recited the Havdalah prayer for Bubba.

How much more do our children gain when they become givers rather than takers! Acts of kindness provide our children with a feeling of fulfillment and newfound joy.

The Joy of Appreciation

Many of life's happy moments are missed simply because we've become jaded. We take our blessings for granted. Who ever asks, "Hey, why is everything going so well for me?"

It is only when you are sitting in a doctor's office, feeling miserable, that you come to genuinely appreciate good health. It is only after weeks of frigid, gray rain that you begin to relish the warmth of the sun and the clear blue skies above.

Take a moment each day and appreciate your blessings. Learn to value your world. Delight in your family. Savor the universe around you. You will find yourself filled with a joy for life. Open up your children's eyes and instill in them, too, the ability to celebrate their world. Let's teach our children to appreciate what they have instead of focusing on what they are missing.

One night, as I was putting my nine-year-old daughter, Aliza, to bed, I noticed her whispering quietly. "What are you saying?" I asked.

"Oh, I'm just saying my thank-yous."

"What do you mean?"

She smiled. "I say thank You, Hashem, for my family . . . for letting me see and hear, for my food and for my clothing . . . for my friends . . . for helping make my body work okay and for all the little babies that I love so much."

Some of you reading this may be thinking to yourselves, Come on, is it really possible for today's kids to speak like this? In fact, parents who attend my classes for the very first time have asked themselves the same question.

Is this really doable with my children? they wonder. Could my child ever be taught to see the world through grateful eyes? Can my child's mind ever be opened to the joy that gratitude brings?

A mom who has studied with me for more than a decade, from the time her children were born, recently shared her *nachas* with me. I have watched her spirited enthusiasm as she has taken our classes to heart. This mom has tried to instill in her kids an ability to appreciate life's blessings, the moments that often go overlooked. These are her children's words, conveyed to me by e-mail:

> "Waiting for a taxi in the pouring rain . . . thank You, G-d, for getting us a taxi."
>
> "Thank You, G-d, for this parking space."
>
> "Thank You, G-d, for kosher marshmallows so that we can still have s'mores."
>
> And I say thank You, G-d, for the way my kids think!

Yes, your kids can speak this way. Right now it may seem unrealistic, but I am here to tell you that it's not. It is all a question of when, how, and if you communicate joy to your children; whether you yourself appreciate your world and then transmit this appreciation to your children.

Children can comprehend gratitude and joy only if we begin to teach them. Teach your children to say thank you before they go to sleep for anything and everything that brings them joy. Express yourself out loud throughout the day so that your kids hear your grateful appreciation—not just for the "big stuff" but even the little things that we take for granted.

Begin to relish, really relish, your world and the gift of life that lies within it. This is where our education of appreciation begins.

We have the ability to help ourselves become happier individuals. Instead of dwelling on emotions of envy, resentment, and anger, we can fill our minds with a positive attitude toward life. As we contemplate all that we have to be grateful for, we develop *menuchas hanefesh*, inner serenity, which is the deepest level of happiness. Setting children on this path is one of your greatest parenting gifts.

Tasting Joy

After graduating high school, my daughter Shaindy spent a year of study in Israel. Although she had a rigorous academic workload, she made time to volunteer on a weekly basis at a Jerusalem orphanage for girls.

One afternoon, Shaindy called me with breathless excitement. "Mommy, you must hear this and please tell the story to Eli and Aliza [her younger siblings]. I took some of the girls out of the orphanage for a treat today. I decided to take them to an ice-cream shop. As we entered the store the girls looked around. Their eyes widened and I couldn't believe what I saw. They began to dance in delight. They laughed out loud and shouted in Hebrew, 'Vanilla, chocolate, strawberry, cookies in cream! What a life! So many flavors, who ever imagined?' You can't imagine the joy, Mommy, just over ice-cream flavors!"

How often do we take our children for ice cream yet never relish the moment? We watch the clock and think about all the errands awaiting us.

How often do our children taste joy? They'll argue over sprinkles, drippy cones, or who has the better flavor. The afternoon becomes soured and we just want to take them home.

Renew your sense of wonder for life. Live with enthusiasm. Breathe in the giggles, breathe in the flurry of activities, and even breathe in the ice cream flavors! Let us resolve not to allow life's blessings to pass us by.

Discover the joy of purpose. Encourage the joy of kindness. Open children's eyes to the joy of appreciation. Think about how much happier we will all be. Think about the joy.

Strategies for Teaching Joy

Smile!

"Shammai says receive every person with a cheerful face" (Ethics 1:15). Can you recall the very first time your baby smiled? Remember the joy?

Think about how great you've felt when meeting someone who's given you a warm hello accompanied with a wonderful smile. Think about the power of a smile.

It sounds so basic, but unfortunately, so many find it difficult to smile. Did you ever walk into a room feeling positive and upbeat only to spend time with someone in a sour mood? Their unhappiness is often contagious and makes you feel down.

Combat moodiness and sadness with a simple smile—even if you don't feel like it. (Of course, I am not speaking about conditions that require medical intervention.) Your smile can radiate enormous joy in a room. You set the tone in your home. When your child returns after a long day in school, greet him or her with a smile. True, you may have had a rough day, your mind may be occupied with various problems. But when you give your children a smile you are showing them that you are happy to be with them. This knowledge fills a child with joy.

Train your children to say hello and address people, even parents and grandparents, with a smile. My *zaydah* would often say in Yiddish, "Give a smile my child, *cost nisht kein gelt*"—it doesn't even cost anything!

Just a simple smile and easy laughter can turn a spiritless home into a truly happy one. We cannot possibly feel happy if we walk around looking blue. You can easily brighten the world that you live in. In fact, we are taught that your face is the one feature that you cannot see. Your face belongs to others.

The latest PlayStation or greatest doll collection does not make a happy home. Build a haven of joy where each person feels loved. Show your children that you cherish time spent with them.

Create Happy Memories

Whenever I teach parents about creating joy, I begin with a simple request. "Take a moment," I say, "and think about your happiest childhood memory." As each participant shares their thoughts, we arrive at an amazing conclusion.

Not one memory is about a specific toy or gift. Every recollection involves a unique time or treasured moments spent with loved ones.

Ours has become the "drop-off generation." We drop our children off to various activities we believe will make them happy. Physical sports, art and culture are important, however, we must balance after-school activities with cherished family memories. Children feel happy when they know that their parents value family time. There is a great difference between keeping children busy and parenting.

Identify your children's loves. I recall spending one evening exploring different colors with my toddler. She had just discovered the world of the giant Crayola box. Each crayon brought new life to her drawings. It may not seem exciting to a parent, but to a child it is most thrilling.

Snuggle up with a good book together, look through family albums, paint a canvas, toss a football, talk to your child about his dreams—you can't imagine the impact that these memories will have for the future. My siblings and I recall our childhood with extraordinary love and laughter. No, we did not live an extravagant lifestyle. We did not possess expensive toys, designer clothing, or take exotic vacations. We had much more than all that. Our parents provided us with a treasure chest of priceless memories that we savor still today.

Don't Lose Your Sense of Humor

You already know that not every day will be your best. There will certainly be days that you're ready to "pull your hair out." The baby wakes up with a fever, the car won't start, and your six-year-old spilled a carton of milk all over the kitchen floor. If you face those exasperating days with a sense of humor, you can turn the situation completely around. Laughter will help you cope.

I vividly recall the day my younger brother and I both woke up with the chicken pox. We looked in the mirror and saw those awful red dots covering our faces. I still remember feeling miserable. We were itchy and bored. Instead of losing it, my mother brought us pink calamine lotion and told us that we could "paint ourselves." Soon the laughter began. My mother turned the situation around and we ended up having loads of fun.

Try and find some humor when your days bring frustration and stress. Don't allow negative circumstances to conquer your spirit. Never lose your ability to laugh. Your children will follow your lead and you will all find yourselves in a happier home.

Appreciation Between Couples Brings Joy Home

Life is filled with daily stress. There are carpools to drive, mountains of bills to pay, and family situations to deal with. We often lose our serenity. We feel overloaded and exhausted. When we also feel unappreciated, there are times when we are ready to explode.

I have met with countless couples who vent their unhappiness. As they speak, feelings of being underappreciated rise to the surface.

"I would do anything for him/her, but at least let me feel that I'm not taken for granted."

Spouses who express gratitude to each other parent with greater joy. Responsibilities and pressures don't seem as daunting if we feel that our efforts are valued. Even the slightest task becomes a heavy load when a spouse is belittled with disdain and scorn. Take time to say thank you. Appreciate each other's efforts. Bring joy home.

The Happiness Trap

As parents, we try hard to create happy families. We seek out the best schools, the most exciting trips, and the latest toys and gadgets for our children. When we hear our children cry or express disappointment despite all our best efforts, we somehow feel as if we've let them down.

We interpret their reactions to mean our own personal failure.

Nancy and Eric were involved parents who wanted to give their kids a vacation they'd remember. After much planning, they decided to spend a week in Florida, at various family theme parks.

Each day's activities were thought out, travel books were pored over, and they left with great enthusiasm.

The week they returned from vacation, I saw Nancy and Eric at couples class.

"How was your exciting week?" I asked.

"Not that great," Eric replied.

"What happened?" I asked.

"I don't really know," Eric said. "But it seemed as if every night ended with one of the kids crying. We didn't really have one good day and I think this might've been our worst family trip. We thought we were being the best parents, taking our kids on this dream vacation, but I have to say, I don't feel like a very good parent right now."

"You know," Nancy added, "we tried so hard to make it special. We got all those souvenirs that kids love, each kid got to choose a first ride for the day, we saw these incredible parades and fireworks, but somehow it was never enough. They didn't want to leave the parks at night so we stayed out way too late. Then, the kids wanted to go on the water rides, even though we thought it was too cold, so they had these huge tantrums . . . and then they kept finding more stuff to buy. I thought this would be our best trip ever. I don't know where we went wrong."

Imagine. Parents plan this amazing family vacation but end up feeling miserable. They try to make their children happy, fulfilling their hearts' desires, but instead of thank-yous, they are met with tantrums and tears.

Nancy and Eric believed that if they'd just buy one more toy, experience one more ride, stay out just a little bit later then at last their kids would be happy.

How often do we take our kids to a game or excitedly plan an afternoon at the circus only to find ourselves left with a terrible headache, feeling miserable? No sooner do we settle in our seats then it begins—I'm thirsty. I want my own Coke. I'm hungry. Let's get some candy and popcorn. Can I have those flashlights they're selling? Can we buy a cap? What about those T-shirts, they look really cute? Look, that guy's selling ice cream bars!

And we think that if we buy it for them, they'll be thrilled and we will feel successful, surrounded by happy children. But they are never satisfied and never thrilled beyond the moment, because there is always one more thing to buy. We believe that if we say no and our kids erupt in tears or show us their disappointed faces, then we've ruined our time together. We mistakenly equate the level of our children's happiness with our capabilities as a parent.

We cannot live in fear of our children's unhappiness. Too often, we knowingly capitulate because we dread our children's reactions. Parents must choose between giving in or standing firm. When a child erupts in tantrums from a perceived lacking in life, that child knows that he can make a parent feel miserable. The child fully comprehends that it is not difficult to cause a parent to feel unsure and unsuccessful. Parents spend a lot of time questioning their decisions, contemplating if they were right or wrong.

Our mistake lies in the fact that we interpret our child's unhappiness as a shortcoming in our parenting skills. We question how it is possible that our child is unhappy if our job as parents is to provide for our child's happiness. We often make the misguided assumption that the child's tantrums are indicative that we have somehow failed them. After all, if we were successful parents, then our child would not be unhappy. This distorted logic is a gross error in judgment.

TOOLS FOR HAPPINESS

We are not responsible for providing children with constant happiness. That's not our job. However, it is within our power to provide the skills necessary to deal with life's ups and downs. It is easy for a child to be happy when he receives the toy of his dreams, but how much more difficult it is to deal with the fact that sometimes he will hear the word no. Disappointments and frustrations will come his way. As parents, it is our obligation to teach our children to accept life's seeming casualties with grace and composure.

If we are able to do this, then we have bestowed upon our children a gift greater than any doll or PlayStation. This is the true measure of success in parenthood. After all, there is no human being who can experience life without encountering disappointment and loss. Ask yourself: Can I teach my child to handle these moments? Will my child maintain his or her inner balance and not "lose it"? Am I able to bequeath to my child the fortitude to overcome sadness and disappointment?

During one parenting class on this topic, a mother asked a very pointed question. "My daughter is the girl that you just described. She's the one lying on the floor, kicking, screaming, and throwing a major tantrum. What do I do? How can I teach her to cope?"

"Even in the Torah," I replied, "our greatest role models had extremely difficult lives. They faced countless disappointments. Our matriarchs, Sarah, Rebecca, and Rachel, could not conceive for a very long time. Abraham was tested intensely by G-d and faced a multitude of arduous challenges. Moses dreamed about the Land of Israel, begged to set foot on its earth but was denied entry. King David, the sweet singer of Israel, had a lifelong vision of building the First Temple in Jerusalem. The honor was given to his son Solomon instead. Throughout all these disappointments, each of these personalities remained steadfast in their faith and love of G-d. Denial is not tantamount to failure or lack of love. In life, we've all learned that sometimes the answer is no. We don't get everything that we desire, and yet, we still know that we are loved."

"And if she still screams?" asked the mother.

"So, she screams," I replied. "Nothing will happen. She won't melt. But if you give in to her screams she certainly will never learn to deal with disappointments. Yes, you can and should display empathy. Equally important, though, is her understanding that the word *no* is not the end of the world. You don't always get what you want in life. And you know what? That's okay. Life goes on.

"If we can teach our children that they are able to deal with the "no" moments, they will feel empowered and successful. They will become confident in the fact that they can make it in life. Isn't that an awesome gift to give to your child?"

It is important that we parents not confuse disappointment with failure. Tantrums and tears can be turned into moments of opportunity to teach crucial life lessons. We can help guide our children to gather inner strength and confront life's challenges. Little disappointments prepare us for the bigger disappointments that unfortunately come our way. Help your child navigate and eventually he will captain his own ship. He need not fear rough waters for the lessons that his parents taught will remain with him for life.

Not long ago, I bumped into a bunkmate from my years in camp. Throughout our summers together, Lea was known for her smiling eyes and sunny disposition. After her marriage, she moved to the West Coast.

Lea suggested that we catch up over a cup of coffee in a local café. As we sat together, the conversation drifted to our families. I was thrilled to hear that she had become a grandmother.

"Let me tell you about my grandson's birth," she began. "I had recently taken a course to become a doula. My daughter-in-law called to inform me that labor had begun. Being that I was now a doula, my children asked me to join them in the birth of my grandchild.

"Of course I was thrilled. What an honor, to witness the birth of my first grandchild! The labor was long but uneventful. I watched as the doctor readied himself for the birth. You can't imagine the excitement. We knew that any moment now, this baby was to make a grand entrance. Finally, we heard that sweet newborn cry. How I was filled with exhilaration! 'It's a boy!' the doctor shouted. The nurses grabbed the baby and began to clean him off. I was elated.

"My son walked over as they huddled over the baby. The nurses started to speak in hushed tones with the doctor. I began to suspect that something was not right. My son then approached my daughter-in-law as I held her hand. He bent down close to her face and softly said, 'Deena, they think our baby has Down's.' I gasped for air. My daughter-in-law gave out a horrific scream.

"'I can't do this,' she cried. 'I can't go on.' She began to sob.

"I was trembling inside, myself. In one moment our entire world had turned upside down."

I looked at Lea. Our conversation had ceased. I didn't know what to say. Lea continued, "Let me tell you about my beautiful son. I've never experienced such *nachas* as I felt that day. My son began to speak. 'Deena,' he whispered, 'I know you're shocked. I'm shocked, too. But if we were chosen to bring this special child into the world, that means that we've been handpicked by G-d, Himself. Not many are trusted with this awesome task. You are going to be the most incredible mother, I know it, and I'm going to be there, right next to you, helping you. This baby will bring us *nachas*. This baby will bring us happiness and we're going to be a beautiful family together.'

"Deena's sobs melted into a soft whimper. They looked at each other with incredible love.

"'Okay,' she replied. 'We're going to make it. We will love our baby and find the strength to get through this.'"

Lea's black eyes were shining as they welled up with tears. But they were tears of pride, tears of joy, not tears of sorrow.

"I called my teenage daughter, Deborah, who was waiting at home for the news. When I told her what had happened, she refused to come to the hospital.

"'Now listen to me,' I said. 'Your brother just became a father. This is your nephew, and not only is he ours, but he is beautiful and he is a miracle. Come now to the hospital and let's be a family.'

"I waited for my daughter. When the doorway opened, I saw that my daughter's eyes were swollen and red from crying. I opened my arms up wide, kicked each leg side to side, and began to dance down the hallway. 'Mazel tov! Mazel tov! Mazel tov!' I sang with all my might.

"'You must be kidding,' Deborah cried.

"'I'm not kidding one bit,' I answered, as I reached her with my final twirl. I took her arms in mine and held her tightly.

"'This baby is our special baby. He is our most precious gift from Above. We will watch over him, we will take care of him and we will love him.'

"We named the baby Simcha, which means joy. And you know what,

Slovie?" she added. "He is our greatest *simcha*. Today he is three years old. He sings, he loves to dance, and from all of my grandchildren, he is the one that the adults run to first. He holds a special place in all our hearts, and most especially, his aunt Deborah's."

Life brings us surprises in many shapes and forms. Lea nourished her family through her own *simchas hachaim*. Her lifelong attitude helped bolster her children through an inconceivable experience. Pain and difficulties become endurable, even a source of strength. Make *simcha,* true joy, your lifelong companion and you will never be forlorn.

FOUR

Communication

It was a scorching, hot summer day. My children and I decided to find cool relief at a local ice-cream shop. As we were walking down Central Avenue, we came upon a large crowd. There were a few police cars with flashing lights and some EMS trucks parked haphazardly. It was apparent from afar that an eerie silence had enveloped the crowd that had gathered. As we inched closer, we heard a woman sobbing loudly.

"Don't worry, Mommy's here. Mommy's here, sweetie. We're doing the best we can. The nice policemen are going to get you out quickly." Evidently, this distressed mother had inadvertently left her car keys in the ignition and locked her two children in the SUV. Advanced technology prevented old-time techniques from opening the Jeep. Her newborn was sleeping peacefully, but her little toddler was hysterical and very frightened. He was frantically banging on the window and obviously couldn't comprehend the directions being called out to him. His mother placed her palms on top of the glass that separated them. She was crying and trying hard to console her child at the same time.

"Mommy, Mommy, open! Open car, Mommy!" the toddler shrieked. Even outside, one could hear the incessant wails of the trapped toddler. You couldn't help but feel a tug at your heart. Who could not be affected by such little, helpless cries? My youngest held my hand even tighter. "When will they get him out already, Mommy?" she asked. That was the question on everyone's mind. Finally, after what seemed like an eternity, the car was somehow unlocked. The crowd broke out in a big cheer. Kids applauded and whistled. Mother and child were reunited as they gave each other tight hugs and kisses. The group dispersed and went on their way.

As I sat down with my children, the scene replayed in my mind. I saw the little child's tiny fists pounding on the window. I heard his mother's soft cries. It then occurred to me that there are times in life that our children are there, right before our eyes, but somehow we are unable to reach them. It feels as if there is an invisible barrier that comes between us. We call out, we may even cry, but our words fall upon seemingly deaf ears. They look to us for help, yet we are ineffective. They may be immersed in terrible tantrums, intense peer pressure, or sullen adolescence. It doesn't matter. We are physically close yet feel frustratingly distant. How can we break down the barrier? How do we extend our hand and touch our children's inner core?

The answer is communication. When we communicate with our children properly, they learn to trust us even if they may not always understand us. Communication is defined in the dictionary as "the interchange of thoughts or opinions through shared symbols." It is all too often that we speak *at* our children or yell right through them instead of communicating with them. Good communication skills enable us to develop a relationship based on respect and honor. Judaism so beautifully offers us the path toward true communication.

THE SECRETS OF THE SHEMA

One of the holiest prayers in Judaism is called the Shema. The word *shema* means "hear"—not simply listen, but concentrate, understand, and absorb. Prior to the death of our patriarch Jacob, his twelve sons surrounded his bedside and reaffirmed their faith by reciting this prayer.

We can gain incredible communicative insights by analyzing its words.

The First Step Toward Good Communication

We begin the Shema by covering our eyes with our right hand. The reason for this is to establish a degree of *kavanah*, concentration and intention. This prayer holds such a high level of importance that we take measures to avoid any distractions that may arise and interrupt our communication with G-d. *Kavanah* teaches us the best way to reach out and develop a strong relationship with our children.

When we communicate with our children, it is easy to seem distracted. After all, phones ring, infants cry, meals need to be prepared, and the responsibilities of life beckon. Good communication translates into not just using the right words but also invoking the right attitude. Speaking to a child while being engaged in three other things conveys a lack of interest. Just think how you feel at the breakfast table while speaking to your spouse and his or her head is buried in the morning paper. You want to shout, "Hello! Do you even hear me? Are you at all interested in what I'm trying to say to you?"

Children return from school with mountains of information to share. They quickly sense our level and span of attention. If we seem disinterested or listen while texting on our BlackBerry, they'll soon shut down. Engaging our children means "I'm interested in you. I want to listen to you no matter what else is going on around me."

Kavanah is the first step toward building a bridge of communication with our children.

Communicating in Our Homes

The Shema directs us: "Teach your children and speak about values to them." This should be done *beshifticha bevaysecha*, while you sit in your house.

As parents, we must think about some crucial questions: What kind of language and tone do my children hear around the house? How do I communicate with my children at home?

Technology that is supposed to draw us closer may in fact pull us further apart. I spoke to a young wife the other day who told me that she e-mails her husband anything of importance because that's the only way she knows he's really listening to her. What kind of verbal communication do you suppose their children are exposed to? Is anyone listening to each other?

Let us examine our conversation, our language, and our tone. Do our words and tone smack of resentment, ridicule, and sarcasm? Do our kids hear us use inappropriate language, slurs, or profanity? Do we roll our eyes as our spouses speak? I've spoken to husbands and wives who meet their spouse's coworkers and friends. "You have such an incredible wife," they exclaim. "Your husband is a doll. What a great guy to have in our office!" they say cheerfully. If they only knew, confides the spouse. This same "doll" loses his or her temper horribly at home over the slightest thing. This "great guy" can talk to the world but has no idea when it comes to his own kids. Good communication begins in our homes with respectful tones and gentle language.

Communicating the Joy of Parenting

"While you sit in your house" also requires us to question how we communicate our feelings to our children. Do we convey our parenting duties as burdensome responsibilities? You can serve the tastiest gourmet dinner, but if it's given with a sour mood or slammed down on the table with resentment, the food will taste like sawdust. Showing our children that we are happy to be home with them is one of the greatest opportunities that we possess of communicating our love for them.

My son Eli was born on the holy day of Shabbos. Jewish law requires that a bris take place eight days later, which means that his bris would occur on the following Shabbos. I returned from the hospital feeling a little overwhelmed. Besides caring for a newborn and our other children, there was a bris to plan. A Shabbos bris meant that out-of-town guests would need sleeping and meal arrangements since Shabbos law prohibits driving or traveling by public transportation. My husband and I began making phone calls. We informed people of the bris while trying to find accommodations for our many guests. One friend offered me these "encouraging" words: "A Shabbos bris?" she exclaimed. "I had a Shabbos bris for my son. Boy, I don't envy you. Here it is eight years later and I still remember the feeling."

"What was the feeling?" I asked. "I felt as if I got hit by a truck," she replied. We finished our conversation and my eyes began to well up with tears. "How will I ever do this?" I asked myself despondently. The phone rang and it was my brother on the line. My voice must have reflected my emotions.

"What's going on? Why do you sound so down?" he asked. "Is everything okay with the baby?" "Yes, *baruch Hashem,* the baby is fine," I answered. "I just can't believe that I'm making a Shabbos bris. I don't know where to begin. The bris will be in my house—I have to arrange meals, put up all these people, and I feel as if I just can't do it all," I said, totally exasperated.

"Slovie, listen," he began. "You are so lucky. Besides having had a beautiful, healthy baby which is a miracle in itself, you're having a Shabbos bris in your home. We know that Eliyahu HaNavi, Elijah the Prophet, attends every bris. This is a once-in-a-lifetime opportunity. The whole family will be together and join you in this great *simcha*. Not everyone is fortunate enough to host such an awesome occasion. If you complain, you're going to lose out on the special joy of the moment. What kind of a bris will this be with a stressed-out mother who can't appreciate the greatness of it all?"

I knew that my brother had just taught me an incredible truth. I'd be missing out on the joy of this most awesome moment, all because of my mood! As we finished our conversation, I thanked my brother for his wise and encouraging words. The rest of the week flew by and I looked forward to Eli's bris with great anticipation. To this day, Eli's Shabbos bris is one of my most endearing memories. It is painful to think that I almost lost this treasured moment because of my attitude.

How often do we exclude ourselves from potentially special moments because of our stress and anxieties? How many times do we plan family vacations or evenings out only to return home disappointed because a bad day on the market ruined our time together? Even ordinary days at home become great sources of conflict as we snap at each other from tension and moodiness. Life's daily pressures can pull us away from mealtimes, story times, or just plain conversations with our kids. If we can succeed in establishing a home with a peaceful atmosphere then we will have communicated to our children our happiness in being their parents.

Recently, my husband and I attended a wedding. We were asked to give a ride home to two twenty-something special-needs brothers. We descended in the elevator and their exuberance over the night's festivities filled the crowded space. "I love weddings! I'm so happy! I'm so very happy to be here!" the boys excitedly exclaimed over and over again. As we were driving home, one brother asked, "Do you know what my mother always tells me? My mother always says, '*Baruch Hashem* for *simchas.*' Thank G-d for joyous occasions."

"Yes," agreed his brother, nodding fervently. "Our mother is always saying, '*Baruch Hashem* for *simchas.*' We are so lucky to be happy. Mr. and Mrs. Wolff, aren't you so happy and lucky, too?" As they spoke, their beautiful and genuine smiles never left their faces. The brothers' innocent enthusiasm for life was most moving. Their mother's message to her sons was truly awesome.

Think about it. There is no question that this mom has had some extremely difficult moments. Two special-needs children along with a large family require constant care and unlimited patience. Instead of buckling under to life's pressures and questioning her fate, this courageous mother had one sublime directive to her children: Thank G-d for joy!

When we make every effort to communicate joy, love, gratitude, and respect in our homes, our children become inculcated with these time-honored values. Their behavior and conduct manifests itself in what we call *menschlichkeit,* great character, as they exude goodness and enthusiasm for life.

Communicating Standards

The prayer of the Shema continues and asks us to teach these Torah values to our children and speak of them, not only while we reside in our homes, but also, "while you walk on your way," *uvelechtecha vaderech.*

Communication does not begin and end in our homes. The Shema prayer reminds us that while we are immersed in our routine tasks of daily living, our responsibility as parents and communicators are not over. Stepping out of our homes does not mean stepping out of our roles. As parents, we consistently impart paramount messages to our children, irrespective of the location. "As we walk on our way" is symbolic of the values and priorities that we convey as we navigate the many highways of life.

There are many parents who would like to build families imbued with traditional values and character, yet they somehow lose sight of these crucial teachings when they depart from their homes. I read a newspaper interview with camp directors who had set down rules of no cell phones in camp, only to find that parents sent two cell phones, in case the first one was found. What does that teach our kids about truth and "beating the system"?

We speak to our children about the importance of honesty. We lecture them about the awfulness of cheating. Then one day we catch our child in a lie. We are naturally concerned. "What will become of him if he already lies at such a young age?" we wonder. "What sort of person will this child grow up to be?" Perhaps we even need to consider therapy.

The moment passes. We forget. We decide to take a long-awaited family vacation. The kids are brimming with excitement and anticipation. As we enter the amusement park, we notice a sign at the entranceway. "Children ages seven and under are admitted at a discount." We take our little one to the side and whisper in his ear, "Listen, if anyone asks, today you are seven."

"But, Daddy, I'm eight," he insists innocently.

"Shhh . . . just listen to what Daddy says," Mommy adds sternly. "Today you are seven."

Our child stands there bewildered and confused at the mixed message he is receiving. All the grandiose lectures, all the solemn speeches extolling the virtues of truth, honesty, and integrity have just evaporated before our eyes. Our children smell hypocrisy a mile away. We spend exorbitant amounts of money to send our children to the finest private schools. We afford our children afternoon tutors and specialized classes. Then they encounter our dishonesty and we are forced to ask ourselves, What's the point of it all?

Life is the greatest classroom and we are our children's greatest teachers. If life's greatest lessons cannot be inculcated successfully by us, then whom can we assign blame to? Our words will cultivate character up to a point, but there comes that moment in time when a child perceives our actions. If we don't take our words seriously, then why should they?

If children observe parents bringing home supplies from their offices that "no one realizes are missing anyway," or a mom who opens snacks in the supermarket but "somehow" neglects to pay for them, then the following is the logical conclusion—our children's vision of what honesty really means becomes cloudy. Children watch and absorb through an osmosis-like process all that we say and do throughout our day. How often do your children notice their parents running into an old acquaintance on the street, greeting each other with feigned enthusiasm?

"I can't believe it! Is that really you after all these years? You look fabulous! We must do lunch and catch up! I'll call you as soon as I get home!" As we walk away, our child questions us. "Who was that, Mommy? Are you really going to get together? Is that your friend?"

"Nah." We wave our hands dismissively. "I just said all that. We'll never really get together. I don't even like her!"

We have attempted to plant the seeds, but have neglected to cultivate the tender shoots. Our distorted actions are like weeds that smother and choke the young seedling. We strongly desire that our children personify kindness and consideration. We remind them to "say please." We find ourselves prodding them to "say thank you." Again and again we request that they "ask nicely for more macaroni, sweetie."

We truly believe that we are teaching them good manners. We have no doubt that we have instructed them properly as they begin to interact with the world and the people around them. And then comes our ultimate litmus test. One evening, we decide to eat dinner out in a restaurant. Once we are seated, each of us studies the menu. Finally, we are ready to place our order.

The waiter listens patiently. Dad would like his meat rare, with an additional side dish added to his plate. Mom requests no oils or additives. Our son needs his steak tender without any of the sauce touching his portion. We wait expectantly for our meals. Finally, the server arrives. As it turns out, most of the orders are completely wrong. "You call yourself a waiter?" Dad sputters angrily. "Can't you even take a simple order without messing up? No wonder you can't get a decent job!"

Our son's ears perk up. He and his siblings are processing every word, every nuance, and every gesture of this encounter. So what that we've labored for years speaking about the proper way of treating others? So much for all the discussions and conversations. At this juncture, all of our lessons are inconsequential. Repeating them is futile as they now begin to fall on deaf ears. When it comes down to it, we have set a dismal example for our children.

How can we possibly influence our children to become all that we hope for if we ourselves fall short? If we deviate from our own course, our kids are left with no choice other than to attach themselves to our misguided route. Why do so many parents scratch their heads in bewilderment when their children mimic their sad behavior?

I have listened as parents ask: "But we've spoken about this a million times. I just don't understand how she could do this?" "How could he speak like that?" "How could she have done such a horrible thing?"

It is time to dig out our mirrors and take a good, hard look at ourselves. Raising children to follow in our footsteps requires strong imprints and an illuminated path. It is not adequate to speak about high expectations if we fail to embody the principles that we cherish. Values cannot be shed like an uncomfortable fur coat in the tropical sun. Our values are nonnegotiable, and must not become values of convenience, easily discarded when the going gets rough. Raising considerate children requires parents who are genuinely considerate human beings. Proper communication is equivalent to truth in both words and deeds.

"While you are on your way" implores us to ask ourselves some pointed questions. Do I continue to communicate my values when we are away from home? Do I live a life riddled with double standards—speaking about important character traits, yet neglecting to uphold my standards throughout my day? How do we treat others who may cross our path—the waiter, the cab driver, the doorman, the person in front of us at the supermarket checkout counter, the driver in the car before us who is moving too slow?

At the conclusion of a lecture that I gave on communication, a young mom asked to speak with me privately. Vivacious and animated, she quickly came to the point. "I drive a carpool for my kids and the past few months have been a nightmare. My eleven-year-old daughter has been sullen and she has begun to talk back in front of her friends. Yesterday, though, was my most awful day. It was cold outside and I felt that my daughter was not dressed warmly enough. The entire car ride we were arguing over her wearing a jacket or not. Finally, we arrived at her school. She opened the door and without giving a backward glance said something so awful to me that I am ashamed to repeat it. I felt as if someone had slapped me.

"As I drove home, I kept talking to myself. 'Where did she learn to speak like this? How dare she? Who does she think she is? What happened to my beautiful little girl?' I was seething. After listening to your class today, I've taken a hard look at myself. . . ." She paused for a moment and I noticed her eyes begin to well up with tears. "This is exactly how I speak to anyone and everyone who gets in my way. When I drive my daughter to school, if the driver in front of me is too slow, I'll honk and scream until he's moved from my lane. If my mother annoys me, I'll just shout at her to stop bothering me and to leave me alone. Even my husband and kids are not spared. My daughter's horrible language . . . I have to face facts. She's just mimicking my angry words. Now, I'm the one who's feeling the sting. I've simply got to rethink the way I speak to people. I just hope that it's not too late."

Our daily interactions are an important means of communicating with our children. Communication is not limited to words but also means the manner in which we handle ourselves when dealing with others. Both words and actions can have far-reaching effects on our family.

Communicating Trust

One evening I was preparing a lecture on just this very topic of communication. My teenage daughter walked into the room and asked me what I was doing. I replied that I was gathering my thoughts because I would be speaking to a group of parents about communicating with their children. "What do you think is the most important aspect of communication?" I asked my daughter. I was curious to hear my child's perspective. "Oh," she replied, after thinking about it for a moment. "I would say that the most important part of communication is honesty." "Meaning what?" I questioned. "Well, like how you and Abba never lie to us, even if it's hard for us to accept. We've learned to trust you because you always tell us the truth. You also taught us never to lie to the younger kids in the family, like to say that we'll do something that we know that we'll never do."

We underestimate the importance of talking with our children—not only talking, but listening to them also. I mean having a real conversation, being interested in what they have to say.

Instead of assuming that our kids understand our points of view, it's crucial to sometimes take out the time and hear their thoughts. Tap their minds and hear what they hear, see what they see. This is especially vital as you raise teens who can easily withdraw into a world of their own.

After speaking with my daughter, I was grateful to know that she was able to comprehend the essence of our family's communication. The key here is honesty and my daughter picked up on that. Untruthfulness, deceitfulness, and hypocrisy cannot be concealed from children. An underlying cause of children's becoming alienated from their parents is the classic double standard of saying one thing and doing another, of words not being honored. The effect of a lack of trust in the relationship that we have with our children can be disastrous.

The basis of any good relationship is trust. Without it we have nothing. Children are unable to trust parents who distort and twist the truth. It is impossible to open your heart to someone who does not stand by his or her word.

On Yom Kippur, the holiest day of the year, Jews all over the world gather together and solemnly chant the Kol Nidrei prayer. The synagogue is permeated with a sense of awe. It is through this sacred prayer that we ask G-d not to hold us responsible for any promise, or vow that we have failed to keep over the past year. We beseech forgiveness for our negligence and carelessness. We are taught that our words are most powerful. They can create or destroy and we must be ever vigilant in how we use them. Our expressions mirror our hearts and minds. If our word is not a word, and means nothing, then where does that leave us and how can we endure? We need to know and our children need to know that our word is something we can all rely on.

Undoubtedly, this is no easy task. A child is sick and shrieks wildly when she hears that she must pay a visit to the doctor's office. Many parents lie and tell the child that they are going to the toy store. As they pull up to the physician's parking lot, the child explodes in wild and uncontrolled screaming. "Well, at least I didn't have to listen to this screaming the entire way here," we assure ourselves. Yet, if we think about it, a car ride filled with hysterical crying and yelling pales in insignificance when we compare it to the breach of trust that has occurred between parent and child.

That parent has just taught his or her child that "my word is not to be trusted." The child begins to ask himself, "If my mom or dad is lying to me about this, what else have they lied about? How can I ever know if they're telling me the whole truth?" This can be enormously unsettling for a child who sees his or her parents as a rock of dependability.

Even if our words result in discomfort for our child, we must know in our hearts that we have told the truth. We have been upfront and that is infinitely better than lying. There are hard and difficult realities in this world, and sometimes the truth can be painful, yet by conveying the truth, our children will grow to trust us and appreciate our honesty.

At the very onset of my father's illness my children felt that something was amiss. As young as they were, the worry in our eyes was apparent. When they asked me if something was wrong I gently explained that Abba Zaydah was in the hospital. Of course I did not elaborate on the private details, but I felt that concealing the truth from them would only increase their anxiety. To fabricate a story that a grandparent is on vacation when in reality he is in the hospital is wrong. Though it was agonizingly difficult for them to accept their grandfather's illness, it would have been exceedingly more troubling for my children to realize that we were being dishonest. Children have a sixth sense when it comes to something not being right. While we have to use discretion when deciding how much to reveal to them, the alternative of hiding our worries and mumbling into the phone while they're in the room only compounds their distress.

Kids will not be satisfied when we say, "It's nothing, don't worry about it." The news we convey may be heartbreaking, but the specter of living with a fear of the unknown can be absolutely terrifying for children.

Communicating Respect

The stories of our forefathers in the Torah help us learn how to communicate respect. Understand that we are not merely learning charming little Bible stories. When we study the Torah, we are studying an instruction manual for life. Our lives and values become uplifted as our perspective on life becomes transformed. We discover how to make our relationships more successful and fruitful. We acquire knowledge in order to assist us in becoming better husbands and wives, better parents and children, better human beings.

In the Book of Genesis, Abraham is told to leave all that was familiar to him and travel with his wife, Sarah, to an undisclosed destination. They would be required to terminate all ties with their country of origin and all past relationships. Familiar cultural activities and their native language would soon fade into obsolescence. After living a most comfortable and prosperous life they would now have to begin all over again in a foreign country.

Abraham was seventy-five years old and Sarah was sixty-five. The prospect of picking up and leaving could not have been easy. The fear of the unknown must have been overwhelming. Traveling long distances in the scorching desert sun must surely have been difficult for such an elderly couple. Our sages make a point of teaching us that throughout their travels, Abraham always pitched Sarah's tent first and spoke to her with tremendous respect.

Abraham and Sarah were not newlyweds. Despite tense circumstances and long decades of marriage, Abraham insisted on honoring his elderly wife. We call such a man a *mensch.*

There will be times in life when we are under a tremendous amount of pressure. Despite our stressed-out state, the Torah is instructing us to exhibit honor and to treat one another with respect. We are being taught that our dignity should not fall prey to life's frustrations. As your children accompany you on the journey of life, let's afford them the opportunity to view parents who are compassionate and kind . . . especially to each other. Permit them a front-row seat in the observation of honesty and love. Sprinkle in doses of humor and laughter. Be generous in spirit. Use your words wisely. Realize the wonderful opportunities of communication that lie in your hands "while you are on your way."

Communicating Throughout Our Nights and Days

The Shema prayer serves as our parental compass as it now points us onto a very specific path. If we heed this ancient wisdom, we will find ourselves in a much stronger position as we build relationships with our children and enhance our communication with them.

The Shema prayer articulates to us: "And when you retire in the evening," *uveshachbecha,* "and when you arise in the morning," *uvekumecha.*

These two times of the day are crucial when it comes to raising our children. Both evenings and mornings bring immense opportunities for us to spend time with our families and nurture the closeness that we so desire. Unfortunately, these are also the times of the day that we find ourselves extremely stressed and unable to communicate and connect in the way we would like.

Evening Moments

Let's begin with late afternoon, early evening. Parents have often voiced to me that the hours between 4:00 and 9:00 P.M. tend to be the most difficult.

Infants and toddlers need to be bathed and put to sleep. School-aged children, preteens, and adolescents expect their favorite dinners and undivided attention. Besides homework that needs to be completed, nighttime activities such as hockey league, tennis, orthodontist appointments, and special tutors demand parents' concentration. Let's not forget the kids squabbling, phones ringing, and at least one child who has suddenly remembered that his science project is due and he has no supplies.

Dad comes home, exhausted from his grueling workload. If there was any problem that occurred in the office he is in no mood for anything but some "quiet alone" time. Whether Mom is a stay-at-home mother or a career woman doesn't really matter. She, too, is feeling the weight of her pressurized day. All the more so, for single moms and dads who bear the burden of supporting their families while trying to maintain their homes and provide quality time. Even if one is fortunate enough to have household help, genuinely involved parents know that there can be no replacement for those individual parent-child moments.

While all this whirlwind of activity is taking place, how can we possibly attempt to find time to converse with our spouse and children?

Let's face it. We are fatigued. We are tired and our patience is tried. When we walk through the door and we are bombarded with the immediate needs of our children, our frazzled nerves are on the brink of exploding. Mom tries to talk to Dad as the kids demand their time and often bedlam erupts. Or Dad returns home extremely late each evening and is met with silence. Sadly, he never has the opportunity to see his kids, let alone eat dinner with them and listen to the happenings of their day. Husbands and wives are too exhausted to communicate. Enter what has been described as "the dead zone."

The night passes. Children tenaciously negotiate and renegotiate their bedtime.

"Please, just one more cup of water, I promise."

"But all of my friends have a ten-thirty bedtime. It's just not fair."

"Do I have to take a shower tonight? I took one last night!"

We are at the end of our rope. We finally snap as we scream in anger and frustration: "Just get into bed *now* before you're sorry! And I mean it!" Forget about reconnecting in the evening; at what point do we begin to connect?

If this scenario sounds familiar, the first thing that we must do is address it in no uncertain terms. We are obligated to inquire within ourselves how we may better resolve our "evening madness." Whether it is rescheduling our afternoons so that dinner and homework are completed at a reasonable hour or discussing a spouse's hour of return so that no one feels shortchanged, evenings must be recognized as time for family.

Many men and women today are in careers or vocations that require them to travel extensively. Fathers, and often mothers, carry a mammoth workload that demands their attention until late into the night. Due to outside responsibilities, some women find themselves unable to be home for their children. Many kids return to an empty house almost every day.

The first moments that a child returns home from school are significant. Frequently, we need only to look into a child's eyes to know that an incident occurred during the day that was hurtful. Many children are slow to open up and share their feelings with us. It is only by seeing them that we get a clear picture of their day. If it is at all possible, let us make an effort to be home for our children without rushing in breathless, blaming traffic or numerous errands as the cause of our tardiness. I have spoken with countless children who have solemnly informed me that they have given up hope of ever finding their mothers home in time for their return from school.

I write this not to induce guilt or assign blame, but rather so that we may gain insight into our children's lives. The sour mood, the unexplained sadness, the senseless squabbling with siblings may all be better understood if we were actually there for our children, in both body and mind. If this is not a possibility, due to financial or familial pressures, let us at least recognize our absence at this crucial juncture of the day. Let's be sure to take a moment out of our busy schedules and call home. This call communicates to your children that they are important to you. You convey your wish to connect with them, hear their voices and listen to them as they tell you about their day. We then impart to our children that their return from school does not arrive unnoticed and that our work does not interfere with our concern for them.

Making Time for Family

We live in a fast-paced society. Many parents are being constantly pulled in several different directions. Our culture has introduced the idea of a weekly "family game night" or "quality versus quantity time" to assuage our guilt.

Judaism has addressed this issue in a deeper, more meaningful way. Thousands of years ago, G-d, in His infinite wisdom, commanded us to "remember the Sabbath day to sanctify it" (Exodus 20:8; the Ten Commandments). There is no doubt that we are busy all week. Business pressures, social obligations, and children involved in their own activities divide the family each night. And then, Shabbos arrives. We put on blinders to all the forces that seem to suffocate us. On the Sabbath we forget about the cell phones, BlackBerrys, video games, faxes, and television. We have eyes only for one another. Mommy recites a blessing and kindles a flame for each soul in the home. The message is clear. We convey to our children that "you, my child, are my light. You have the potential within to illuminate the world. Despite the tensions and difficult moments that our week together may have brought, you will forever be my fire, my spirit, my joy. You are my blessing."

Daddy may have been distracted all week. Perhaps he came home short on patience and long on problems. He seemed preoccupied and unable to listen to you properly. Friday night, though, is unlike any other. We sit together, joyously, as a family. Daddy recites Kiddush—the sanctification over the wine. He sings "Shalom Aleichem," a warm welcome to the angels who accompany him home from the synagogue to ensure a peaceful Sabbath. As the glowing candles dance before our eyes, each child stands before us, in age order, anticipating his or her own personal blessing. We place our hands on their heads. To each son we whisper, "May you be like Ephraim and Menashe, the two sons of Joseph. These two brothers never harbored a moment of jealousy toward each other. They have become the symbol of peace and harmony. May you, my son, follow in their footsteps and always look kindly upon your siblings."

We draw our daughters near. We place our hands upon their heads and recite a blessing. "May you be like Sarah, Rebecca, Rachel, and Leah," we whisper. "The matriarchs of Israel faced life with courage, strength, and compassion. You are not simply Jaquelyn, Debbie, or Arianna. You are daughters who continue the legacy of a life filled with purpose and meaning." As we recite our blessings, we have an opportunity to wish our children any hopes or private blessings that lie within our heart.

Our home is filled with love. Can any moment possibly replace this cosmic connection with our children? As we stood at that little mountain called Sinai in our first moments of nationhood we were endowed with the ultimate treasure called Sabbath. This built-in gift of purposeful time together is our weekly guarantee that our families will survive.

After attending a few parenting classes in the city, Alyssa decided to join our couples class with her husband. Together they embarked upon a path of study. A wonderfully sensitive couple to begin with, Torah study solidified their relationship.

Alyssa sent me this note:

> I did not grow up celebrating Shabbos, so I did not know how to create a Shabbos. You created a class especially for me. I took every note I could and hung on to your every word. I was truly given such a gift.

Each Friday night my whole family looks forward to Shabbos dinner. It is the only night we eat as a family; unfortunately my husband works late. It is a time we cherish. We talk and share with one another. Everyone is so happy and together.

Thank you for all the lessons and for our Shabbos. I am so lucky.

The message of Shabbos remains with us all week. We yearn to find time with family and friends, we long for the spiritual tranquility of the day. When you speak to those who have kept Shabbos for years, you will find that they never tire of it. Each week they anticipate the moment of lighting their Shabbos candlesticks once again. Shabbos brings renewal to the soul.

And even those students of mine who have just recently begun to embrace Shabbos, gathering their children round the glow of their Shabbos candles and offering their blessings and prayers, gratefully find a peaceful solace they never knew possible; never knew existed. Shabbos is our ladder as we connect heaven and earth.

We must begin by finding special time together as a family. Coupled with an aura of spirituality, we bequeath to our children a priceless treasure for life. Begin by discovering a starting point, a courageous desire to step onto the first rung of the ladder. You will find these moments to be sources of strength and security as your family grows.

Meaningful time between parents and children are a requirement for families to flourish and become reinvigorated. It is incumbent upon us, as parents, to finally set aside real, permanent moments for our family to come together, to unite and bond under the mantle of true peace and serenity.

Communicating Tranquility

Nighttime can be overwhelming for all of us. As we lie in our beds our fears tend to confine us. Whether we are an adult or a child, we understand the powerful and gripping emotion of fear. Whatever it was that disturbed us during the day remains in our minds as we attempt to fall asleep. Nighttime then becomes the prime time for us to spend intimate moments with our children. We share their fears, relieve their burdens, and enjoy some lighthearted moments from their day.

We often ponder the questions: "How, exactly, can we set aside all the stress and help our children feel that we are there for them? How can we help our children feel safe and loved?"

We are given a special bedtime Shema prayer to recite before we go to sleep. This prayer is a unique gift that was bequeathed to us and one that has been cherished for thousands of years. It is like a soothing balm that covers us after a long and emotional day. Newlyweds are often given this piece of advice: Never go to bed angry with each other. The eternal wisdom of the Torah conveys this priceless piece of advice in a universal sense. No one should ever go to bed with feelings of anger and rage toward others, whether he or she is family, a friend, a coworker, or anyone we happen to encounter during the day. In a place where anger resides, there can be no peace and that place can mean our hearts and minds as well.

There is no question that a calm evening with both parents sitting together at the dinner table as each child joins them would be ideal. We should certainly make an effort to strive for such perfect evenings. It is my hope that through studying the Torah's methods of raising children we will all be able to create the best childhood that we are humanly able to give. But we know that not every day are we granted true bliss. In fact, there will be many days when we will not recognize bliss if it hits us on the head. There will be nights when we are overwrought and emotionally worn down. There will be evenings that we tuck our child into bed and find a tear trickling down her face. Let us be consoled with the bedtime Shema. We have the understanding that evening brings forgiveness and resolution. Forgiveness brings strength to face tomorrow.

The bedtime Shema begins with a prayer of forgiveness. This is a most beautiful lesson for us to transmit to our children. It teaches us to extricate all of the short-tempered moments of the day and to erase any traces of anger. We are telling our children to forget the irritation and anger of the day. We are telling our children that we love them and that together we will complete the night with a message of hope and healing:

"Master of the Universe, I hereby forgive anyone who angered or antagonized me or sinned against me . . . whether he did so accidentally, willfully, carelessly, purposely, through speech, deed, thought, or notion . . . may no man be punished because of me. . . ." Even if you incorporate just a few of these words into a bedtime prayer with your children, you'll teach them that forgiveness and forgiving others is our final message of the evening. Tomorrow is a new day. We will start fresh. If we pay close attention to this prayer we will begin to see a major attitude adjustment both in our children and ourselves. We never simply send our children off to bed. Instead we can take our children to a higher level and soar with them. The Shema creates a permanent memory in our child's mind that speaks about healing and forgiveness. The final words that our children hear are not shouts of "get into bed or you're going to be in huge trouble!" Rather, we take leave with an acclamation of faith and forgiveness.

When I would put my newborns to sleep, from the very first night, I would cradle them with the words of the Shema. As my children grew, they began to look forward to our evening moments spent together. We would speak about our day, share a book or story, giggle a little, and then chant the melody of the Shema together.

And if I close my eyes, I can still hear my father's gentle voice, as he would recite the Shema prayer with me. I can still hear my mother singing to me the beautiful words of this majestic prayer, and to this day I am comforted.

Each year our family gets together on the *yahrzeit,* the date of death, of my *zaydah.* My family, together with my siblings and their spouses, nieces, nephews and their children, join my mother in her home for a special evening of family unity and remembrance. This past year, all the children and grandchildren gathered around my mother's dining-room table. Sweet babies were being passed around and held by their aunts and uncles. Excited cousins exchanged stories and laughter. I noticed my mother glance from face to face and take a breath. Each child represented a piece of her very being, her inner soul. My mother began to speak with great emotion.

"After the Holocaust, we lost so much family. My *zaydahs, bubbas,* all my aunts and uncles, my little cousins . . . they were all gone. As I look around this table I want to first express my gratitude to Hashem for allowing me and your *abba* the opportunity to rebuild our family. I look at all of you, my beautiful children, and I can't believe the *chessed,* the kindness and compassion, of G-d. I want to tell you all something now. I am going to share something that I'd like you to carry forever in your hearts. And one day, when you will become *bubbas* and *zaydahs* yourselves, with G-d's help, I ask that you tell your children and grandchildren this story."

My mother continued, "The Holocaust was finally over, but our sadness did not end. Zaydah, Mama, my two brothers, and I were taken to Switzerland and put into displaced persons camps. For some reason that I will never comprehend, we were once again separated as a family. Parents were put into one building and children were sent to yet another residence. The days were agonizing but the night brought fear that is impossible to describe. . . ."

My mother grew silent for a moment. The room was hushed as we waited for her to continue. "The fear at night, *kinderlach,* was not to be believed. Orphans would be crying out in their beds, calling into the night, 'Mama, Tattah, where are you?' They would scream wildly. Your uncles and I were terrified. After everything that we had gone through, how could we be denied the simple touch of our parents? How is it that again we would be divided from all that we had remaining in this world? Each night we would lie awake in our beds. Our hearts would pound furiously. The chair in the corner, the dresser on the side, why suddenly, in the black of night, they would look like Nazis! We would shout from our beds and scream in terror, 'Don't let them take us away again! We'll be good children, we promise!'"

All of us around the table, children, grandchildren, even the little great-grandchildren sat in complete silence. After all these years, my mother's pain was still raw as it enveloped the room.

My mother went on: "Somehow your *zaydah* received permission to visit us in the night. He would take a moment and stop by each bed. He would softly comfort the children and hold their hands. 'Shhh . . . ,' he'd whisper to them, 'it's going to be all right.' Then Zaydah would come over to me and my brothers. '*Zeesa kinderlach,* my sweet children,' he would say gently, 'let us say the Shema. Never be afraid. You have no one to fear. G-d is watching over you.'"

My mother continued. "Zaydah had suffered enormously. He was beaten savagely and received a lifetime of scars and pain. He had witnessed his father walking into the fires of the crematorium while holding a holy Torah scroll in one hand and an infant grandchild in another. With all that, my children, Zaydah never lost his ability to love. He held on to his Shema and sang it for me and all the children beside me each night in the D.P. camp. As Zaydah would be forced to leave, he would lean over to me and softly say into my ear, 'Mein tiera kind, my precious child, remember these words: venafsho keshura benafsho, and his soul was bonded with his soul. Our souls are forever connected.' With that, my father would leave us until the next night's Shema."

My mother began to cry. "So all of you, my tiera kinderlach, never forget your zaydah's Shema. It has sustained me and carried me through some very difficult and painful moments. My soul will be forever bonded to your souls. Each and every one of you."

Even through excruciatingly difficult circumstances, the Shema has survived the centuries and comforted children throughout the darkest of nights. It has empowered us with the ability to forgive and to find the strength to face our tomorrows.

THE POWER OF OUR NIGHTTIME RITUALS

In our home, nighttime rituals were very special and enduring. When we were small children, my parents would tell us a bedtime story and then recite the Shema prayer with us. We did not go to sleep hearing about Hansel and Gretel or Goldilocks and the Three Bears. Instead, my parents would weave colorful tapestries in our minds. We became enraptured with tales describing the giants of our people. We discovered the kindness of Abraham and Sarah, the leadership of Moses, and the courage of King David. We were touched and inspired by these stories of greatness and nobility. Before closing our eyes, our night had been filled with an abundance of possibilities of what one's potential may accomplish in this world. We could reach the stars!

As my children grew, I retold these same stories to them. I watched as their eyes widened with awe and amazement and I observed their hearts and minds being stretched. One evening, my nine-year-old daughter, Aliza, summed it up with her one-word reaction. She smiled at me and said, "Awesome." What a magnificent path for us to be guiding our children on!

Our children will forever remember the powerful messages of their parents. Who knows in which direction life will lead our children? They may traverse a path that will lead them to be distanced from us. Perhaps they will be faced with personal struggles that may be difficult to overcome. Know that the power of your bedtime ritual will remain with your children forever.

• • •

One of the first American rabbis to set foot inside the concentration camps at the conclusion of the war was Rabbi Eliezer Silver. Once there, he did not know where to turn. Survivors who did not appear to be human were actually living corpses. Among the six million were one and a half million children. How does one man stand amid the graveyard of human decency? How does one breathe in the stench of death and exhale hope?

Amazingly, Rabbi Silver heard about some Jewish children who were being reared in French monasteries. They had been hidden during the war and baptized by the monks who were raising them. Rabbi Silver decided to seek out these last remaining children. When he arrived at the monastery he was told unequivocally that there were absolutely no Jewish children residing inside. Combing the list of youths, Rabbi Silver recognized some names that sounded Jewish.

"No," he was told emphatically, "these are all German children." Rabbi Silver refused to curtail his search. He was determined to rescue these little souls. He returned that night and insisted on speaking to the children himself. The rabbi entered the room. "Listen to me, children," he said as he began to sing the Shema. Suddenly, sweet little voices could be heard, joining together with the rabbi's, chanting the words in unison. The prayer had lain dormant within their hearts but was never forgotten. Their parents and grandparents may have parted from their children physically but their spirit lived on. The children returned with Rabbi Silver and rediscovered their roots. The shining legacy of their parents remained.

We sometimes wonder if all of our toils really make a difference. Raising a child with soul requires enormous effort. It would be much easier to simply put our children to bed. There is no doubt that these bedtime rituals infuse our children with significant directives that become an intrinsic part of their lives. Our words resonate within their hearts. In fact, the first paragraph of the Shema says, "These words that I command you today should be placed upon your heart."

What does it mean to place words upon your heart? The Kotzker Rebbe responds so beautifully and assures us that there will be times that you feel as if you are not getting through to your children. You may grow despondent and think that you are talking to a wall. You begin to doubt yourself. Understand that even words placed on the heart eventually enter through the slightest opening. When children's hearts are ready to open, the words that we have spoken, so delicately perched on their hearts will slip right in. We must never resign ourselves to defeat or failure. All of your many heartfelt words and prayers echo within your child's very being. It may take some time, but eventually you will see the fruits of all your labor.

The Blessings of the Angels

After 9/11, I received numerous calls from parents who attended my classes. The natural fear that all of us felt was palpable, however parents voiced their concerns to me that their children were experiencing tremendous fear and anxiety, especially during the nighttime hours. Adults themselves felt uneasy and had bouts with insomnia. They asked if there was anything in particular that I could suggest to allay their nighttime fears. Perhaps some would cynically suggest a quick fix of tranquilizers for the adults and therapy for the kids. Instead, I introduced the parents to a most poignant prayer, one that is also part of the bedtime Shema. It is the prayer of the angels. We tell our children that we call upon G-d and His ministering angels to protect them during the darkness of night.

"*Beshem Hashem*. . . . in the name of G-d, may the angel Michael be on my right, may the angel Gabriel be on my left, may the angel Uriel be before me, and may the angel Rephael be behind me and above me is the Presence of G-d." These words convey to our children that the angels above, along with G-d, love them as much as their parents and protect them at all times. Our children never feel alone.

Mothers and fathers took leave of our class with a sense of empowerment and transmitted this when they returned home to their children. They told their kids that at night, when we lie in our beds, we are surrounded by angels and never have to feel alone. Each evening these parents added this prayer to their children's nighttime ritual. As time passed they felt more at ease and happily informed me that their children felt additional peace and solace.

You have taught me to sing the Shema to my children. My older son had major sleep issues. I went to every sleep therapist and nothing worked. I never spoke to you about my son's sleep issues, but after hearing you at one class discuss the importance of this prayer, I sang it to him that night. He slept. It was unbelievable. He was finally comforted. No matter what, no matter where I am, I call home and sing it to my children. I have not missed a night in six years. They love it and depend on it.

· · ·

Do children really absorb your words and efforts? Recently, my family was blessed with the marriage of my daughter, Shaindy. Preparations for the wedding included meetings with the band's coordinator to discuss the music. We sat around our kitchen table, mulling over the details. The conversation turned to the music to be played during the *chuppah* ceremony.

"What song would you choose as you walk down the aisle, Shaindy?" the band coordinator queried. Without a moment's thought, Shaindy replied, "'Beshem Hashem.'" "Ah, that's a beautiful melody," responded the arranger approvingly. After he left, Shaindy and I spoke. "Mommy, do you know why I want to walk down the aisle to my *chuppah* with this song?" Shaindy asked me. "Tell me, my Shaindelah," I responded. She looked at me for a moment and said, "*Beshem Hashem* were the words with which you put me to sleep each night. You sang these words at my bedside as far back as I can remember. Now that I am beginning a new life, I want these words to accompany me . . . I want your *tefillos,* all your prayers, to always be with me. These are the words that I want to hear as I walk down the aisle."

A few weeks later, we walked down the aisle to the *chuppah,* Shaindy, my husband, and myself. Our hands interlocked with hers as the music began to play. "Beshem Hashem," the prayer of the angels escorted us as we approached one of the most meaningful moments of our lives. I stood beneath the white wedding canopy and asked G-d to safeguard this young couple. I felt sure that as my daughter would begin to build her own *mikdash me'at,* the prayers of the angels would always protect her.

Morning Communication

We conclude our guidance for communication based on the Shema's wisdom: "And when you arise in the morning"—*uvekumecha.*

There is no doubt about it. Our mornings can be extremely over-whelming. Whether you've had a most difficult night with an infant who seemed to wake you every time your head hit the pillow, or a child who kept you up as you coped with his fever, illness, or nightmares, evenings without adequate sleep make for tough mornings. When we compound that with the times in our lives that we must also deal with mounting personal pressures, just climbing out of bed becomes a seemingly insur-mountable task.

Financial problems, relationship difficulties, struggles at work, health issues, worries about our children all rob us of our peace of mind. We of-ten wake up in the morning with a sense of unease. Even if we've had our sleep, we are still physically and emotionally exhausted. It seems easier to just remain in bed.

Even days that do not hold any daunting personal challenges still re-quire stamina and positive thinking. We attempt to manage our morn-ings well, but despite everything we can still become easily frazzled. There are carpools to drive, school buses to catch, breakfasts to give, and, at times, a crying infant howling in the background.

It doesn't take long before you feel the pressure escalating. Your son decides to pour his own cup of juice and ends up spilling it all over the morning paper. Drops of juice are trickling onto the floor. His pants are sticky and wet. Your daughter begins to wail. Her favorite outfit is in the laundry. She refuses to get dressed. Someone's schoolbook sits on the counter, left out from the previous evening.

If you're raising teenagers, you're anxiously watching the clock and hoping. Your daughter finally emerges and announces, "There's nothing to eat in this house." It's now 8:03 A.M. You have exactly seven minutes to get everyone out of the house. You are ready to explode. In a total frenzy, you grab each child and attempt to get them moving. It is only after they have left and the door slams shut that you have a moment of silence with your now cold cup of coffee. You realize that you've been screaming for the last half hour. It dawns upon you that your children did not even receive a hug and kiss, never mind a smile. There's got to be a better way.

Judaism guides our day with wisdom and a profound knowledge that steers our course from the moment we open our eyes and watch the sun hit our coverlets until the last hours of the day. As parents, we seek to es-tablish noble families. As human beings though, we all have our flaws and there is not one of us who is infallible. Parenthood does not endow us with instant wisdom. G-d who created us, and who was also cognizant of our limitations, bequeathed us with fundamental ordinances, which guide us through our everyday lives. These mitzvahs have been transmitted from generation to generation and recorded in the Code of Jewish Law.

This code begins by teaching us a mind-set as we awake in the morning and attempt to begin our day. We comprehend that we are responsible for the peace and well-being of our children. Parents who snap and scream cannot possibly provide an atmosphere that prepares our children to face their day happily. We obviously need direction.

Morning Mind-Set

The Code of Jewish Law provides us with guidance and instructs us as follows:

> As soon as one awakes he should acknowledge G-d's compassion, in as much as the soul which had been faint and weary was restored to him renewed and refreshed. Every morning man is like a newborn living being and for this he must thank G-d with all of his heart. While still in his bed he should say: "*Modeh ani lefanecha*, I gratefully thank You, G-d, for restoring my soul within me with compassion."
>
> CODE OF JEWISH LAW, 1:2

The moment we open our eyes is the moment we say, "Thank You, G-d, for my life."

We mentioned this prayer when we spoke about raising children with gratitude. Mornings are perfect opportunities for us to give our children this sense of thankfulness. Just as I sang "Shema" with each child in the evening, I swaddled my newborns with the words of *modeh ani* each sunrise. As they grew into toddlers this was the first phrase they heard as they awoke. We begin our day with gratitude. We become cognizant of the fact that our lives are a gift not to be taken for granted. A grateful person is a person with soul.

If we begin our day with gratitude our entire attitude is transformed. Instead of grumbling about our problems and feeling weighted down by our responsibilities, we greet each day with a renewed sense of awe. We have been given a gift; the gift of life. We should know in our hearts that each day is a new opportunity for us to grow, to give, to accomplish. If we are able to savor this taste for life then we are able to take on our days with enthusiasm and even a sense of reverence. The challenges that we face become opportunities for self-discovery. If we can handle our daily pressures with dignity then we have transformed ourselves. We have overcome our weaknesses and summoned up the strength to rise to any occasion. When we reach out to our children with love, despite our personal hardships, then we have painted our world with bold, beautiful colors. As we discipline ourselves to curtail the explosions of anger and communicate with patience, our children learn the definition of compassion. Modeh Ani, our morning thank-you, puts us in the proper mind-set and allows us to appreciate this daily astonishing experience called life.

I sometimes tell parents to look at themselves in the mirror every morning. Not glance but really look. Observe the angry brows. Ponder the scowling face. Probe the dark eyes. Would you want to spend time with this person? Would you desire to wake up to yourself? Before you take on your children and responsibilities, take on yourself. Establish a positive attitude.

My father would frequently quote the Breslover Rebbe, Rabbi Nachman. He would say, "Put a smile on your face and G-d will give you something to smile about." You may not feel like it, it's true, but a happy countenance is one of the greatest gifts that you can transmit to your child. When a child finds a happy parent who handles the morning's pressures calmly he will act in a more self-composed manner himself.

You may feel like shouting and having a tantrum, but before you do, ask yourself what you will have accomplished. After your children are out the door and you remain with only yourself, you will be left with pangs of guilt, disappointment, and sadness as you become aware of your lack of self-control. Speak to yourself silently as you are on the brink of losing it. Whisper two words that can transform you, "*Modeh ani.*" "Thank You, G-d, for granting me this day."

I am not naïve enough to believe that mornings will not be stressful anymore. The juice will still spill, favorite shirts will still be in the laundry, buses will still be missed. Certain situations cannot be prevented. What can be prevented though are our angry and negative reactions. We are in control of our emotions and our attitude is in our hands. Will we be even-tempered and stable or will we have a meltdown? Will we become agitated over spilled milk or will we hand our child a washcloth and turn the moment into a valuable teaching experience? "*Modeh ani.* Thank You, G-d, for granting me this day."

. . .

A beautiful couple approached me at the conclusion of one of our monthly couples classes. We had been discussing marriage and relationships. They exuded warmth and a sense of deep closeness with each other. After speaking for a few moments, they introduced themselves as Nicole and Andrew, young professionals living in New York City. Nicole confided to me that for the past two years they had been going through the challenge of a lifetime. Their beautiful three-year-old son, Zach, had been diagnosed with leukemia. He had undergone chemotherapy, lost all his hair, stopped attending school regularly, and had suffered both physically and emotionally.

"We are finally seeing the light at the end of the tunnel," added Andrew. "Zach will have his bone marrow test this month and we pray that he will be given a clean bill of health." Nicole's and Andrew's eyes revealed emotions that spoke volumes. "People ask me," Nicole said in a soft voice, "if I remember what it felt like from the onset of Zach's diagnosis . . . the fear of watching your little one face a life-threatening illness. The challenge of waking up each morning and facing another day. The dry mouth and pounding heart as the doctors disclose Zach's test results. The sheer terror of what could be . . . now that Zach is so much better we are slipping into a sense of normalcy, which, believe me, we are so grateful for. But I really don't want to lose that sense of appreciation for each day. It shouldn't take a dreadful disease to give us an awareness of making each day count. How can we hold on to that feeling without being afraid? Is it even possible?"

What an extraordinary couple! I thought to myself. "You have been through a life-transforming challenge," I responded. "Instead of becoming enveloped in self-pity and bemoaning your situation by crying out, 'Why us, why our innocent little boy,' you have faced your pain with courage. You stepped up to the plate, stared adversity in the face, and have walked away strengthened. Your question is inspiring. I would answer that each morning, the moment you open your eyes, say, '*Modeh ani.*' Thank G-d for the gift of life. Appreciate the moments that each day brings. You are right on target when you say that it shouldn't take a frightening illness to teach us this incredible lesson. Grasp the feeling of awe and anticipation for each day. Hold on to the delight of being blessed with good health. Be sure that Zach remembers to thank G-d for each day, too. It's just two words, thank you, but these two words are life-changing. As Zach grows you will all retain the positive emotions this challenge has brought you."

"You know," Nicole said, smiling, "I, of course, would never have requested this illness. I realize, though that we have experienced a spiritual makeover these past few years. If *modeh ani* allows us to preserve this newfound strength, then we will gladly celebrate our lives through these two words each day."

Many parents mistakenly believe that communicating with children is defined only by their words. Unfortunately, they neglect to glimpse beyond their conversations and realize that each day presents bountiful opportunities to silently speak to our children. The Shema so eloquently teaches us that we impart crucial values to our families through our very being.

The very manner with which we speak to each other conveys tolerance. As we journey through life's numerous way stations, our conduct becomes a paragon of understanding and moral clarity. If we only so desire it, our evenings allow us those precious and intimate moments with our children. Teachings of forgiveness, the blessings of the angels, as well as stories of towering biblical figures infuse us with unwavering spiritual strength. Despite our many pressures, beginning our day with a positive and cheerful demeanor inculcates within our children an appreciation for life and an ability to remain calm and even-tempered.

Dark clouds may lie ahead. There is no life that is free of troubles, but as our children take notice of our genuine appreciation for all of life's blessings, they will gain an absolute can-do attitude. Our legacy of *modeh ani* helps soothe our weary souls. We begin each day with our spirits revitalized.

Late one Sunday evening I received a call that affected my inner core. It was after 10:00 P.M. and I was inclined to let voice mail pick up and take a message. I then noticed that the caller ID displayed COLUMBIA PRESBYTERIAN HOSPITAL. Who could be calling? I wondered.

The receiver was cradled on my shoulder as I tried to make sense of the muffled cries on the line. It sounded like gibberish that began to amplify with each moment. It's probably a prank call, I decided. I was about to hang up, but then realized that someone was attempting to call my name. Now who could this possibly be?

"Hello?" I asked into the receiver. "Hello? Hello?" There was a second of silence. I heard my name called out again and then I heard sobs. Heart-wrenching, uncontrollable sobs. "Slovie, it's Melanie! I don't know what to do. Help me." "Melanie?" I shouted into the phone. "What's going on? What happened?"

Certain individuals walk into your life and touch you through their ability to radiate instant joy. Laughter accompanies them the moment they enter a room. A quick joke and easy smile are always on their lips; their mere presence brightens the atmosphere. This would most certainly describe Melanie; a delightful, glorious young mom with a bubbly and effervescent personality. The only characteristic greater than her radiant smile would be her heart of gold. Melanie and I connected easily after she attended a parenting class given near her home. How could this be her on the line, crying hysterically?

"Melanie, I'm here but I can't understand you. Take a deep breath and talk to me," I said. As Melanie spoke, her subdued voice conveyed awful fear. I could barely hear her. "I wasn't feeling well over the weekend," she began. "Then I felt a weakness in my arm. I started to slur my words. One side of my face began to droop. We called my doctor and he said that we must go to the hospital immediately. He thought I was having a stroke. You know my husband, Steve. He rushed me here and stayed with me as they ran a battery of tests. Oh, my G-d, they just came in and diagnosed me. It's not a stroke at all. They told me I have MS! I have multiple sclerosis!"

Melanie began sobbing loudly and uncontrollably. I was shocked. How could this be?

"Listen, Melanie, I'm coming over to see you."

"Tonight's too late, it's past visiting hours," she replied, as she tried slowly to get the words out of her mouth. "Please, come tomorrow."

As we hung up, Melanie continued to cry. Throughout the next day Melanie remained on my mind. After teaching and putting my children to sleep, I found myself wandering the halls of Columbia Presbyterian Hospital, in search of Melanie and Steve. I opened the door and found Melanie in her hospital bed. She was curled up in a fetal position, a blanket covering her head. Steve sat on an uncomfortable chair, adjacent to her.

"Melanie?" I whispered softly.

"Oh, Slovie." She gave out a deep sob. Her tears were endless. "I can't go on. My life is over."

"That's just not true," I countered. "I see the same beautiful Melanie that I've come to know and love so very much."

She remained enveloped by her covers. I sat on Melanie's bedside and embraced her.

"I didn't brush my teeth, you know. I'm a mess. I need a shower, too. I don't think you want to come so close." We laughed.

"Are you kidding?" I asked. "I'm not going anywhere, so let's talk."

Melanie, Steve, and I spent the night talking. We spoke about the dark storms that life sometimes brings our way. We spoke about the joy of children, the responsibility of family. We explored the definition of commitment to one another, no matter what. As best we could, we addressed the age-old question of "why do bad things happen to good people?" I tried to imbue Melanie and Steve with the Torah wisdom of my parents and grandparents while we grappled with the challenges of life.

Steve spoke up. "I want you to know, Melanie, that I have never loved you more than I do at this very moment. I have never been more committed to you and our kids than right now. We're going to beat this thing. It will not beat this family. We are going to emerge from this stronger and better than we've ever been. I'm actually looking forward to the challenge. We are going to make it and be better than ever."

Melanie stared at Steve intently. A tiny tear trickled down her cheek. I had just witnessed family at its best.

"Where do I begin?" Melanie asked me in a hushed tone. "Right now, life seems so impossible."

"Let's start with the moment you open your eyes in the morning. The first words that I want you to say are, '*Modeh ani.*' The first thought I want you to think in your mind is, 'Thank You, G-d, for another day.' No one knows what tomorrow will bring. No one knows what even the next hour will bring, but one thing that we do know is that our attitude allows us to endure. While it's true that illness is not in our hands, we do know that our reaction to this challenge is up to us. Your kids will get firsthand knowledge of what the definition of true courage is. You will teach them the power of a smile. You will educate your family and friends as you connect to G-d through daily prayer and increase your fortitude."

"But I'm clueless when it comes to prayer. I've never really prayed in my life." Melanie's eyes filled.

"I know that, and that's exactly why I'm giving you these." I opened my bag and handed Melanie various Hineni prayer cards that I had brought for her. We discussed the words and concepts behind our prayers.

"I like that." Melanie gave her first smile of the night. "What about our kids? I don't want them to get down and glum. They'll be coming to visit me. What can I do while I'm stuck here in the hospital, waiting for more test results?"

"Well," I replied, "we've been taught that when faced with darkness you can either curse the night or illuminate the blackness that surrounds you. What will it be?"

"You know my answer. I'm going for the light. Steve, are you in with me?" Melanie asked.

"You bet I'm in. So, what do we do?" Steve asked.

"This week, for the very first time, Melanie, you will kindle the Sabbath candles. Just a little bit of light pushes away the darkness. You and Steve will bless your children. As you sit here in the hospital and celebrate Shabbos with your family, you will bring joy and blessing into this room. And Melanie, the next time I see you, you'll be showered, perfumed, and all made-up with your gorgeous smile on your face, ready to roll."

One of my mother's favorite teachings is, "In a desert, it is true that the sun always shines. You never come across a storm. Yet, nothing grows. Flowers will bloom only in a place where there is rain."

Melanie and Steve understood that they were now charting unconquered territory. The course of their life would take them across a stormy sea. Faith, prayer, commitment to family, and true joy were all required for triumphant survival.

I have had the privilege of watching Melanie and Steve grow together. Of course, we are not simple Pollyannas who perceive life through rose-colored glasses. We recognize the harsh realities of life. Sure, there have been tough days, but allow me to share with you the magnificent flowers that have bloomed.

Melanie's parents and in-laws spotted her prayer cards one morning and requested their own. The extended family has learned to acquire a deep appreciation of living each day to its fullest. Each week Melanie's Sabbath candles brighten her home and extinguish the darkness. There have been both good days and some more difficult days. Melanie's unyielding faith, strength of character, and spirit have served as a beacon of hope for her family throughout this entire ordeal. Melanie and Steve have redefined their dedication to each other. They are committed to their marriage and children.

Not only has Melanie never missed a parenting class since her diagnosis, but she has reclaimed her inner spark and indefatigable zest for life. Her humor continues to bring us laughter and joy. She is a courageous warrior in the battle for life. Recently, Melanie put it to me this way:

"My morning prayer of Modeh Ani is my starting point. Without it, I really don't know where I'd be today. I may not always know where I'll end up in life, but at least I have the wisdom of knowing where I must begin."

COMMUNICATION DO'S AND DON'TS

The Jewish people were liberated from the land of Egypt and encamped opposite Mount Sinai in the desert wilderness. The Torah describes their travels till then, their thirst for water and their pangs of hunger. They complained bitterly about the lack of meat and bread.

After overcoming and conquering their physical battles, the time had arrived for the beleaguered nation to become spiritually strengthened. G-d desired to bestow the greatest gift ever given to humankind, the Ten Commandments. These commandments would solidify the moral foundation upon which man's every footstep would tread. The existence of the world would depend solely upon the acceptance of these commandments. Effective communication between G-d and every single man, woman, and child who stood at Sinai was a must. How would G-d reach the heart and soul of each individual?

Our sages teach us that two distinct groups would be addressed, each requiring their own manner of communication. Moses is told that when teaching the commandments to the Jewish women he should "*say to them*" implying a softer form of speech, suited to their feminine nature. Then, Moses was instructed to "*relate to the men*," as he would educate them in a firmer, more masculine manner. This is a priceless lesson in communicating with our children. Individuals have inborn distinctive natures. Different personalities require personalized methods of contact. In order to reach out and connect with your child you must first gain a comprehension of "what makes this child tick?" Ask yourself,

"How can I best create a link with this child so that our relationship can flourish?"

Do Identify Your Child's Particular Disposition

Be mindful that each child is unique. Some children best respond to a soft tone while others need a firmer word or look. In vain do we attempt to communicate with our kids if they do not listen or run out of the room in tears. We could have the most incredible wisdom to share, we could possess undisputed knowledge of proper discipline and child-rearing, but if we are not being heard then we are not communicating. We may be giving fabulous speeches but we may as well be talking to a wall.

If each day I find myself saying, "Sarah, come for dinner," or "David, take a shower, now," or "Adam, do your homework," over and over again, yet I'm still not listened to, then I must realize that I have failed to communicate effectively with my children. I may be a world-class orator, but nonetheless there is a glaring problem with my ability to be an effective parent.

Beyond repeating one's self to the point of frustration, parents should recognize which mode of communication works best with each child. Different natures require disparate communication techniques. Knowing this, we can then best communicate effectively with our children.

Do Communicate Early

Oftentimes parents are under the erroneous assumption that infants lack any kind of formidable perception. They believe that their babies are unable to differentiate between caregivers: "He's just a baby, he doesn't know the difference, anyway." Studies have shown that newborns recognize their parents' voices and scents. Singing and speaking to infants while creating a nurturing environment definitely does make a difference.

The Talmud relates that as an infant, Rabbi Yehoshua was brought by his mother to the house of study. She would bring him in his carriage so that his ears would hear the words of Torah. She did this, despite the hordes of detractors who admonished her for bringing a baby into a house of study.

"Why are you bringing this child here?" they would ask.

Little Yehoshua grew up to become Rabbi Yehoshua, an illustrious teacher and a great tzaddik, a great and most righteous man. In *Ethics of*

Our Fathers it is written of him: "*Ashrei Yeladato*—praised is the one who gave birth to him." His mother brought him into a sanctuary of spiritual holiness even as an infant because she had a fervent desire that words of Torah enter his soul. Even if he could not comprehend the learned discourses that swirled around him, she knew that communication begins at this early stage of life. Her dream became a reality. Imbued by holiness as an infant, her child grew to become a spiritual leader. Not satisfied with bringing forth physical life, this mother insisted on touching her child's soul even as an infant. Our words and surroundings immeasurably impact our children. If this holds true at such a tender age, then imagine the responsibility and opportunity in the hands of parents as our children grow.

My husband and I would often return to my parents' home with our small children for the Sabbath. In the middle of the night, my youngest at the time would inevitably wake with his or her wails. So as not to disturb the rest of the household, I would carry my infant in my arms, soothing him all the while. As I would approach the kitchen, I would find my father in his favorite chair. Spread across the table were his beloved holy books. He would softly hum as he studied Torah, engrossed in every word. His sweet, melodious voice permeated the air. His body would sway back and forth as he concentrated on the deep teachings. My father was immersed in great sanctity, oblivious to the late hour.

The moment he felt my presence in the room, he'd look up, and a magnificent smile would spread across his lips.

"And what are you doing up, my *shayfelah*?" he'd ask.

"The baby woke up," I'd mumble as I yawned, half asleep.

My father would open his arms wide and gesture for me to hand him his newest grandchild.

"But, Abba, it's so late. You must be exhausted, too!"

My father would laugh out loud.

"Slovelah, do you know why babies wake up in the middle of the night? To remind their parents and grandparents to study Torah. My learning will be so much sweeter with this baby at my side. He will study together with me, this *zeesa neshamah*, this sweet little soul."

And so our babies were raised. My father would sing the words of the holy Torah as his grandchild would nestle in his arms contentedly. Though, sadly, my beloved father has passed from this world, he created a bond with his grandchildren that is recalled with enormous adoration until this very day. The genesis of this bond was formed in infanthood. As these children grew, there was no love that could ever replace the love of their special *zaydah*. The love that was communicated in the stillness of the night, as words of Torah floated above, remains steadfast in their hearts and minds.

Early communication allows us to create powerful bonds with our children. When Moses was an infant, a decree was enacted by Pharaoh. All Jewish males born in Egypt were required to be thrown into the Nile River and drowned. Yocheved, the mother of Moses, gently placed her baby into a wicker basket by the bank of the river, praying for his very life. Her little daughter, Miriam, stationed herself at a distance and watched over her brother.

Pharaoh's daughter, Batya, went down to bathe by the river and noticed the basket among the reeds. She opened it up and was startled to find a little infant inside, crying. The baby refused to nurse from the Egyptian women. Miriam ran out from her hiding place and offered help.

"Allow me to get a wet nurse from the Hebrew women who will nurse the boy for you," she said.

Pharaoh's daughter immediately agreed. She had taken pity on the child. Miriam, of course, brought Yocheved, the mother of Moses who nursed him for a lengthy period of time until he was returned to the palace.

Our sages teach us that events were arranged in this way so that the future leader of Israel would be nurtured by his mother. Not only did she nurse baby Moses, but Yocheved instilled within her son Jewish beliefs during the most impressionable years of his life. She nourished him with her deep convictions and mother's milk of never-ending faith. G-d Himself, is teaching us the importance of early infancy communication.

As your child grows, convey to him or her the beauty of your world, the delight of your beliefs. Each Friday night after I had lit my Sabbath candles, I would take my young children by the hand. Together we would watch the flames of the candles dance. My infant would be burrowed in my arms as I would simply whisper, "Shabbos, Shabbos," in hushed tones. The luminous light would reflect in my children's eyes as the beauty of our Shabbos made an indelible imprint on their souls. Joyous memories can be created with even the youngest of children.

Do not hesitate to communicate your love for this universe of ours, even to your smallest infant. Describe the dazzling ocean hues as you sit by the seashore. Point out the diamond icicles that hang magically from the bare branches of the trees in winter. Take a moment to sniff the scent of a rose or savor a slice of sweet watermelon as the juice drips down your kid's chin. Children love to hear your thoughts and share your imagination.

On a bright spring day my children were playing outside. My daughter Shaindy was just four at the time and enjoying our new swing set. As she pumped higher and higher, she leaned her head back toward me and exclaimed:

"Mommy, I'm so happy that Hashem gave me eyes to see this world! It's so beautiful!"

Could a four-year-old really be grateful for "eyes to see this world"? Is this for real? you may be thinking.

If you communicate your love for this universe to your children from an early age, if you express your thoughts and share your wonder for G-d's creations, then of course this can be your child's voice, too.

Just listen to this mom's words as she described the way her young children see the world in an e-mail to me:

> When we were in St. Barts we saw a rainbow and Max said, "Look what G-d created for us, it is so beautiful!"
>
> At SeaWorld, Jack said, "Look how many animals G-d created, each one different!"
>
> Ally woke up one morning and said, "Mommy, I prayed to G-d last night to make me feel better and I feel so much better today."
>
> "Mommy, why did G-d create fire?"

A butterfly in flight, the brilliant hues of a sunset, the splash of a waterfall on a hot summer's day, the delicious array of colors with which G-d created the fruits of the earth, the fact that we can run with the wind; all are miraculous wonders waiting to be shared with your children.

• • •

Communicate with your children from the time that they are born. Don't discount their ability to learn about our world despite their tender age. Educate them in your faith and beliefs. Nourish them in an uplifting environment. Touch their souls as only a parent can and build that strong connection from birth. As they grow, continue to invest in their essence of being.

Do Communicate Love Tangibly

Sometimes, we know deep inside that we love someone, but we tend to neglect tangible displays of our love. It is easy to show affection to an infant. We are either holding him, feeding him, or playing with him. He smiles and coos at us. We reciprocate and smile back. Even when our baby is upset, he doesn't answer back or give us attitude. As our children grow and become independent, our interactions change. We direct and instruct more, dote and enjoy less time together. We get annoyed more frequently. Children misbehave and challenge us. Somehow, affection becomes an afterthought; given if remembered. Many children wipe away our kisses and distance themselves from physical contact. Without realizing it, we gradually become physically removed from our children.

The Torah describes the physical affection that our patriarchs displayed even as adults. Upon revealing himself to his brothers after years of separation, Joseph kisses them and weeps. Joseph is also described as giving his father, Jacob, one last kiss before his passing. When Isaac desires to bless Jacob, his son, he requests that Jacob approach him for a kiss. Even though our father Isaac was elderly at this juncture in time, he taught us that age should not impede parents and children from displaying (appropriate) love for each other. The Torah is showing us that physical affection is not only limited to mothers; fathers, too, have the responsibility to display this kind of love.

Judaism instructs us that any objects of holiness should be revered. Our holy Torah scrolls that we carry, prayer books that are read, mezuzahs (the scrolls containing the Shema prayer placed on our doorposts) that we pass by—all should be touched with a kiss in order to give physical expression to our love and reverence.

Our sages teach us that our children are literally living Torah scrolls. They physically embody our holy teachings. As we behold our children we realize that they represent the paradigm of innocence and purity of spirit. It is incumbent upon us to infuse their hearts and minds with goodness. It is our responsibility to cultivate the infinite potential of their souls.

A kiss and hug convey just how precious our children are to us. Our kids then comprehend how very much we cherish them. Generally, teens are reluctant to ask for a demonstration of your love, as they might interpret it to be childish or infantile, especially during a time when their independence and eagerness to be an adult is growing by leaps and bounds. Despite their protestations, we as parents cannot allow their lives to pass before us without displays of affection. Don't permit them to become "touch starved." We all require concrete knowledge that we're loved.

Children who feel loved are encouraged and strengthened. They become more willing to share their innermost thoughts with us. They dare to reveal intimate fears and failures, venture to disclose their dreams and aspirations. This ultimate trust between children and parents occurs when love is communicated in our relationship with them. A day should not go by without giving your child some expressions of love such as:

> *"I love you."*
> *"I'm so happy that you're mine."*
> *"I know you can do it."*
> *"I know that wasn't easy, and I'm really proud of you."*
> *A reassuring pat on the shoulder, a warm smile.*
> *Hugs and kisses in the morning and/or before bedtime.*
> *Notes in backpacks and peeking out from under children's pillows,*
> *inscribed with a smiley face, heart, or needed words of*
> *encouragement.*

Take your pick! (It is also a great idea for spouses to keep these expressions of love alive with each other as years of marriage go by.)

If we neglect expressions of love during most of our children's young lives they will be unable to communicate love adequately to their own children. We must understand that we are not only raising our children but we are raising generations to come. How can our children "love" if they have not been touched by our love—the love of both mother and father, love given to both infants and youths?

There are times when we find ourselves at a loss for words, unable to know just what to say. Sometimes physical contact and touch can comfort us in ways that words cannot.

We may have no idea how to express our feelings adequately, but a kiss or reassuring hug says it all.

Consider a husband and wife who rarely display affection for each other. One day, the wife asks her husband, "Do you love me?"

"Of course I love you. You know that!"

"How should I know?" she replies.

"It's in my heart."

"But I cannot know what is in your heart! I need to hear it, see it, feel it," she responds.

There is no difference with parents and children. We all need to hear it, see it, and feel it!

After a lecture on communicating with our children, I received an e-mail from a participating parent:

> Slovie, somehow your talk on communication struck a chord within me. I began to cry, not knowing exactly why. I realized that throughout my adolescent years, my mom, who was definitely a good mother, never told me how much she loved me. She never kissed me good night or hugged me as I grew older. I guess we all thought that older kids didn't need this type of affection. The only loving memory I really have is my mother stroking my hair as she'd speak to me. This makes me feel so sad. Thank you for enlightening me as I raise my own children.

After my father passed away our family dedicated a new Torah scroll in his honor. Our entire family—my mother, my siblings and I, along with our spouses and all of our children—joined our Hineni family as we marched the Torah into the sanctuary of the Hineni building. There was a grand and glorious procession down West End Avenue in New York City. Bright blue balloons were flying as festive music played. Along the route, the holy Torah scroll was passed into the arms of different people to carry. As the procession came to a conclusion, my brother spoke these beautiful words: "Some people ask, 'How do I carry a Torah? Isn't it heavy?'" He searched the crowd and then gave his reply. "I'll answer you—carry it as though you are carrying a baby. Pick it up, hold it tight, and give it a kiss. Once you hold it, it's not heavy anymore."

Many of our weighted loads can be lightened through the power of touch. Our children will experience our love for them even if they can't always understand our actions. At the end of the day, we will have communicated our love—the most powerful communication of all. As we attempt to raise our children, with all of the heavy burdens that are entailed in doing so, we will find that we possess an inner force that we never knew existed. We discover that this internal strength was within us all along, just waiting to be tapped and communicated. It is the mighty power of love.

Do Use Positive Language

When we were small children, we spent many a Sunday afternoon together with my cousins at my grandparents' home. Theirs was a tiny apartment. Inevitably, some of the children would bicker over various toys. My grandfather would never lose his temper with us. In fact, I can not recall him ever raising his voice. Instead, he would come over to us with a genuinely pained expression on his face. He would simply say in Yiddish: "From you? This is not worthy behavior of such a special child." That was it. No shouting. No shrill screaming. No insulting descriptions of our behavior. It wasn't necessary. Zaydah expected more from us. We knew that we were good children who could do better. And we *were* going to do better.

When communicating with children you will reach greater heights if you pick them up rather than push them down. Speak to them using positive language even while attempting to convey a negative situation. Always give children an ideal to aspire to instead of digging a deep hole into which they will descend.

A parent relayed a conversation that her husband had with her school-age son. The discussion upset her tremendously. Her son, Benjamin, brought home a disappointing report card. He did poorly in various subjects and failed his foreign-language course. As they sat around their kitchen table, her husband turned to their son and said, "Benjamin, you brought home an awful report card. You failed. I think you should drop the foreign language right away."

Her son answered, "But, Dad, I really tried. I want to learn this new language. Please, let me try again."

"Why? So you'll fail again? You'll end up showing your mom and me exactly what you can't do. You'll just do poorly again, so what's the point?"

Their son began to cry.

"Prove me wrong, Benjamin, prove me wrong!" her husband shouted as he stormed out of the room.

The mom caught up with her husband.

"Why did you say that to Benjamin?" she asked.

"Because," her husband replied, "I want to challenge him. I want him to prove me wrong."

After she related her experience, we spoke about what had occurred. "Tell your husband," I said, "that instead of saying, 'Benjamin, prove me wrong,' he should say, 'Benjamin, prove me right! I believe in you and I know that you could do better. Prove me right!'"

Believe in your child. Who should believe in him if not you? Grant him hopes and dreams. Allow him vision. Never doom him to failure. We must be so careful with our words. Our sages teach us that words can build and words can destroy. Speech is a potent tool, especially in the hands of adults. Your negative words can cause your child to self-destruct beyond repair. Conversely, your positive words allow your child to construct a tower of fortitude upon which he can climb and reach tremendous heights.

Even in the Torah, G-d was careful to use positive language. When describing the sense of aloneness that Adam felt before the creation of his life partner, Eve, G-d could have said, "It is really *bad* that Adam is all alone." Instead, G-d said, "It is *not good* that man is alone." This language is called *lashon nekiyah*—clean, positive language.

The message is that while expressing ourselves or even when conveying a negative situation, we should accustom ourselves to positive language.

For example, instead of "You're such a liar! You're a cheater!" try: "You're not telling the truth." Instead of "You're an awful slob, what a mess! Your room's a disaster." try: "You can be neater and cleaner. Your room needs to be put in order." Instead of "You're always starting up with your sister! You're always fighting!" try: "You can get along much better with your sister."

• • •

After graduating teachers' seminary, I taught elementary school. Before one particular start of the year a previous teacher called and asked if I'd like a rundown of the children. I politely declined and responded that I'd prefer to make my own judgments. "They're a tough bunch," she warned. "And you'd do better knowing which kids to watch out for and which ones are prone to failure. Why waste your time?"

I never did meet failure that year or "kids to watch out for." I did encounter children who took my positive words to heart. They tried valiantly to fulfill my bright expectations. Sometimes they struggled with their studies, but they never gave up on themselves. As the year came to a close I don't know who felt more fulfilled—I, the teacher, or my students. As we said our good-byes I knew that the greatest teaching I could ever have given them was a positive belief in themselves. If that was just one year in the life of a student, envision the impact you can make as a parent in the lifetime of your child.

Do Not Communicate in Anger, with Empty Threats

A life filled with regrets is excruciatingly painful. I have spoken to countless parents who express sorrow for their harsh words; words spoken in anger, in the heat of the moment. When passions rule, we communicate our feelings without thinking first. Our tone of voice is biting. We say things we don't mean and mean things we don't say. In our fury we ask unanswerable questions:

> "Why don't you ever listen?"
> "Why are you the one who's always fighting?"
> "I just don't understand you. Where did you come from?"
> "Why can't you be like your sister?"
> "Why are you such a baby?"
> "What's the matter with you?"
> "Are you nuts?"
> "How could you be so stupid?"

What should our children reply to these questions? Our words ring in their ears; our acrimonious expressions echo in their heads. We notice the hurt in our child's eyes. Their cheeks flush beet-red as their faces droop in shame. What exactly have we accomplished?

There are times when we are at the end of our rope. We shout empty threats that we know will never be kept. Our children absorb our inconsistencies.

> "I'm never taking you on a vacation again!"
> "This is the last time I'm taking you guys out to a restaurant."
> "That's it, no more videos or Game Boy for the rest of the month."

Who are we kidding? Now our children know that our discipline doesn't carry any weight. Our attempts to set limits are a sad joke. When we lash out in anger our children usually retreat. They withdraw from us physically or emotionally recoil. The message we have tried to transmit, whether discipline or a life lesson, becomes moot. Instead, a child is now left with anger or confusion about our furious outburst.

I was invited by a young couple for dinner in their home. Their children joined us excitedly. The meal began comfortably, but one child began to act up as the hour grew late. She grew restless and began to misbehave badly. Her parents were furious with her. In their anger they began to shout, "What's the matter with you? Why can't you ever sit like a normal human being? Go to your room, now! You're never eating dinner with the adults again!"

The child pushed her plate away and ran from the table. The eyes of her siblings grew wide. They took it all in—the embarrassment, the empty threats, and the shouts of anger. Dinner was ruined.

We will discuss discipline and the proper way of handling such a situation in chapter 7. For now, let us understand a fundamental rule of communication that will change your life and the lives of your children. *Never* speak in anger. King Solomon teaches us: "Words of the wise are transmitted in calmness" (Ecclesiastes 9:17). If you wish to be a successful parent, speak to your children intelligently. When you are composed and collected, you speak with wisdom. Your words will be respected. However, if you allow your fury to overpower you, who knows what you are capable of saying? Your words and actions will bring you heartache that can last a lifetime. Your attempts to communicate with your children will be rejected.

Learning self-control while in the depths of anger can become a life-transforming metamorphosis as you communicate with your children. You will find yourself more articulate, clearer, and better focused. Your words will be held in higher regard. Besides your children's respect, you will have gained self-respect, a most important achievement.

Do Take Time Out to Communicate Your Values

There are times when we wish to communicate to our children the vast emotions that lie deep within our hearts. Significant occasions call for important and well thought-out directives. We often become mired in the laborious details of the event and we tend to overlook the opportunity that awaits us. These events can include the first time a child goes away to summer camp, consequential religious milestones, momentous birthdays, wedding days—all are life-changing experiences for both parents and children.

Instead of simply busying yourself with the multitude of details of the day, take a moment to share your thoughts and emotions with your child. Sit down in a quiet spot with just a paper, pen, and your thoughts. Transcend time and transmit your hopes, your convictions, your wisdom, and your love. Your communication will be remembered and cherished forever.

I spoke about this topic in one of my parenting classes and noticed one young mom with excitement written all over her face. At the end of our session she told me that soon she would be celebrating her daughter's bas mitzvah. She had never thought of it as an opportunity to communicate but decided to utilize my advice.

The following month she couldn't wait to speak with me before class began. She could hardly contain her enthusiasm.

"Slovie, as soon as I got home from our last class I bought a beautiful album. I called up my parents, my in-laws, even my aunts and uncles. The album traveled from Long Island to New York City to Miami Beach. Everyone was so excited to be a part of my daughter's bas mitzvah. They all had such beautiful messages. On the 'big day,' we presented my daughter with her album and read parts of the letters out loud. My daughter loved it. Our friends and family were moved to tears. It was the most beautiful gift we could have possibly given her. The best part is that she'll have our words in her heart always."

Some teens may not immediately appreciate the offering of words that you've compiled. They may mumble a casual "Thanks" or not even that. They may not realize the value of the gift that they've received.

It doesn't matter. The day will come when they will open up their book of memories and gingerly turn the pages with love. What's important is that you have conveyed thoughts and prayers along with hopes and blessings. The message has been imparted. Your child will grow to understand and foster a gentle tenderness for your communication and all the love expressed.

The many stages of growing up bring us great opportunities to reach out and touch our children with our words. We can offer our children guidance and prayers as they travel through the many seasons of life.

As my oldest daughter was about to embark upon her married life, I thought intensely about composing my own letter to her. The night before her wedding found me with pen and paper in hand as soft tears moistened my notes. There was so much within my heart that I wished to convey.

Could it be that my little girl now stood as a young woman ready to embrace the next stage of life? Where had all the years gone? We had just cheered her first baby steps, shared in her delight as she discovered fireflies under the summer stars, and wondered at her courage as she befriended those who were friendless. Delicious memories filled my mind; this child had moved me so. Life was beckoning, but I didn't want my child to move on without my words. I wished to give her "food for the way."

I wanted to present my daughter with an understanding not only of our deep love for her, but also an appreciation of her unshakable roots. These roots would sustain her as they had sustained me. Though she had witnessed the faith and love of my parents' home and the living legacy of our own family, I wished to put it all on paper for her to take along as she set out on her new journey. I longed to impart insight into the life of her *zaydahs* and *bubbas*. Not only had they lived for Torah and goodness, but they died in sanctity, still tightly clinging to their long-held beliefs and principles. We raised her with their vision in our minds. I wanted my daughter to hold on to this vision. Forever.

So on that night prior to my daughter's wedding, I wrote like I've never written before. I shared our love, our thoughts, our prayers, and our legacy for life. And I know that with G-d's help, my letter shall accompany my daughter along the corridors of life. Forever.

A Final Communication

King David wrote a letter to his son, Solomon, before he passed from this world. Solomon was just twelve years old at the time. He was faced with the loss of his father and a kingship surrounded by jealous siblings and difficult circumstances. How could he bear it all?

As Solomon sat on his father's throne he was able to read his father's words. King David relayed his wisdom so eloquently.

Don't mourn for me and my years. It is our nature as human beings to eventually die. Death in itself is not tragic, but it is a part of life. This is the way of the earth. I completed my task in life. Now it is time for my soul to return to G-d. This is how G-d created us.

But if it is your own loss that you grieve, accept my words of advice and encouragement. You will not remain in the world alone. G-d will always be there for you. Everything I gave you came from G-d and so now just turn to Him directly and He will never forsake you. Take the strength that G-d has given you and use it properly. Understand that before you rule over others you must first rule over yourself.   I KINGS 2:2; ME'AM LOEZ

How powerful are these words! I find it incredible that this, a final communication from a father to his young son, has survived the centuries. We have, each day, thousands of moments and infinite opportunities to communicate all that we hold precious to our children.

FIVE

Self-Esteem

No parent ever wants to hear their children utter these discouraging words:

"It's impossible. I can't do it."
"I'm going to fail."
"I'm just too stupid, okay?"
"Nobody likes me."

We aim for children who are confident; who possess a can-do attitude toward life. We strive to raise children who will grow into successful young adults. We wish to give our children self-esteem. But how do we accomplish that?

OUR BIG MISTAKE

Many parents are under the mistaken impression that the key to self-esteem is praise. In fact, they believe that the more they praise their child, the greater that child's self-esteem. The assumption is made that greater self-esteem is linked to feeling good about oneself and gaining self-confidence.

Once a child is self-confident we trust that he will succeed in life. But will he really?

How often do we open up our morning paper and find tragic headlines about some of the most successful people on the planet? Hollywood's brightest stars, superb athletes, business magnates, brilliant scientists, and astronauts somehow crumble on a path toward self-destruction. Why would a person at the apex of his career risk it all and find the need to turn to drugs, alcohol, and scandalous behavior? How could an individual who possesses self-esteem lie in a heap of reckless desperation? Didn't these great stars receive mammoth doses of praise as they climbed the ladder of success and beyond? Why were their achievements not adequate enough to bring about a sense of value and fulfillment to their lives? Through their phenomenal achievements, wouldn't one assume that these would be the most self-confident people on earth? Self-confidence must surely breed an appreciation of one's life. What is so sorely lacking here? Instead of self-confident spirits we find self-deficient souls.

Obviously, we must reexamine our definition of self-esteem or self-confidence and the road to achievement. When we view the world through the eyes of Torah, we are given the ability to contemplate life in a manner that allows us greater depth perception. Truths become apparent and unequivocal.

The Book of Genesis begins with the creation of Adam, the first man. Surely, G-d could have formed Adam together with Eve. Or perhaps G-d could have created a ready family or even an entire civilization of people to inaugurate the world? We know, however, that just one sole individual—Adam—was called into being. Why was an entire universe created for just one man?

Our sages teach us that the fact that man was created alone, with the vast world before him, is a monumental life lesson for us. Understand how vital you are! Each one of us is told that it is correct to say, "The entire world was created only for me," therefore we must justify the world's creations through our good deeds (Sanhedrin 37a).

Instead of giving empty praise to bolster our kids' sense of confidence we must teach our children the importance of their life's mission in this world. Most children's self-esteem is hardly based on any true life accomplishments. I've observed parents gush over their children's appearance or go on and on about their kids' karaoke skills. I've even heard parents shout triumphantly, "Great pumping, Adam!" as they watched their son on the swings in the park.

We use words such as *awesome, amazing, incredible,* and *the best* to praise our children and what they do. We are under the erroneous impression that we've got self-esteem covered by the utilization of these words, but we have to guess again. The fact is that there will always be someone out there who is richer, smarter, prettier, or better at sports. Then what? How will our kids respond to those who are more incredible, more awesome, and more amazing? How will our children handle the loss of having been nudged from the top of the world that we have created for them?

We look at their drawings and exclaim, "What an incredible artist you are!" We cheer their Little League games and shout about their "unbelievable catch." Compliments may have a nice ring in our child's ears, but we are shortchanging their souls.

We must teach our children about the value of their actions. Even young children can impact this world through their mitzvahs. Each time you achieve virtue you have brought *tikkun olam* into this world. This is the ultimate purpose of creation and brings about a true feeling of self-worth. If we can teach our child that he or she is unique and able to leave his or her individual handprint on this world through his or her deeds, then we have established a legacy for him or her to live by. Our child will comprehend that even his or her seemingly small acts of kindness can make this world a better place. His or her talents are not an end unto themselves; rather they are means through which he or she can make a difference in people's lives. (As we discussed in chapter 3 the ability to give to others enables children to feel happier and more vital.)

A smile can brighten up a room. A phone call to Grandma elicits joy. A colorful picture radiates sunshine indoors. A shared snack creates friendship. An invitation to join a game at recess dispels loneliness. The possibilities to create blessing in this world are endless.

Heaping praise on our children is not sufficient, but rather we must help them find meaning and purpose through their words and deeds. We then teach our children that they can make significant contributions and thereby make a difference in this world. We let them know in no uncertain terms that their presence matters. Judaism teaches us that the value of a person lies not within his accomplishments on the baseball field or his academic performance. We are taught that each one of us possesses an intrinsic self-worth that lies within.

Our children require proper guidance and tangible opportunities to build their concept of self. I was once asked to speak in a suburban community center, not far from New York City. After discussing the appropriate path toward building our children's self-esteem, one mother raised her hand and asked to speak. She wished to share a child-rearing tip with the audience.

"My husband and I have discussed the importance of confidence in our children from the time my son was an infant. We want our Noa to feel great about himself. One day, we heard a very famous politician lecture about himself and his success in life. He said that from the time that he was young, his parents always stood up and applauded the moment he walked into the room. We've adapted this great idea and each time our little boy, Noa, enters the room we shout, "Hooray for Noa," and clap. He always feels as if he's getting a standing ovation."

She looked at me expectantly, thrilled with her innovative idea.

"I'm sorry to tell you this," I replied, "but that is one of the greatest mistakes in raising children that I've ever heard. You are doing your child and yourselves a great disservice. We cannot applaud our children for walking into a room. We cannot shout hooray each time our child breathes. We must not allow our children to believe that their mere presence merits accolades and a standing ovation. Yes, we love our children. Of course, we cherish them. But we must teach our children to dig deep inside, to give of themselves, to grow. And let me tell you, once Noa goes out into the real world, he will come to expect constant applause and praise, but he will hear thundering silence. Teach him that he has a real mission in this world. Applaud his mitzvahs. Shout hooray each time he is able to overcome his selfishness. Clap for each small kindness. Cheer each seedling of honesty that he plants. Give him a standing ovation for courage. Watch him grow and realize his ability to bring light into our universe. But please, I beg of you, don't root for emptiness. You will create arrogance. You will watch a child grow into a young adult with no sense of purpose. It's not fair to your child's soul."

SHLICHUS—THE MISSION OF YOUR LIFE

As a young man, Moses fled Egypt to save his endangered life. He became a shepherd in the land of Midian. One day, G-d called to Moses from amid a burning bush. Moses was commanded to return to Egypt and transmit G-d's message to the powerful Pharaoh: Send out My people and they shall serve Me! *Ve'eshlaacha.* "And I will send you on a mission, and you, Moses, will be My messenger to the Jewish people and help lead them out of Egypt."

Moses was apprehensive. "Who am I?" he asked. Moses felt inadequate. G-d replied that He would perform miracles and the Jewish nation would believe Moses.

Moses was still not convinced. "Please," he insisted, "I'm not a man of words. Not since yesterday, not since You first spoke to Your servant, for I am heavy of mouth and speech" (Exodus 4:10).

Moses had a speech impediment. The great leader was a stutterer! In the future, Moses would be called upon to bring the Ten Commandments to the world and teach Torah to the Jewish nation. Why would G-d choose a man who had a speech defect as his charismatic messenger? Wouldn't it seem logical for G-d to heal Moses before he spoke?

G-d refuted Moses. "So now go! I shall be with your mouth and teach you what you should say."

There are times in life that our children feel inadequate. "I just can't do it," they say. "I'm going to fail."

Moses felt the same way. He had real reason for self-doubt. A speech impediment is not the quality you would expect in a world-class orator. G-d, however, did not allow Moses to use his speech impediment and deep humility as a reason to feel unworthy of fulfilling his destined life-work. Instead, G-d explained to Moses that he had a mission in life. Moses would never feel abandoned as he journeyed on his mission. He was assured that G-d would never desert him.

The encouragement given to Moses is a great directive on self-confidence. Self-confidence is fortified when we are able to overcome the limitations of our nature. For example, a child who confronts her timidness by acting boldly; a selfish child who tries hard to share; a child who performs publicly despite his shyness; a temperamental child who attempts to control her outbursts—each of these children will feel strengthened and emboldened. By ensuring our love, we encourage our children to find their particular *shlichus*, or mission, without fear of failure. Pinpoint your child's weakness and help him to overcome it. Support him with your love.

Our guidance toward our children must be twofold.

Do Not Allow Your Children to Feel Sorry for Themselves

Whether it is a physical or social difficulty, a real or imagined problem, do not join your child in a self-pity party. Give strength and encouragement to your child, as G-d did for Moses. If not, you will create a miserable child who is constantly putting him or herself down.

Seek out the uniqueness within his or her own soul. Each child is created with a matchless quality that is his or hers alone. No two people are exactly alike. Just as each of us is created with our own unique fingerprint, we are also given our own particular "spiritual fingerprint" with which we may leave our mark in this world. Discover your child's "exceptional remarkableness" and encourage him or her to touch the world in their unique way. Concentrate on the positive and withdraw the negative emotions that strip away self-esteem.

When I speak about "exceptional remarkableness" I am not referring to a brilliant IQ or out-of-this-world talent. I am, in fact, addressing the beauty that makes each child the individual that she or he is. Take a moment and look at your child. Really look at him or her. Delve beyond the exterior appearance and see his or her inner core. Help him or her to appreciate "the gift of being me." It could be a generous spirit, a kind heart, the ability to make friends easily, or even an infectious laugh—the majesty that lies within.

From the time that my son Eli was an infant he was always an explosion of energy. When he was six years old, our family went on a ski trip. In the early morning, we'd walk through the village to the slopes. Most people ventured quietly, still trying to wake themselves up. Eli would joyously skip and sing at the top of his lungs as a huge smile graced his little face.

One man stopped us. "Hey you!" he called out. "I've never seen a kid so happy. Never lose that smile, it's terrific!" Eli has always been our lively spirit, ready to inspire and exhilarate. A child who is full of life is a gift from G-d. It is incumbent upon parents to recognize this. It is crucial that we find ways to channel our children's qualities in order to bring *tikkun olam*. Once you appreciate your child's uniqueness, teach him to recognize his individual fingerprint. Eli knows that he can be a source of joyous spirit—what an awesome mission!

Ours is a generation that has become spiritually impoverished through a lack of understanding of our own self-worth. We fail to consider our innate blessings. We overlook the greatest source of self-respect that we can bestow to our children. We don't realize the heights that can be achieved by channeling our talents and capabilities.

For example, a child who enjoys drawing can give her pictures and cards to a classmate who is ill, elderly neighbors, or family. A child who is artistic can create treasured memory scrapbooks that bring joy to friends and family. A child who excels in math can tutor or help siblings. A child who loves to tell jokes can bring laughter and good cheer to those who feel down. A child who possesses leadership qualities can include unpopular kids. A child who loves to bake can create goodies for a family struggling with hardship or help out a mom who would welcome an extra hand.

When children feel vital they will discover the spiritual dimension of self-esteem. It is our mission as parents to help guide our children as their true self-worth is revealed.

Each of us is born *B'Tzelem Elokim*—in the image of G-d. There is a distinctive characteristic of G-dliness that lies within. Bolster your child's sense of vitality and discover the magic that is embedded in his or her soul.

Once children are able to contribute to others using their special characteristics, they will look upon themselves more favorably. They will take pride in who they are and not feel the need to put others down in order to feel self-worth. They will see their lives as a blessing.

Show Your Children That You Believe in Them

Our sages relay to us the inspiring story of Rabbi Akiva. When Rabbi Akiva was forty years old he was just a simple shepherd known as Akiva.

Akiva was in the employ of one of the wealthiest men at the time, Ben Kalba Savua. Ben Kalba Savua had a lovely daughter, Rachel. Rachel noticed this young shepherd who tended her father's sheep. Although Akiva was unlearned, Rachel discerned an inner spark waiting to be ignited. She was moved by his character and modesty. One day, she imagined, this man could become a great teacher in Israel, if only he was given the chance. Something about him was unusual and touched her soul.

Rachel disclosed her dreams to Akiva and he was stunned. "How could you believe that I could achieve greatness at this point of my life? I am forty years old and I don't even know the Hebrew alphabet. It's too late."

One day, Akiva noticed a huge rock by the river. Somehow, a hole had bore into it. Akiva grew hopeful with his observation.

"Each day drops of water fall onto this rock and slowly, over a span of time, a deep hole was bored inside. Our Torah is compared to water. If water can pierce thick stone and create an opening, surely Torah's words can enter my heart and penetrate my soul. All I must do is take the time to study, and perhaps I will achieve greatness."

Akiva and Rachel were secretly engaged.

When Rachel came of marriageable age, she refused the finest suitors and best marriage proposals. She finally revealed her secret engagement to Akiva, the shepherd. Her father disowned her in fury.

Rachel left her affluent lifestyle and took on menial jobs. She sent her earnings to support her husband as he began to delve in the wisdom of the Torah in a distant yeshiva. Rachel lived simply and was subject to many insults and mean jokes about herself. She was told that she was a fool to have put her faith in such a man. Despite all this, Rachel never stopped believing in Akiva and the investment she made in him. During this time, Akiva grew to become a great Torah scholar who completed learning the entire Torah.

One day, Akiva returned. He was surrounded by twenty-four thousand students. The same people who had mocked Rachel now pushed hard among the throngs to catch a glimpse of this outstanding scholar. Rachel went to greet Rabbi Akiva. She was dressed in rags. As she approached her husband, people shoved the unknown woman away.

"Do you know who this is?" Rabbi Akiva asked. "All my wisdom and all of your wisdom comes from her. Everything I am and everything you are stems from this woman." Rabbi Akiva went on to become a great leader of the Jewish people. Ben Kalba Savua reconciled with his daughter Rachel and said, "You had the wisdom to love this righteous man" (Avos D'Rebbe Nosson).

Rachel's father eventually came to see that which lay hidden within Akiva's soul. Greatness that his daughter Rachel recognized as dormant became an inspiring reality.

Rachel teaches us the power of believing in another's potential. She had firm convictions in the reality of Akiva's soul. Her faith unearthed hidden possibilities that became actualities.

Rabbi Akiva was known for saying, "Love your neighbor as yourself; this is a great principle in the Torah." Rabbi Akiva is teaching us a profound lesson in self-esteem. If we are to love others as ourselves, we must first learn to love ourselves. Self-respect leads to the respect of others. If we don't value ourselves we will be unable to comprehend the value of others. Self-esteem means that I love myself, not in an arrogant fashion, but I love myself because of the enormous potential that lies within me.

I cherish my abilities to do good in this world and so I cherish my life. I have genuine gifts to offer this world. I can give of myself—this is the ultimate road toward self-esteem. Rachel endowed Rabbi Akiva with this understanding of his intrinsic worth through her steadfast belief in him. Her faith in him allowed Rabbi Akiva to transmit this awesome teaching to us.

Later on, Rabbi Akiva tragically lost thousands of his students in a devastating plague. He easily could have said, "This is impossible for me! I've failed. I just can't do this anymore." Instead of throwing his hands up in despair and giving up, he decided to build his yeshiva anew when only a few primary students remained. He had to attend thousands of funerals of students he had loved as sons. The emotional toll must have been excruciating. Irrespective of his personal suffering, Rabbi Akiva had the fortitude to start all over again. Rachel's unwavering belief in her husband allotted him the courage to reconstruct his life's work.

As we raise our children, it is crucial that we impart a profound sense of belief in who they are. True success is not measured by the brand of sneakers you wear or the model car that you drive. Success is defined by your ability to rise above life's obstacles that may come your way. Genuine strength is not found in the gym or on the football field. Rather, it is the capacity to overcome weakness and self-distrust.

Self-confidence is born within when our children realize that they can be builders in this world. Our children will not be afraid of failure because they know that as parents we have granted them the realization of innate self-worth. Above all, our children know that no matter what, their parents love them and have faith in their abilities despite all the hardships that life holds.

Who Are You?

If we are to transmit a feeling of self-worth to our children, then we parents should examine our own feelings of self-regard. Unfortunately, today's world measures men and women by their financial success and achievements. This attitude has impacted our children's image of success. Children are privy to their parents' conversations as they discuss OPM—other people's money.

"Did you hear about their vacation?" "Did you notice her diamond ring?" "Wow, did you see their house?" "How much do you think they spent on their kitchen?"

I've heard children parrot their parents' discussions as they speak about their friends' success in the stock market, down to exact numbers. If these are the values we're transmitting then, of course, our children associate materialism with self-worth.

"I need the Juicy sweatshirt, Mom!"

"I've got to have the latest iPhone, Dad!"

We've taught our children that the more we have the better we feel about ourselves and that what we have must be the latest and the best. What happens when you strip away the latest electronics, expensive sneakers, and brand-name bags? What are you left with? Ask yourself, "Who am I, really?"

I posed this question to a group of young parents who attended a parenting seminar. One mom raised her hand. "I'll tell you the truth, Slovie, I feel better about myself when my son is well dressed. I love seeing him in his little Todd loafers and designer jeans. I love wheeling him down the street in his Bugaboo with all this great stuff. I know he doesn't need it." She smiled sheepishly. "I do it for me." The other parents nodded their heads in agreement.

"But then what?" I asked. "You've got to think about where you're going with all this. Is it only the latest great stuff that ensures your self-confidence and makes you feel good? What will you do, keep getting more stuff to maintain this feeling? How do *you* think your kids will grow up? What will happen if you can't always give them everything they want? And what about yourselves—ask yourself, who are you? Of course all this stuff is nice but what creates your self-worth? Is it your home, your salary, your designer shoes? Isn't there more to you than that? If you want children who feel good about themselves, their feelings of self-worth must transcend all this 'stuff.' It must, however, begin with you."

When my children were little, one of their favorite times was spending Shabbos at my parents' home, together with their cousins. The house was filled with children's chatter and laughter as the adults piled in, carrying overflowing suitcases and baby gear. We sat around my parents' table as the warmth of Shabbos drew us near. Although it was crowded and we had to squeeze together, the love in the room overcame the small space. After the meal, all the children would gather together in their pajamas, lying on makeshift beds and blankets. Wherever you turned, there was another child peering out from under his coverlet.

My father would sing the Shema with his grandchildren. His melodious voice filled the air. I listened in from the kitchen and even as an adult, I felt the soothing sounds balm my soul. "Tell us a story, Bubba," the children exclaimed when my father completed the nighttime prayers. "Tell us about when you were a little girl."

My mother would sit down surrounded by all the children. No matter how exhausted she was, she was full of life as she wove together her childhood memories. "When I was a little girl," my mother would begin, "Zaydah was the chief Rabbi of our city. We had many guests and visitors. Mama always had the most delicious cakes and cookies coming out of her oven. . . ."

My mother described the loving home that she grew up in . . . the visits by horse and carriage to her grandparents' home through the deep snow as the winds of war blew over Hungary. Many times she relayed her experiences as a little girl growing up in the shadow of the concentration camps.

One of my children's most requested stories was my mother's description of Shabbos in Bergen-Belsen. Each day, my grandfather would set aside his meager portion of stale bread. Friday night he would bring his children close, together with Mama.

"'Close your eyes, *kinderlach*,' he would whisper. 'Close your eyes and imagine that you are home. It is Friday night and Mama has a beautiful white cloth on the Shabbos table. The candles are lit, the flames are dancing. Mama's delicious challah is warm. The house is filled with light.' . . . Zaydah would then share his hidden crumbs with us."

The grandchildren sat up in their beds, spellbound.

My mother continued. "We heard the soft melody of 'Shalom Aleichem,' welcome to the angels of Shabbos, as Zaydah began to hum. We would join in song and for a few minutes forget that we were living in so much darkness. One week my little brother called out as Zaydah was singing. 'Tatty,' he said, 'you are singing welcome to the angels, but where are they? I don't see any angels here.' Zaydah began to cry. He looked at us for a moment and then he spoke. 'You, my precious children, are the angels.'

"And you know what, children?" my mother asked. "Each morning, I had to stand at roll call. My head was shaven and I was dressed in rags.

I was shivering from the cold. My stomach was empty and I was starving. Across from me stood the Nazi soldiers. They were marching in their shiny black boots, dressed in their fancy uniforms, all neat and perfect. But to me, they had nothing. I had everything. I was a *malach Hashem*— I was an angel of G-d. I would never in a million years want to be them. I would never want to stand in their shoes. I'd rather be barefoot and freezing but still be me, the daughter of Zaydah and Mama, an angel on earth."

My mother's stories molded my children's souls. It's not the shoes, the house, or the latest electronic toy that defines you. It's your spirit, your soul, your understanding of who you are within.

Ask yourself as a parent: Who am I? What defines me? Be sure to transmit the answer that reflects profound truth to your children as you build their self-esteem.

MEET THE INCREDIBLES

Time and time again, I meet parents who describe their children as incredible. They can hardly imagine that there is anyone else who could possibly have given life to such an amazing being. They take their cue from actors and actresses who compete in giving the most unusual names possible to their children. Everything the child does is noted, observed, and analyzed. It begins innocently enough in infancy:

> *"Look at how she nurses so well, it's amazing."*
> *"Look at how alert he is, wow, he must be very intelligent."*
> *"Watch her! She's starting to walk. She's really quick and she's only*
>   *ten months old."*

As they grow, these children come to quickly dominate their parents' lives. When their grandparents visit you can be sure the attention is focused solely on these kids. They control the room, constantly interrupting adult conversations, knowing that life revolves around them. These children can never be "just average kids"—I call them "the incredibles." As they grow and start school they meet other "incredibles." To their teachers they are mostly all just good, average kids. Some are good in spelling, some are better at math, others are great at jumping rope—but none are truly "incredibly amazing" super kids.

These children who were led to believe that they are the greatest thing that ever happened, whose every first sound and step was video-taped and posted on the Internet, arrive at school and discover that they are really like all the other kids in the room.

What have we done? Why do we find the need to produce these "incredible" kids?

Perhaps we look at our own lives and feel that we've never really excelled the way that we thought we would. We had so many dreams of what we would accomplish and who we would become, but it just never seemed to happen. We are secretly disappointed. Now we have in our hands a new opportunity to produce excellence—our children. They hold our dreams and our aspirations. All our visions of success lie within their very being. If they are incredible then so am I—after all, I did produce this child. Here is my child upon whom the sun always shines, and so I must be standing under the bright lights together with him.

We have staked our self-esteem upon the knowledge that our children are unusually amazing. The realization that they may be just average kids becomes a painful image of our own ordinary selves. If we haven't become accomplished at least our children will be great achievers.

Channah is a woman whom we meet in the Book of Samuel. She was childless and desperate to conceive. "Just one child, G-d," she pleaded. "You created the entire world. You hold the key to all souls, isn't there just one for me?"

Channah made a vow and said, "G-d of Hosts, if You will look at my pain and remember me, and give me a child among men, then I will give the child to G-d all the days of his life."

"A child among men," Channah begged. Our sages teach us that Channah asked for a child who would be average among men. She requested that he be not too tall, not too short, not too clever, and not too simple. Wouldn't Channah have asked for the most brilliant child? A world-class athlete or pianist? An amazingly beautiful child?

Channah knew the truth. What makes a child extraordinary is not his appearance, his skills, or even his high IQ. None of these constitute greatness. It is not the physical attributes that this child possesses that will be the arbiter in deciding if he is special. Rather, it is the potential for incredible goodness that makes a child great.

Channah promised that she would propel her child toward a path of G-dliness. More than anything she would nourish his soul. Channah gave life to a son whom she called Samuel—"For I have asked him of G-d." She kept her word and educated Samuel in the Torah's path. He grew to become a great prophet of Israel.

Even today, it is "Channah's prayer" that we recite as we light our Shabbos candles each week and pray for our children. Each child enters this world bearing a spark of holiness within. Our job as parents is to help him unearth his hidden potential. If I can teach my child to feel extraordinary not because he was born special, but because he lives his life with meaning and purpose, then I have perfected my mission. Children come to understand that they can affect the world and accomplish greatness in the truest sense of the word. And *that* is incredible.

JEWELS ON LOAN

Our feelings that our children's accomplishments are intrinsically tied to our own encourages us to push our children to achieve and when we push, we push hard. We rush to enroll them in the "best" nurseries so that they will be accepted into the "best" grade schools . . . we even contemplate how this choice will affect their college plans. After-school activities abound, leaving no time for simple play. As soon as school is out for the day there are yoga classes, music and art appreciation, chess lessons, swim classes, gymnastics, karate, and ballet. We think about the best age to enroll our children in Mandarin. After all, that is the future.

The pressure grows. It's difficult for our children not to feel competitive in such a driven environment.

"I'm going to the toy store and you're not."

"We're going to Disneyland and my mother said we don't have to wait on the regular lines."

"We're going skiing and having a *special* instructor. Where are you going during vacation?"

"My father has a huge office in a big building. Where does your father work?"

We need to take a step back. We must remember that our goal is not to fill our children's days with the most sought-after classes or to have the tallest trophies crowd their shelves. Children are not given to us so that we may feel better about ourselves through their achievements or to despair when they fail. They are on loan from G-d and we are the guardians of their souls. Perhaps we wouldn't push so hard if we kept this thought in mind. In fact, breaking away from the pressured environment we have created would be liberating.

When I was a teenager, my father shared a Midrash, an explanation of our sages, with me that moves me even today. After my father passed away I discovered that he had preserved the story among his many papers. I share with you my father's words:

> While Rabbi Meir was holding his weekly discourse in the House of Study one Sabbath afternoon, his two beloved sons died suddenly at home. The grief-stricken mother carried them to her room and covered them with a sheet. (There is no mourning or burial on Shabbos.) When Rabbi Meir returned after the evening services, he asked his wife, Beruriah, about the boys whom he had missed in synagogue. Instead of replying, she asked him to recite the Havdalah service, marking the departure of the Sabbath. When it was over, Beruriah turned to Rabbi Meir and said, "I have a question to ask you. Not long ago some precious jewels were entrusted to my care. Now the Owner has come to reclaim them. Shall I return them?"
>
> "But of course," said Rabbi Meir. "You know the law. Naturally, they must be returned."
>
> Beruriah then took him by the hand, led him to the bed, and drew back the sheet. Rabbi Meir burst into bitter weeping. "My sons! My sons!" he lamented. Then Beruriah reminded him tearfully, "Did you not say that we must restore to the Owner what He entrusted to our care? Our sons were the jewels which G-d left with us, and now their Master has taken back His very own. G-d has given, G-d has taken, may G-d's name be blessed."

We are blessed with precious children. They are our diamonds; their many brilliant facets reflect their inner light. But we are not their true owners. Ultimately, they are on loan, given to us for safekeeping.

Our children are gifts from G-d, entrusted in our care. We set their standards. They live our values. This means that there are times when we must confront ourselves. Conveying self-esteem compels us to question our self-identity. Who are we? What do we hold dear? What is our definition of success? When we equate financial success with the "ultimate self-worth" we are destined to lose the most vital part of "self." When we push our children hard so that we may feel self-pride, our children's inner spark is diminished. Remember, poverty of the soul is the saddest poverty of all.

ARROGANCE VERSUS SELF-ESTEEM

In our quest to raise confident children it is easy to fall into the trap of creating children who possess an inflated sense of self. Kids who have had their egos stroked as far back as they can remember sincerely believe that they deserve a steady stream of compliments and attention. They float through life pumped up with praise like overfilled balloons, ready to burst. *The Wall Street Journal*'s Jeffrey Zaslow wrote an article entitled "The Most Praised Generation Goes to Work." He described the difficulties that bosses and spouses face as they live with those who require constant acclamation. One large company has a staff member who throws confetti and hands out helium balloons to employees. Another gives praise every twenty seconds through "Celebration Voice Mailboxes." Many employees receive accolades for simply showing up to work.

Young adults and college students are described in research studies as more self-absorbed than in previous generations. Imagine being married to such a self-centered individual whose ego requires constant care. As parents we are responsible for preparing our children to become mature young adults who will thrive in future relationships.

Adults who need praise for showing up to work will not survive the difficult long nights and many thankless moments of parenthood. Genuinely dedicated moms and dads find no allowance for selfishness as they take on their many responsibilities. Parenthood is a 24/7 position where we give of ourselves both physically and emotionally, despite financial pressures, exhaustion, emotional turmoil, and daily stress. Self-absorbed children become self-centered adults who are unable to devote their heart and soul as they form their life bonds. Family life requires unselfish dedication.

These children who have been lavished with praise easily grow into arrogant kids. They have learned never to accept criticism and find fault with everyone but themselves.

You will hear: "My teacher is boring, the coach doesn't like me, the other kids started first." Even the alarm clock is guilty for not waking him or her up on time.

Over and over this child will proclaim:

"It's not fair."
"Why are you blaming me?"

"What did I do?"
"It's not my fault."

"Whatever," he says as he rolls his eyes at you. Pure arrogance, yet this attitude is often learned at home:

"That teacher doesn't know how to teach."
"Your principal doesn't know what he's talking about."
"This coach is an idiot."
"Forget about it, your school has the most ridiculous rules."

A parent I know called the parents of a child who punched and bullied their seven-year-old on the school bus. Their reaction was: "We don't get involved in our children's business and why does your child allow himself to get bullied, anyway?"

When children are constantly defended and never allowed to take responsibility for their actions, we do them a huge disservice. They lose touch with an inner voice that teaches them right from wrong. They are *always* right, the rest of the world forever wrong. Apologies and remorseful tears are humbling and necessary as we attempt to develop our children's character and refine their soul.

One evening, as I was about to begin teaching my young-couples class, a parent asked to speak to me privately.

"I am still in shock over an incident that occurred in my daughter's school today," she said, "and I'd just love a moment of your time to tell you about it.

"I picked up my six-year-old daughter from school this afternoon and one of her friends asked if she could tell me a secret. As I crouched down beside her, she spit a huge gob of saliva into my ear. I looked at her, shocked. I just could not believe it." She took a breath and continued.

"I turned to her. 'What did you do?' I said. 'That's so mean and horrible, what did you do?' I even had a small tear in my eye, I was so hurt and taken aback, but in her eyes I saw nothing. She just looked at me. No remorse, no sense of regret. She absolutely refused to apologize. What is so surprising is that she comes from such an educated and involved home. I honestly am still shocked. I know that if I'd call her parents they somehow would never accept that their daughter acted so horribly. So what do you think?" she asked.

"I think that this is great proof of everything we've been speaking about in our parenting classes," I replied. "A child who can spit in the ear of another person and not feel shame is behaving horribly and sad. But a child who can spit in the ear of an adult and refuse to apologize shows a tragic deficiency in character. This is the absolute zenith in arrogance. For six years this child has been made to feel self-important. Her entire sense of self is inflated and she's clueless when it comes to the feelings of others. Her heart is filled with arrogance; there is no space for remorse. As she matures, her parents who created this 'amazing child' will often find themselves at wit's end, the brunt of her disdain."

We cannot allow our children to walk through life with a sense of haughtiness. We are told that G-d, Himself, cannot remain in the presence of an arrogant person (Arachin 15b). The conceited individual is so full of himself, there is no room left for G-d. It is easy for children to place themselves in the center of their universe and think only of their personal needs and wants. Very quickly it becomes "all about *me*."

"I'm sorry" and "please forgive me" become phrases that are removed from their vocabulary.

King David was a royal king of Israel, known for his victory against the giant Goliath while he was still a young boy. After he led his forces and conquered the holy city of Jerusalem, it was named Ir David—the city of David. King David had a right to feel pride, yet when the prophet Nathan admonished the king for a lapse in personal judgment, King David did not fall back upon his past glories. He was overwhelmed with disappointment in himself and overcome with grief. King David responded with two words: "*Chatasi laHashem*, I have sinned against G-d." There is no question that King David could have come up with a thousand excuses and each one would have been accepted because of his royal stature. As king, he could have dismissed the prophet in a fit of rage and self-righteousness. Instead we learn that David's remorse was genuine and complete. His regret completely shattered his heart and his response was devoid of arrogance.

When the prophet Nathan completes his rebuke, there is a space in the text before we find King David's reply. The space represents a moment of hesitation by King David. "Perhaps I'm not to blame," King David rationalized for just one second. This is human nature. "It's not my fault," we say. "It's my job pressure, it's my bad marriage, it's my neglected childhood that's making me act like this." Or we excuse our children and say, "It's not my kids, the teacher is the real problem, it's those other kids' bad influence." We convince ourselves and our children that the shortcoming lies everywhere but here. King David courageously overcame the pull of human nature that compels us to place the blame on others instead of confronting our own deficiencies. His sin was immediately pardoned.

King David became known as "the sweet singer of Israel." He would rise at midnight and compose heartfelt psalms as the air of Jerusalem would stir his soul. King David did not inscribe his psalms for himself alone. He meant these words to be an everlasting source of strength for future generations. Even today, the world turns to the Psalms of King David for encouragement and consolation. It was in his humility that his greatness was born. King David confronted himself and did not allow a curtain of conceit to obstruct his view. He discovered his inner depth through sincere remorse and introspection.

Our sages teach us that this is the true quality of greatness—being able to admit the truth despite the shame of embarrassment. No excuses, no ifs, ands, or buts, but rather taking full responsibility for our actions.

We raise our children and want them to feel good about themselves. We shower them with words of encouragement and often become blinded to their faults. Many times we permit them to get away with unacceptable behavior. No apologies, no regrets.

They become accustomed to our words of praise and begin to speak with a condescending attitude. Maintaining a balance of humility with self-esteem must become a parent's priority. Self-discipline, compassion, and gratitude are all qualities that are unable to flourish amid a pompous soul.

A parent recently called me for a word of advice. Her eleven-year-old son and his best friend spent their Sunday afternoon together, making annoying phony phone calls to their neighbors. When she found out, she was understandably upset. She confronted her son and he admitted the truth.

After calling the other mom, this parent was left with a dilemma.

"I told her about our parenting classes," she said. "I told her about the importance of teaching our children sensitivity and responsibility for their actions. I said that I want our boys to apologize to our neighbors, and she refused."

"Why?" I asked. "What's the problem?"

"She said that if her son apologizes, he's going to feel embarrassed and she doesn't want to affect his self-esteem. But I know that we just spoke about the importance of teaching our children to apologize. Don't you think my son should say he's sorry?"

"Of course," I replied. "How will this child ever know right from wrong if he never takes responsibility for what he's done? How will he not grow conceited if he's never told that he did something wrong? You don't have to scream at him or humiliate him in order to teach him. And you can tell him that you know this is difficult. But that doesn't mean that you can just ignore the times you need to discipline him because you're afraid of affecting your son's self-esteem. A child who never apologizes becomes arrogant."

●   ●   ●

It is crucial for us parents to acknowledge the little things in life that our children do. As we notice and point out the small acts that require backbone, our kids will be more likely to continue on this path.

Realize that apologies take real effort, sharing a prized possession or dividing a favorite snack is not easy. Elicit thoughts from your children to bring them to think about what they do, and help them visualize the effect of their actions.

When we encourage our children to take little steps that build and form their character, we can help them climb lofty heights and achieve nobility of virtue. Self-esteem is the product of such achievements.

Teaching Humility While Maintaining Self-Esteem

Some people think that in order to teach humility, a person is required to deny his feelings of self. However, this is not our goal. We want our children to recognize their capabilities, yet not become consumed with arrogance. I don't want my child to feel inadequate; rather, I want my child to feel blessed. If your child has an ability or talent, speak to him or her about the wonder and sense of accomplishment he or she can acquire by sharing this gift properly. Distance him or her from feeling egotistical—"I am so great because I can . . ."—instead, have him or her realize that "I am blessed with this great talent and feel so grateful to be me." Help him or her understand that talents are G-d-given gifts that allow us to color our world with joy.

Moses became the greatest leader of the Jewish people, yet we learn that he was the humblest of all men. This is not a contradiction. Know your strengths and capacities but recognize their Source. Tell your child: You are a most capable athlete, you have an incredible voice, you are amazingly popular, a born leader, you are a whiz in math—whatever it is that your child is gifted with—but none of this is your own doing. You have been blessed with a gift from G-d; now let's think about how you can use your gift to endow our world. How can your talent make someone's day better? The truly humble person possesses great self-confidence and sees his gifts as an awesome responsibility. He sees no need to mock others or to feel jealousy, because he believes in himself. In fact, we find that most bullies hurt others because they suffer from low self-esteem. They push others down in order to increase their own sense of self-aggrandizement.

If you teach your children to feel secure in their sense of self, the achievements and possessions of others will never cause them to feel threatened. They will come to feel satisfied and happy with themselves. Self-confidence maintained by the knowledge that one's gifts are blessings from G-d creates the needed balance between self-esteem and humility. Help your children comprehend that their natural fortes are G-d-given gifts accompanied by great responsibility. Instruct them to be aware of their strengths and to seek opportunities to use their endowments to achieve their life's mission, their personal *shlichus* in this world. Any individual, adult or child, who feels vital, wakes up each morning with a sense of purpose and lives life on a higher plane.

HELPING OUR CHILDREN GAIN DAILY DOSES OF SELF-ESTEEM

Children who lack self-esteem will be reluctant to attempt new experiences or take on challenges that can benefit them. They often grow up to become adults who lack confidence. They fear rejection and limit expressions of true emotions in their relationships. Low self-esteem can affect marriages, friendship, careers, and the way one parents his or her children. Knowing this, it is important for us to find the proper channels in our daily lives to help build our children's real sense of self. Many moments that can affect self-esteem are not earth-shattering events, but rather, common daily occurrences that pass us by unnoticed. Let us try to take advantage of these opportunities that come our way.

Convey to Our Children Our Own Attempts of Tikkun Olam

We want our children to realize that it is their mitzvahs that help make them special. The latest sneakers, clothing, and electronic gadgets may come and go, but the essence of my soul is everlasting. What better opportunity is there for kids to gain this understanding than by witnessing their parents' actions that attest to this truth?

Find avenues to "accomplish good" in your life. Seek out opportunities to help others. Express out loud your feelings of gratification as you act upon your good intentions. For example, tell your children: "I'm so glad that I got a chance to spend time with Grandma and Grandpa today," or "I had such a wonderful day volunteering in the school's resource center. It was a great feeling helping a child learn to read."

Instead of just hosting guests, communicate your joy as you open your home. "I'm so looking forward to Friday night. We're inviting a new family that just moved in to join us for Shabbos dinner."

Share your pride with your children as your spouse accomplishes his or her mitzvah.

You are not bragging; rather, you are introducing your children to the joy of tikkun olam, being a source of goodness in this world. Let them see how content you feel as you "do" for others. Your kids will quickly absorb this wonderful lesson of life. Help your children develop their spiritual self-esteem as you cultivate your own spiritual character.

Purim is one of the most joyous Jewish holidays. We give gifts of food to friends and neighbors while we prepare for the festive meal that marks the culmination of the day. Growing up, my siblings and I would help our parents pack countless packages of homemade goodies for the many families of our synagogue. We would load the car and gingerly pile mountains of baskets on top of one another. Finding an empty spot to sit in became the next task. My father would drive us down every block of the neighborhood, and we'd run in and out of the car with our deliveries in hand. After a few hours, we'd return home to find that my mother had prepared many more baskets and we would begin the entire process all over again. My parents would always be sure to include lonely widows and families undergoing turmoil, even if they were not members of the congregation.

It was hard work for all of us—the packers, the *shleppers,* and my father, the exhausted driver. One thing I can tell you—I will never forget the expressions of joy on the faces of so many as they opened their doors and received our little baskets. I experienced the thrill of giving and overheard my parents express their own sentiments of delight as they gave of themselves throughout the day. These moments impacted me more than a thousand lectures ever could.

Now, years later, one of my children decided to give Purim baskets not only to his friends but to some children whom he thought would be lonely over the holiday. As he ran back to the car after handing over his gift, he had a huge smile spread across his face. "Mommy," he said, "I feel as happy as if I hit a home run!"

Be a Great Example When Things Don't Go Your Way

Sure, it's easy to stay calm and feel good when everything is perfect. But when you don't succeed, how do you react to disappointment? Be sure to convey that there are times in life we may fall short, but that doesn't mean we're a failure. It just means that we will try harder next time. It may be a little occurrence, like working on a recipe for two hours and then having it burn in the oven, or misplacing the keys and missing an appointment. Perhaps a bigger event occurred—my PC crashed and I lost my files, I was passed over for a promotion at work, we lost out on a bid for the house we so wanted, or my stock portfolio crashed.

It doesn't matter. What *is* important is my ability to show my child that no event can strip me of my self-esteem. I remain who I am, my essence intact. This moment defines my definition of success to my child. It's not the burned cookies, the missed promotion, or the bid on the home that I so desired yet lost. I am still the same person formed *B'Tzelem Elokim,* in the image of G-d. No event, no portfolio, can ever alter that fact.

> L. was about three years old and I had just taken your class on how to build self-esteem in children. One of the examples that you gave was showing children how you react in situations and I remember you gave an example of when you were about to begin a family vacation and the plane got canceled.
>
> So there I was, driving in the car, getting ready to pull into a parking spot after waiting for one to open in a full lot and it was raining.

And the spot opened up right in front. And this woman swerved in and took it.

At that moment I said to myself this is a perfect moment to teach my child a lesson. And with that I explained how even though that was frustrating, there is no need to get upset. There will be another spot.

L. always talks about that moment. Remember when that woman took our spot and we just walked away and didn't say anything ? He uses this example in his life, like whether a child is nice to him or in other situations.

I always think to myself, that woman actually did me a favor. Anyway, L. was three, so this was three years ago and it still resonates for both of us.   EXCERPT OF AN E-MAIL I RECEIVED

When I studied about the Great Depression in school, my mother commented that as a young girl she was always shocked when she learned about this chapter of American history. "How could grown men with families jump out of windows because they lost their fortunes?" she wondered. Here she was, a refugee who arrived penniless to this country with her parents and siblings. Everything they had was suddenly snatched away—their home, furniture, clothing, bank accounts, even living family members. Not even for an instant, though, did the thought of ending one's life enter the picture. Life was too precious, there was too much to live for. There was yet so much that remained to be accomplished.

No matter what, we still own our most vital assets—our spirits, our souls, our future. Failure is the lack of strength to try again. Success is the ability to hold on to the force of life and maintain one's sense of self. Your children will mirror your definition of success and failure.

The Power of Children

Children often feel powerless. They require help with almost everything. So much is out of their reach. They are "little people" in a "big people" world. When they are able to contribute, their self-esteem grows. Everyone has a need to feel vital and independent. Give children responsibilities they can handle. Allow them to tend the garden of life and watch their offshoots sprout.

Instead of just waiting for dinner to be served, kids should be encouraged to be a part of the meal preparation. When a newborn sibling arrives, allow older siblings to help. Younger kids can help bathe or sing to the newborn. Older siblings can give a bottle or gently rock a baby to sleep. Have children create welcome signs when grandparents or guests visit. Let them help set up the guest room. They will enjoy watching people's reactions to their hands-on hospitality. Keep a charity box in your home. Have your kids contribute. Even pennies add up and make a difference. When the box is full, count it together and decide to which charity you would like to contribute it. As children grow older, discuss which responsibilities they'd like to take on.

A student of mine called to tell me that her son was studying Hebrew. She and her husband did not know how to read or even recognize the Hebrew letters. The first evening her son returned from class, he excitedly showed his parents the first letter, *aleph*. "Don't leave it at that," I told her. "Tell him that he is your Hebrew teacher." She later informed me that his eyes lit up when she conveyed this idea. Her son comes home each week enthused to share his newfound knowledge. His ability to contribute has provided him with a whole new dimension. Children should feel essential.

Encourage children to pray. Judaism teaches us that the prayers of innocent children are pure and cherished. They are indispensable to our world. The Book of Esther describes a dark time for the Jewish people. Haman, an evil advisor to King Achashverosh, was given royal permission to annihilate the Jews of ancient Persia. Queen Esther, a Jewess, had not revealed the origin of her faith. She spoke to Mordechai, a leader of the Jewish nation and Esther's uncle.

"Go, assemble all the Jews that are to be found in Shushan and fast for me," she begged (Esther 4:16). She would speak to the king and plead for her people. There was just one condition. Esther asked that Mordechai gather the nation for repentance.

Mordechai cried bitterly and tore his garments in mourning. He spoke publicly, with a heavy heart.

"Beloved brothers, we have no prophet to beg for us and show us what to do. We have no land, no city to run to. We are like sheep with no shepherd, a ship without a captain. . . . We have only G-d" (Artscroll Megillas Esther).

Mordechai then assembled the children and sat them down on the ground. They wept and studied Torah. He asked them to pray on behalf of their people.

Each parent felt that their child's presence made a difference. And each child understood that their prayer was crucial. The edict was over-turned. Days of sorrow were transformed into days of joy and gladness. The holiday of Purim was declared. This is the power of children.

Show Your Child That He or She Is Important to You

Each child should feel loved and cherished. Chapter 4 on communication speaks about maintaining and strengthening the parent-child bond. Try not to multitask when your child speaks to you. Eye contact is an important medium that demonstrates an appreciation for your child's words. Mumbling "Okay," or nodding distractedly to your child's words as you speak on the phone doesn't create an atmosphere of caring.

One mother told me that once when her son was speaking to her she was so preoccupied that it was only after he left the house that she realized he had asked her permission to go somewhere—the problem was she had no idea where!

There are times that a child's performance will conflict with your work schedule. If you are able to reschedule in order to be there, your child will remember your commitment to him or her as one of his or her most special memories. My children know that when we read a bedtime story, are having dinner, or if we're in the middle of a discussion, I will not answer the phone. Our time together is most important.

Our facial expressions significantly manifest our love: "Rabbi Yochanan says it is greater to show the white of your teeth than to give someone a glass of milk" (Kesubos 111b). A smile is more beneficial than a glass of milk. There is nothing like a great smile to nourish your child's soul. I can still clearly visualize my parents' enthusiasm each time we'd visit with our children. "My gorgeous *kinderlach*," my father would say with great joy, his arms spread wide, a beautiful smile spread across his lips. "Look who's here," my mother would sing and an expression of delight graced her countenance. We were showered with kisses and felt immensely loved.

Develop Your Own Self-Image

Self-esteem is contagious. A child easily picks up on a parent's lack of confidence and self-assuredness. Children model behavior after their parents. One of the greatest components toward developing a child's self-esteem is his observing a parent who embodies a positive self.

Ask yourself these questions:

How do I see myself?
Do I feel confident?
How do I act toward others?
How do I react?
Do I lose it over small slights?
Do I like myself?

See yourself in certain situations:

If I am not invited to a certain party, do I go on and on about how
   offended I am?
If someone cuts me off in traffic or if a clerk doesn't give me
   immediate attention, do I become agitated?
If someone insults me, do I rant and rage? Do I hold on to my anger
   and not forgive easily?
If I am unhappy with the last few pounds I gained, do I feel down?
   Do my kids hear me complain about my poor body image?
If I face a financial loss, do I feel a loss of self-respect?
Are other people's words able to upset me easily?

My self-respect should not be dependent upon other people's words, the reading on a scale, or my bank account.

The laws of *lashon harah*, the prohibition of speaking gossip and slander, includes the fact that one may not speak badly about oneself. We are not to destroy our self-image, for aren't we all created in the image of G-d Himself? "Rabbi Shimon says do not judge yourself to be a wicked person" (Ethics 2:18).

Parents should never put themselves down in front of their children. Not only are you teaching your child to disrespect you, but you are exposing your child to "self-hatred." Watch that your children do not hear you articulate phrases like:

"I hate myself, I got so fat."
"I can't believe I'm so stupid."
"I don't know what's the matter with me; Mommy's or Daddy's so
   silly."
"I'm such a loser."

Well, what does that make your child, the son of a loser? Who wants to be that?

Create a Family Legacy

Names in Judaism are very significant. We believe that a person's Jewish name is closely related to his life's mission. The root of the word *neshamah* is *shem,* or name, because one's name and one's soul are inextricably tied.

The Midrash recounts a fascinating event that occurred at the beginning of creation:

> When G-d desired to create man, He consulted with the ministering angels.
>
> "Let us make man," He said.
>
> "What will be his nature?" the angels inquired.
>
> "His wisdom will be greater than yours," He replied. G-d presented the angels with all the animals in creation. He asked the angels to name the animals but they were unable to do so. Then He brought the animals before man. One by one, G-d asked him, 'What will this one be called?'
>
> Man replied. "Ox, donkey, horse, camel," to each one. (Each name had great significance towards the animal's characteristics in the Hebrew tongue.)
>
> "What is your name?" G-d asked him.
>
> "It is fitting that I be called Adam, since I was created from the *adamah,* the earth," he replied.
>
> "What is My name?" asked G-d.
>
> "It is fitting for You to be called the L-rd since You are the Master over all of Your creations," replied Adam.
>
> BEREISHIS RABBAH 17:4

Adam named himself Adam because he was created from the earth, *adamah.* Adam perceived that a name is not merely given because of pop culture, or you like the way it sounds. Rather, in Judaism, a name is holy and represents one's essence.

Our sages explain that just as the earth yields its fruit and sprouts forth goodness after much hard labor, so, too, does the life of man. Man accomplishes in life through hard work and self-betterment. Beneath the earth lies great potential waiting to be tapped. Oil, precious stones and metals, diamonds, and gold must be mined deep below the ground. A farmer tends his soil from early morning until dark, for countless hours before he realizes its fruits. So, too, man. This is our very core, the key to our existence. We must dig deep and strive to accomplish. This is our mission. Teach your child the lesson of Adam. Discover the hidden qualities within. Find the inherent attributes through which your child may shine.

A child who is popular, talented, or intelligent will easily feel self-assured. But what about the child who does not feel good or special enough? Do not allow him or her to fall into the role of seeking negative attention that he or she finds preferable to no attention at all. Seek out a unique quality that lies untapped, beneath the surface. Adam's lesson still speaks to us today. Discover the hidden character traits within. Help your child excavate and explore the depths of his or her soul. If you tend your garden well, the fruits of your labor will be so sweet.

To help better understand their family legacy, I encourage my students to explore the meaning of their Jewish names. As they bestow Hebrew names upon the next generation, they give the matter much thought because we are taught that one's spiritual destiny is contained in one's name. Each name's definition contains deep personal meaning. Once their children receive a biblical name, it is valuable to share with them the beautiful birthright that they have received. They will love to hear about and then feel connected to these great personalities for whom they've been named. Our Torah introduces us to those who launched the noble qualities that are so lacking in our world today.

Abraham and Sarah embodied kindness, Joseph withstood the pressure of an immoral society, Rachel taught us the true meaning of selflessness, Miriam never allowed her faith to die, Daniel displayed courage in the lion's den. As we study, my students are awed by the beauty of it all. They seek out names through which they hope to spiritually impact their children's lives. Biblical heroes and heroines endow us with an everlasting legacy of moral strength, conviction, and faith that has survived the centuries. Their story becomes our story as we cultivate their character traits within our personal lives.

Your child will take pride in his or her deep roots and gain a personal role model for life. It is true that "the apple doesn't fall far from the tree"—but the tree needs hardy roots to endure wind, storms, and harsh conditions. When we give our children a foundation upon which to stand, when we provide a personal history, we lay the bedrock from whence they draw inner strength. These children will find it easier to embrace life with dignity. They will find direction and purpose as they move forward because they have grasped tightly on to their past. Knowledge of their roots fortifies them. What a great journey to take with your child!

Too often we move away from the heritage of our previous generations, as we become enthralled with the culture of today. Only too late do we regret the priceless treasure we have so easily discarded. We remain with empty souls and meaningless refrains. Endow your child with a spiritual inheritance. Rediscover your roots. Provide your child with a narrative to live by.

There is a time-honored tradition in Judaism that teaches us to name our children for one who has passed from this earth, usually a relative or a known righteous individual. The soul of that person is now intrinsically linked and bonded to his or her namesake. We pray that his or her merit continuously accompanies the infant. The newborn is given a lifelong legacy even through its very name.

If your child has been named for a relative, explore the wonderful character traits that individual possessed. Encounter the beauty of previous generations. Strengthen your family's bond.

All of our children were raised with an understanding of our family's noble legacy. Righteous and great rabbis, together with their wives and children, they were known for their Torah knowledge and kindness. A rabbinical dynasty was bequeathed to us. Our family traces its roots back to King David. Each child is inspired by the legendary figure for whom she or he has been named.

My son Akiva Chaim received the name of my father's nephew, Akiva HaLevi Jungreis. He was an outstanding Torah scholar who perished during the Holocaust. He was anticipating his bar mitzvah when he was taken away, together with his parents and small siblings. They were never heard from again.

When we reached the momentous occasion of my son's bar mitzvah, we could not leave the remembrance of our dear cousin behind. As my thirteen-year-old bar mitzvah boy rose to speak, he carried the legacy of his name so gracefully.

His young soul bore witness to the ancient faith of our people. His sweet voice rang through the room as echoes of the past could be heard. Our Akiva concluded his bar mitzvah message with these words: "I dedicate my bar mitzvah to the memory of my cousin, Akiva HaLevi Jungreis, who died, *al kiddush Hashem*, sanctifying G-d's name, and to the thousands of bar mitzvah boys whose voices of Torah were cut off in their childhood. *Menesharim kalu umearayos gaveru*—they were swifter than eagles and stronger than lions to fulfill the will of their Creator."

Don't Raise a Praisaholic!

We've heard about shopaholics, alcoholics, workaholics, even chocoholics. Now, we have created a generation of "praiseaholics"—children who have been raised on words of constant glorification. They have become "praise dependent." They cannot function without proper acclaim.

I was sitting on a park bench, speaking to a set of parents seated beside me. Every few moments, one of them would turn and shout out to their son enthusiastically:

> "Wow! Look how you climbed up the slide! You are amazing!"
> "You are the best jumper ever!"
> "That ball you threw went so far. What a great ballplayer you are!"

Each time this little boy landed at the bottom of the slide, he needed to hear how wonderful he was before he could move on.

We all want to raise confident, self-assured kids. Yet constant praise is not the formula for success. Our children grow to expect praise. Like the child in the park, they cannot move on without being celebrated.

Give the Right Type of Praise

It is not only constant praise that is detrimental to our children's well-being. Even the *type* of praise offered can affect our children's self-esteem.

It is much more beneficial for a child to hear his efforts praised and encouraged than listening to "you're so smart" or "you're so amazing."

When you praise a child for his intelligence or for being "the best," or "unbelievable," you are setting him up to fear failure. What happens if the next time he's not "the best"? Let's say he's not "amazing" when the subsequent challenge comes his way.

Why try, if I'm already "the smartest," "the best on the team," or "the most talented of all"? There's no place left for me to go but down. Why bother?

CLIMBING JACOB'S LADDER

When our patriarch Jacob departed from his parents' home and traveled on a long journey of exile, he laid down to rest on Mount Moriah. This was the exact spot where the Jewish Temple would later stand in Jerusalem. The Torah tells us that Jacob had a dream, a vision.

> And he dreamt, and behold! A ladder was set earthward and its top reached heavenward; and behold angels of G-d were ascending and descending on it.   GENESIS 28:12

Jacob's ladder is a beautiful metaphor for our lives. We are charged to strive toward the heavens and live each day with an ultimate goal as we climb the ladder of life. Just as a ladder requires us to ascend, so, too, does a person rise, step by step, moment by moment. We don't begin on top by being the smartest or the best, but it is through our good deeds and efforts to grow that we are able to bridge heaven and earth. Sure, there will be unexpected obstacles that may pull us down. We may even miss a step and fall. The beauty of man is that we have within us the G-d-given ability to pick ourselves up and rise again. We possess the fortitude to overcome. One just has to draw upon his inner strength. We should never become paralyzed by self-doubt. Instead, Jacob taught us to always have a lofty goal in mind. Strive higher and higher and if mistakes are made don't be ashamed to try again.

This then, must be our attitude as we watch our children map their course in life. Our purpose is not to praise our kids and plaster their bulletin boards with easily obtained awards and stars proclaiming their slightest accomplishment. We can teach our children to soar and build their own personal ladders through real effort and the pains of labor.

It is not enough for us to aim for kids who are satisfied with their status quo, afraid that the next step may bring a lower grade or inferior standing. Content with "merely being" doesn't propel us to move ahead toward a higher direction.

If we praise effort—genuine attempts at mastering skills and subjects—our children will grow more confident in their abilities. They will not fear failure or mistakes. They will dare to achieve that which seems so difficult in their eyes. Praising and appreciating our children's efforts means that no one can ever disparage the force of their exertion as they try to reach their goals.

Be careful not to make the common mistake of parents who confuse praise with encouragement. They are not the same. Children need your positive reinforcement, knowledge that you believe in them, and unconditional love. In other words, encouragement. They do not require consistent accolades, exuberant compliments for their most minute achievements, and a steady stream of commendations. This would only devalue your words of real, truthful, hard-earned praise.

It is important not to ignore character achievements, which, unfortunately, are easily overlooked. When we were kids the first grades my parents would search for on our report cards were those for character. The message was clear. You could have the greatest marks, but without good character your grades are meaningless. We were told over and over: *Derech eretz kadmah laTorah*—ethics and good character must precede your studying of Torah . . . for what is the purpose of all your studies and great test scores if you do not know how to behave like a *mensch* in life? I have seen intelligent kids who attend the most elite private schools wound parents, teachers, and peers with their sharp, hurtful words. In vain do we praise grade-point averages and extracurricular activities if our children fail to spiritually strive. Judaism impresses upon us the belief that every effort one makes toward living a life filled with value and every mitzvah that is accomplished is a priceless achievement. Show your child that you appreciate his strength of character.

Put yourself in your child's shoes. Perhaps the A in history came easier to him than the B- in math. He tried his hardest in math. He studied for all his exams, but struggled with his math problems. If Mom and Dad only focus on delighting in the A and questioning the B, they have disregarded his efforts. They see the ultimate grade as the measure of success. Why should I endeavor if my efforts are not realized as an accomplishment?

Rabbi Tarfon transmitted to us in *Ethics of the Fathers* a life-transforming teaching. "You are not required to complete the task yet you are not free to withdraw from it" (Ethics 2:21). It's easy to become overwhelmed and discouraged when faced with challenges in life. Don't worry, Rabbi Tarfon implores us. You are not expected to carry out all of your obligations perfectly. You are only required to do as much as your capabilities permit; just don't extricate yourself from your responsibilities. At least make an attempt and give it all you've got. Climb Jacob's ladder. Don't be afraid to stumble, there's always another rung to climb.

Allow Your Children to Face Adversity; Allow Your Children Independence

Many times we attempt to shield our children from difficulties. Parents don't want to see their children struggle. We believe that we must protect them from adversity and provide them with exclusively happy experiences. This is an impossible mission to fulfill. No matter who you are, no matter your status in life, there will unfortunately be sadness and adversity, trials and tribulations. If you create a stress-free zone around your child he will be unable to handle any experience out of his realm. He will lack the coping skills that are crucial while dealing with everyday life. Life's little mishaps will set him off balance—I'm not even speaking about a genuine, full-blown crisis!

We have become overanxious and overinvolved:

"What do you mean the coach sat you on the bench?"
"You didn't get to be in the class with all your friends?"
"You feel as if your teacher doesn't like you?"

Instead of allowing our children to work out these situations independently, we respond by telling them: "Don't worry, we'll make a call." Perhaps you've seen it described as helicopter parenting: mothers and fathers who hover and can't seem to let go.

"I can't believe Amy said that to you. I'm calling her mother and giving her a piece of my mind."
"You're too tired to do your homework? I'll write a note."
"You fell off the swing? Don't move, I'm coming to carry you away."

We are the Purell generation. In an instant we are able to wipe away any "bad stuff" that may be lurking nearby. But we cannot protect our children from the many disappointments that life has in store for us. We cannot deny our children the functional skills needed to deal with life's unpleasant moments. We are raising children in their own world of virtual reality. They are unable to navigate beyond the secure borders that we have drawn. We try to protect our kids from challenges. We expect them to absolutely succeed; yet their success or lack thereof takes place on the turf that we provide.

Very rarely do we allow them the taste of defeat or even the struggle of completing a task. It is more important to us that our children receive an A or make honor roll than be labeled as a B–. How many times have we come to a school fair only to find that most of the parents had completed their children's projects? Reports and papers are passed on from sibling to sibling or parents wind up pulling all-nighters and writing the reports themselves.

Children whose parents are overly involved and manipulative are unable to handle independence. They cannot manage their time well. They get bored and frustrated easily. A twenty-minute homework assignment requires an hour's worth of time. Simple tasks bring on whining and complaining. Tutors and therapists are sought after and recommended. We not only shelter our kids from the storm, we shelter them from the basic elements. The magic of learning through one's mistakes is lost.

Children mirror our emotions. If we are overly anxious they will reflect our apprehension. On the other hand, if we remain calm and secure our kids will develop an attitude that is absent of fear and equivocation. They will behave in an assured and confident manner.

Practically speaking, if your toddler falls down while running and cuts his or her chin, you have a choice. Either you can rush over and scream in a voice filled with panic or you can calmly hold a cloth onto the wound and in a soothing voice survey the damage. Screaming with panic will only cause your child to become terrified, as he or she will reflect your emotions. Speaking in a calm demeanor lets your child know that there's no need to become hysterical even if stitches are required.

The same concept applies to children as they grow older. There will be emotional issues with friends, difficulties in camp and school. If we overreact or micromanage our children's lives, they will never learn to cope on their own. Every bump on the road becomes a major mountain to climb. Children who are exposed to various life situations—some joyful, some sad—learn the art of endurance. They grow confident in their abilities to triumph over life's challenges.

It was early morning when my phone rang. Laurie and Jeff, a young couple who attend my classes, were on the line. Laurie's dad had passed away during the night. Although he was elderly and frail, his death was sudden and unexpected.

"We're not sure if it's appropriate for our girls to attend the funeral," Laurie said. "We think they may become traumatized by the whole death thing," Jeff added.

Laurie and Jeff were treating their school-aged children as if they were fragile pieces of glass. Any pressure would cause them to shatter.

"I appreciate your concerns," I told them, "but life is not Disneyland. Besides the proper honor that is required to be given to their grandfather, your girls must experience life. No matter how you cut it, death is unfortunately a part of life. We cannot protect our children forever. This is a perfect time to teach your children about the body and soul. Spend time putting together a beautiful memory journal about Grandpa. Permit your daughters to observe that sometimes parents cry and experience sadness for those we love. It's okay. Reassure them that we also find comfort with time and don't cry forever. We feel happy again. Memories remain in a special place, deep within our hearts, forever."

Life brings many challenges. While we are not required to seek out difficulties, we should not shield our children and provide a Teflon coating from all of life's struggles. Instead, we can teach our children how to better handle adversity. We need to give our children the tools to maneuver and work through various situations. Our goal is to raise children who are ready to face challenges with courage, fortitude, effort, and faith. These are the kids who have acquired true self-esteem.

Begin When Your Children Are Young

A disciple approached his rabbi, the renowned Baal Shem Tov. "Each time I feel that I am approaching G-d, I find myself farther away than ever."

The Baal Shem Tov replied, "When a father wishes to teach his infant how to walk, he waits until his child is able to stand on two feet and then places himself nearby. He stretches out his arms within a few inches. Even though the child is afraid, his father's presence encourages his child to take a step. After the first unsteady footstep, the father retreats a bit, his arms still beckoning his child. Seeing his father still within his grasp, the child moves one foot forward. With each retreat comes one more step.

"'What's happening?' the child wonders. 'Every time I try to reach my father he retreats. I move closer but he is farther away.'

"Your situation is quite similar," concluded the Baal Shem Tov. "G-d wants you to travel a distance and grow as you seek Him. Learn how to search for G-d and you will find that G-d is there, right in front of you."

Our relationship with our children is similar. We want to teach our children independence. We desire that our children learn to be self-sufficient. If we always carry them they will never master the skill of walking on their own. There will be times in life that we need to step back. It may be painful for parents to retreat and watch their children stumble. If children feel their parents' confidence in them, they will find the inner fortitude to stand again on their own two feet. Parents may remain unseen, but their unwavering faith is felt within as children take their first steps toward independence. Even when he leaves home, he always finds his parents' images before him, giving him the courage to go forward in life.

Begin when your children are young. Small children get frustrated easily. Instead of rushing in and correcting the situation, see if they can remedy it on their own. The puzzle piece that won't fit, the noodle that keeps slipping off the fork, the shirt put on upside down are but a few examples that may impede a young child throughout the day.

Step back for a moment. Offer words of encouragement, even guidance, but allow your children to discover their own path toward fixing their problem. Parents find that older kids come to them and say things like: "I'm starved," "I'm bored," "I can't do this homework," "I can't find my shoes." You may be tempted to prepare a snack, present activities, sit down with the homework problems, or find the lost item. Step back. Ask your child a question: "What could you do to help yourself?" Give your children the ability to come upon a solution of their own instead of spoon-feeding them.

A father and mother complained to me about their toddler's constant whining. They couldn't handle the screeching and often lost their tempers. We spoke about the proper response to whining. After implementing the steps discussed, they were delighted to find that their daughter's tantrums diminished over time. One afternoon, their child began to whine but caught herself in this undesired behavior.

"Mommy, Daddy," she exclaimed, "I almost cried hard, but I stopped all by myself. I'm a big girl now!"

Their child felt proud of herself. She had achieved self-control on her own. This little girl was on the road toward healthy independence.

She was thrilled with her newfound maturity. Her parents observed their child's self-esteem blossom as they stood at a near distance.

Angels Never Fall

No one wants to see their child in pain. We want our children to be content and lead happy lives. When our children are excluded and made to feel unpopular, we hurt for them. I have spoken to countless parents who ache inside as their kids lie on their beds, crying from being left out of the clique. These are kids who were shut out of sleepovers, baseball games, weekend get-togethers, or huge birthday parties that everyone else seemed to be attending.

Then, there are the physical turmoils that children face. Problems as they grow discovered during doctor's checkups, chronic conditions and illnesses, learning disabilities, or exhaustive medical procedures all take an emotional toll on our children. Our hearts pound as doctors lay out various options. We hope and pray for the best. We look at our children's innocent faces and ask that G-d spare them from any pain. "It's not fair!" they cry out. Somehow, we feel their hurts, both emotional and physical, more than our own.

Suffering is difficult. It is even more difficult when we watch our children in pain. Though we cannot always remove the source of distress, we can give our children an attitude for life when faced with struggle. This attitude can transform their challenges from a source of misery to a source of spiritual growth.

Judaism teaches us that every situation one finds himself in is custom-made by G-d in order to develop one's inner self. There is no such thing as a random event, a senseless happening. Our mission is to find meaning in everyday events. The Jewish view of suffering is that it is a process of self-birth. If my pain has no meaning then I am just a victim of unfortunate circumstance. However, if I contemplate my struggles and grow from this experience, painful as it may be, I can develop my inner being. Now there is a purpose to my suffering. *Purpose* changes the entire picture. It is the difference between a random shard of glass that cuts me versus the pointed jab of a doctor's needle that vaccinates me from disease. If I realize that there is validity to my pain, I can endure.

The point is not to ensure only lighthearted moments in our children's lives, but to help our children find purpose in their life's challenges. Deep within our souls lie vast potential that remain untapped. Our mission is to unearth character traits such as sensitivity toward others, compassion, and faith that may be realized through life's challenges. My responsibility as a parent is to help my child face adversity and discover his or her capacity for greatness. We tend, though, to indulge our children's feelings of self-pity as they face their struggles. We miss a major highway toward developing our children's character. How much of our children's souls lay wasted, unrealized potential waiting to be tapped?

Our sages call this situation *yissurim shel ahavah*—afflictions of love. We are to go through certain difficulties in life, because G-d wants us to realize that there is more to us that lies dormant than we can possibly conceive. Just as grapes are pressed and trampled upon to produce wine, so, too, there are times we will be pressed to produce our vast, hidden potential. Adversity is a great teacher.

Abraham and Sarah brought knowledge of G-dliness and spirituality to a world that had none. They were also sorely tested in their lives. As this couple taught others about G-d and watched these families flourish, Sarah herself remained barren. They went through crisis, trauma, and pain. Finally they were blessed with a precious son, Isaac. They then faced new challenges and moments of deep sacrifice.

And so went the lives of all of our patriarchs and matriarchs. They faced great difficulties and various hardships. Our sages teach us that these struggles forged a path for us, their children, to live by. Their encounters created spiritual genes for future generations to transmit until today. We possess the ability to endure despite persecution, to sacrifice and strive, to achieve beyond the mundane. We were given the desire to endow kindness to mankind based on this spiritual legacy.

Struggles continued for the twelve sons of Jacob. They settled in the land of Egypt and grew into a small nation. There, they were enslaved, beaten, and assigned tortuous labor. All male Jewish babies were to be thrown into the Nile River. The children of Israel are described in the Torah as afflicted and embittered.

When we were finally taken out of Egypt we traveled in the desert for forty years. There were times when the Jewish people complained bitterly. They stumbled and sinned. Through all the traumas and crises, the nation picked themselves up, summoned their strength, and, finally fortified, accepted the holy Torah.

We are taught that angels never fall. They are always standing and are never challenged. They remain upright.

Man, on the other hand, can stumble but he can also rise and reach great heights. These are the moments that propel us forward. These are the challenges that develop an inner core. We draw upon our hidden reservoir of character as we withstand the tests of life.

BUILDING CHARACTER THROUGH ADVERSITY

At Sinai we were given the Torah with all its commandments for time immemorial. One mitzvah in particular that was given builds upon the experience of our suffering in Egypt. "You shall not taunt or oppress a stranger for you were strangers in the land of Egypt. You shall not cause pain to any widow or orphan" (Exodus 22:20–21).

The Torah is teaching us to be sensitive to those who are vulnerable and hopeless. Our sages expound that we should be aware of the emotions of any newcomer—even to a neighborhood or school. Anyone who may feel ill at ease in strange surroundings requires extra-special sensitivity. We are cautioned not to forget our past, when we ourselves felt vulnerable and anguished. We are instructed to use our pain as a vehicle for bettering our society instead of becoming bitter.

When your children are excluded and pained, know that you can now teach them to feel the pain of others. Besides helping them cope and finding other friends or experiences that will develop their self-esteem, focus on their souls. Children who are cast aside by their peers can grow embittered quite easily. They often seek revenge, many times with their parents' encouragement: "Arianna didn't invite you, now *we'll* make a sleepover and not invite her," or "Jordan left you out of his swim party, forget about inviting him to our pizza party."

You are just encouraging your child to act in the same unkind, cruel manner as that of the other child. Why not teach your child to take the higher road? This is a perfect opening to widen your child's heart and teach him or her to become a more compassionate human being. What a great opportunity to explore feelings of kindness, goodness, and tolerance despite the meanness of others!

Good-heartedness is not developed by talk or by being responsive to those who oblige us. Rather, by showing our children how to live with dignity and not fall into the trap of reflecting the mean-heartedness of others, we can develop our children's characters. We can teach them to utilize the pain they feel as a springboard toward expanding the depths of their souls.

Tell your child to remember this feeling, remember for always how you ache. Now tell him or her, "Try to be forever sensitive to the feelings of others. Don't inflict this pain in the hopes of becoming popular. Don't shrug your shoulders with indifference as you exclude other kids." Watch your child's sensitivity grow.

The physical challenges our children must endure are indeed painful to observe. We cannot comprehend why G-d sends illness or handicaps to children. I do not pretend to hold the key toward understanding G-d's hidden ways. I can only hope that through my words, we can instill in our children the courage to carry on with faith and deep-rooted joy. It is up to us to create spiritual footsteps so that our children may walk through life, sensitive to the pain of others.

Rebecca and Daniel began to study with me in our young couples class. Whoever met them was touched by their genuine goodness. You could tell that this couple was indeed "a match made in heaven." They were blessed with two beautiful children, a perfect family to behold.

Their six-year-old daughter, Sarah, began to complain of severe stomachaches. After her symptoms grew more serious, Sarah was sent for testing. She was given the diagnosis of celiac disease. Sarah would now need to be ever vigilant with every bite of food for the rest of her life. Birthday parties, school lunches, vacations, and simple play-dates would all be affected. Rebecca called, quite upset.

We spoke about our children and their struggles. We discussed the heartache parents feel as we watch our child in pain and the potential for good that can be drawn out of our child's struggle. Much time has passed since that first difficult day. I asked Rebecca to share her thoughts and emotions with you and the impact on her child's essence as seen through her eyes.

My six-year-old daughter suddenly exhibited signs of illness. Physically and emotionally, I could not make sense of it. It was the first time in my life that I truly felt helpless. I watched her suffer through physical symptoms. She had gastric pain that kept us on the bathroom floor through the night. Pains in her legs, inability to eat, severe nose-bleeds . . . but even more painful for me was watching her suffer emotionally.

A new, overwhelming anxiety had taken over. She was afraid of school; she had become withdrawn, and was left out of activities. Afraid to be snatched, she wouldn't sit on our doorstep. Sadness had replaced her spirit and sometimes a strong anger set in. I looked at her and saw a small frame. She was pale with thin hair. For the very first time in my life I began to feel heavy sadness, the kind that comes when someone you love and protect is suffering. I had no control. My firstborn was falling through my fingers and I just couldn't lift her.

Was it emotional? Physical? My fault? I didn't know. The doctors didn't know. I was Torah-parenting and it was supposed to go just fine . . . but my baby was sick. During one conversation with my teacher, Slovie, we talked about fear.

"Fear is unproductive," she said. "Torah says that everything in life should be purposeful." She asked me to try and save up my fear all day and then take time before bedtime to pray. "Channel your emotions toward prayer. The gates of tears, we are told, are never closed."

It became my ritual, Psalm 20 each night. I sobbed through each beautiful word.

We found a doctor and a diagnosis. Celiac Disease is a multi-system autoimmune disorder. As our doctor told us, "The best one to have, it is completely controlled by diet." It was a protein in grain that her body was attacking and causing her digestive system to shut down. Physically, she would be fine. Spiritually, I was more confused than ever.

My teacher, Slovie, and I discussed why some souls need to struggle. She told me that every child has something to struggle with; some physical, some emotional. We discussed how struggle refines a soul. Sarah would know what it was like to live without. She would always have to think before she acted—which was actually a Torah formula for living. In my heart I knew that one day she would bene-fit. We would know how to give a little more, plan ahead, and be im-perfect. I would never have imagined what was to come.

My mother and I shared my daughter's diet, wanting to share her burden. Sarah called us a team. She began to understand that every-one has a challenge, some she couldn't see. Feeling so helpless has al-lowed us to feel more compassion. Often, Sarah tells another child, "Don't worry, I have something, too!"

She has become strengthened. She can sit at the table, with adults who will not limit themselves in any way, and she enjoys what she can. She has learned how great her inner fortitude really is.

One night my husband was overwhelmed with inspiration. "If she can do this," he said, "surely I could be kosher." He has now be-come strengthened.

Just this week, Sarah was offered a really delicious-looking doughnut. She asked, "Can I take it for my brother?" While driving home I looked at her through my mirror. She was holding his doughnut.

"Sarah, it is so difficult to bring something to someone that you want so much to enjoy yourself. It is the ultimate kindness. You are so young and you inspire me to be kinder. I am so proud of you." She is surely strengthened.

At the time of diagnosis I had wondered: Why after so much growth, a kosher home and Sabbath, why had this happened? Sarah would never be able to enjoy a normal cake, pizza, or cookies. And what about our Sabbath challah?

It did not take long for our questions to be answered. During the High Holidays, we decided that even Sarah's safe foods must be kosher to be brought into our home. Within weeks we found a woman who baked beautiful gluten-free challahs. As my mother said, "I see a miracle every day." She, too, has become strengthened.

Our personal miracle. That which was once heartbreak now makes our hearts sing. I do not feel that G-d allowed this challenge in spite of our hard work. Rather, He gave us this gift because of our hard work. We have all learned courage, self-discipline, and faith. We have learned to be sensitive and caring toward others. Sarah has a challenge. It has strengthened and refined her, and all of us in her life, and we thank Him.

A Plea for Shalom Bayis—Peace Within the Home

After all is said and done, nothing nurtures our children's self-esteem more than *shalom bayis*—peace within our home. Kids who grow up in loving homes feel connected to their families. They don't need to look elsewhere for love. One can live in the most magnificent house with every accessory one's heart desires, but in a place where *shalom bayis* is lacking, there is zero blessing.

No one wants to be part of a home mired in strife. Couples sit across from one another in stony silence or use their words as sharp daggers that inflict emotional wounds. Over time these hurts defy all attempts at healing. Husbands and wives may live together but it is a lonely life. Children would gladly trade away the most luxurious lifestyle for a solid and sound family unit.

There is no greater blessing to offer those we love than peace. Moses was commanded to instruct Aaron and his sons, known as the Kohanim, concerning the Priestly Blessing. This prayer would be their birthright. They were given the obligation of conveying this blessing to the Jewish nation for all time, even until today. The prayer speaks about being blessed with prosperity, spiritual blessings, and G-d's compassion. This beautiful supplication concludes with the plea: "May G-d establish peace for you."

Our sages teach us that you may have all the physical blessings in the world with no desire of yours left wanting. Yet, if you do not have peace, all that you have is worthless.

Therefore, the blessings are sealed with the gift of peace.

This gift is in our hands. Parents meshed in marital conflict are often weighed down emotionally. Stress and fighting bring on feelings of depression and anger. Often, one parent "abdicates," leaving children feeling sad and puzzled. Some children blame themselves for their parents' contentious behavior. "If only *I* could get my parents to stop fighting," they wish silently. The fact that they are unable to bridge their parents' gap causes children to feel insecure. Kids may even feel guilty, mistakenly believing that the conflict is their fault. They begin to doubt themselves and feel less assured in the stability of their homes.

Children pick up on their parents' unhappiness. Study after study has shown the detrimental effect of depression and sadness on children. These kids often exhibit a higher chance of developing depression or a psychiatric disorder themselves. Parenting is difficult enough—how can one possibly parent while in the throes of such pain? Your destructive emotions are bound to impact your child's well-being.

There are times, of course, when the situation is so detrimental, or even dangerous, that separation is the only viable recourse. I am not speaking about such extreme conditions. I am addressing the daily hurts, the biting words, and insensitive insults that serve to slowly unravel the hallowed bond of marriage.

Throughout my years of teaching I have met with countless couples who live a life together filled with agonizing pain. As time passes, they disconnect. "How did we become like this?" they wonder aloud, meaning unhappy, depressed, short-tempered, easily annoyed, unable to carry on without some sarcastic comment or criticism that mars their family time. Their question hovers above their blackened horizon: "How did we ever become like this?"

Many times kids hear their parents arguing over their care. Think how they must feel.

"How could you let him eat that junk? You know I don't allow snacks before dinner!"

"Look what you did, you made her cry!"

"Can't you even read a story right?"

"Why are you putting him to bed, I just came home?"

The accused parent lashes back in anger.

"Oh, please, what's the big deal?"

"So you do it, okay, I'm not getting involved anymore."

"That's right, I'm always doing everything wrong, you're always right."

The fighting escalates.

"Don't you dare speak to me like that ever again!"

"You know, you're just like your mother/father."

"I can't take you anymore, just leave me alone!" Slam.

What is a child to think? What is a child to feel? Beneath all the anger lies incredible pain.

A ten-year-old girl asked to speak with me privately. "Slovie," she began, "what does it mean if my mother cries at night into her pillow? She thinks I don't hear her but I do. And why does my daddy say, 'Tell your mother this,' and my mommy says, 'Tell your father that,' if they're both in the same room together?" She began to sob. "It's a really bad thing, right? Why can't my parents just be nice to each other?"

The greatest joy is a happy home. Husbands and wives who live together in harmony bequeath the most priceless gift to their families. Children grow with treasured memories and an understanding of relationships based on love and mutual respect. They feel connected and anchored to an invisible bond that defies time and distance. A home filled with a peaceful atmosphere is one that invites Heavenly blessing inside.

We need to stop the hurt. We need to realize that we are both on the same side. Once and for all, let us understand that eroding one's spouse's sense of self is a harmful act of sabotage against one's own self. Ask yourself: Would my left hand ever be angry at my right hand? We are each other's right hands. We are here to build a life together. When we shatter our spouse's self-worth, fissures form in our marriage bond. Destructive emotions in our home extinguish all that is holy and sacred in our lives. The light within begins to dim.

There are no winners, only pitiful losers. The home is devastated. The beautiful *mikdash me'at* has been razed by our own hands. What have we done?

One of the most tragic moments that I have ever witnessed occurred at a funeral I attended. A young mother had passed away suddenly. Her children huddled together on the uncomfortable wooden benches in the chapel. They were sobbing out loud uncontrollably. Their father rose to speak.

"Lisa," the man began, "You have been my wife for the past fifteen years . . . you were a most wonderful mother, a patient and devoted wife. I am ashamed to admit this but I must. During our years together, I did not appreciate you. I did not value your dedication. I took your love for granted. I hurt you. I spoke unkindly. I did not understand you . . . I am left now with deep regrets and a searing hole within.

"I ask you, Lisa, in front of this entire room, for forgiveness. As you approach the gates of heaven, I publicly ask for your pardon."

There was but one sound heard at that moment. Sorrowful wails of the children joined the cries of each mourner. The tragedy of the moment was too much to bear.

The loudest wail of all, though, was emitted from this young husband and father. He remained with only his regrets to ponder and live with for the rest of his life.

SIX

Compassion

Mommy, you've got to read this." My son held out an article in his hand. "I think this is really horrible," he added.

The story that caught my son's eye was about a Little League championship game played by nine- and ten-year-olds. It was the bottom of the ninth inning. There were two outs and a runner on third base.

The article describes what happened next.

Up to bat is the team's star hitter, Jordan. After him on the roster is a scraggy kid, waiting on the sidelines. His name is Romney. He is a young cancer survivor who takes human growth hormones and has had a shunt put into his brain.

The coach decides on a "brilliant" plan. His team would walk the star hitter and thus bring out the frail little boy who would surely strike out. It would be an easy win.

Guess what? That's exactly what happened. As the victors celebrated that evening, Romney cried himself to sleep.

I discussed the story with my sons. "You know what I'm thinking, Mommy?" my son asked. "I'm thinking about that story that happened in our school . . . I can't believe the difference."

My son was referring to a baseball game that touched the hearts of so many. The story spread and set the bar for compassion both on and off the field.

RUN, SHAI, RUN

The fifth graders in my son's school joined together on the field to play baseball during recess. The game became intense. They were at the bottom of the ninth, bases loaded.

A young boy, Shai, stood up to bat. Shai was a child with special needs. He could scarcely hold the bat properly. The pitcher threw the ball. Shai's swing was out of control. There were now two strikes. The emotions on the field deepened.

The pitcher drew closer to the plate. Unexpectedly, two boys walked over to Shai. They put their arms around him and, together, held the bat. Once again, the pitcher threw the ball . . . gently. *Smack.* This time the ball rolled past the third-base line. The third baseman watched the ball pass him by, willingly. He made no attempt to dive for it. The boys began to shout, "Run, Shai, run!"

Shai ran straight past first base. Another boy ran up beside him and propelled him toward first. He pointed out second base and yelled, "Go!" As Shai touched second and then third base, kids on both teams began to scream, "Run, Shai, Run!" Shai finally reached home. The boys picked him up on their shoulders and carried him off the field.

"You won the game, Shai! You won the game!" they all cheered. Shai's heart was bursting with joy.

Rabbi Yaakov Bender, my son's Rosh Hayeshiva, the head of his yeshiva school, witnessed this incident from afar. The boys had no idea that their principal was watching. Their actions were natural and spontaneous, from their hearts. Years of Torah education combined with constant spiritual teachings to be sensitive created the beauty of this moment.

These boys have consistently been molded into fine young children who live with Torah values and priorities. Sure, they love to win. Yet, they comprehend that the real definition of "winning" goes far beyond the score of the game.

After recalling that game together, my twelve-year-old son, Eli, turned to me. "But, Mommy," he said, "What's the big deal? Whenever there's a kid who's challenged, he's always included. That's how we play ball."

Some may say I'm asking for too much. When there's a major game you need to play hard. Besides, kids just want to win. To them, I'd like to respond, ask yourself who the real champions are. Isn't it possible to teach kids to have a little heart? Is an easy win ever more important than bashing down a hard-hit soul? What does it mean to raise a child of whom you can be proud?

We have done a great job instilling in our children the desire to come out first. After all, "winning isn't everything, it's the only thing." Right?

We measure our children through their success on and off the field, their popularity, and their grades. If they do well then we believe that we are raising successful children.

We are wrong. We are raising one of the most selfish generations to have ever lived.

"Why should I pick up the phone, it's not for me, anyhow?"
"I didn't make that mess, why should I clean it up?"
"Why isn't supper ready yet? I'm starving!"
"Mommy told you to carry in the bags, not me."
"What did you buy me, Grandma?"
"Why do I have to sit next to Grandpa?"
"I don't want to invite her to my party, she's such a nerd."

Ask yourself, when was the last time your child gave of himself to someone else? When was the last time your child sacrificed—really sacrificed, and gave of his time, a material possession, or even gave up his seat? What about feeling someone else's pain? Did your child ever hurt for another, cry for another? Did he ever shed tears for someone else's sorrow?

A few years ago, a Special Olympics took place in Seattle, Washington. A group of Down's syndrome children stood at the starting line. The signal sounded and the kids began to run. Each step was a personal triumph. Just a few moments into the race, though, a little girl fell down. She sat on the track and began to cry. The children who were running ahead heard her cries. Together, they turned around and returned to the fallen child. Hands extended, they helped her stand on her feet once again. All the kids then linked their arms and in unison walked to the finish line in exhilaration.

Think about it—who really is the disabled one here? Perhaps it would be too much to ask that one turn around during a competition, but how many of us would even pause for a moment in our busy day to give a hand to someone in need? We race through life oblivious to the heartbreak of those around us, too occupied to even give an encouraging word or a smile. And so, too, do our children, who have become spiritually callous and indifferent.

Turn "Me" into "We"

Babies are born into this world with their fists tightly clenched. Some of their first words are "no," "mine," and "give me!" As parents, we must open their tightly closed fingers, one by one.

As they grow, children become obsessed with themselves and the excessive materialism that surrounds them, "their wants and their needs." In pursuit of their own desires it becomes easy to overlook the needs of others. Children are so self-immersed, there is no moment set aside to ask, "What can I do to help?" Let us strive to raise children who are not completely self-absorbed. Let us teach our children to become givers and not merely takers.

My father once told me that he was shocked when he first arrived to this country and began to study the English language. "How could it be," he thought, "that the only pronoun that is capitalized is I?" He had never heard of such a thing.

The time has come for us to take the focus off *I* and include others in our circle of vision. Our responsibility is to help our children remove their blinders and observe the need in the world around them.

It is not adequate to nourish their bodies; we must also provide food for our children's souls. Helping our children develop empathy for others is a primary way for us to influence a young soul. Children have the ability to grow and become more charitable, kinder individuals. It is incumbent upon us to teach our children to give, to feel for others, to become sensitive and compassionate beings. In Judaism we call such a person a *baal chessed*.

Abraham and Sarah were each known to be a *baal chessed*. They brought a profound vision of G-dliness to mankind. Along with their newly discovered faith came a personification of *chessed*—kindness. They not only spoke about compassion, as many do; they lived it. Their desert home was open on all four sides so that they could invite guests inside, from all directions. They established a universal moral code through their genuine concern for all people.

Abraham performed the commandment of *bris milah*—circumcision. He was an elderly man who had just undergone a major operation, in excruciating pain. Yet he sat in the scorching desert heat, searching the bare horizon for potential visitors. He yearned to find someone onto whom he and Sarah could shower their hospitality. He actually felt pained that a day would pass by without their exhibiting kindness to another.

How could Abraham and Sarah have mastered this ability to be compassionate? Why did they yearn so for an act of benevolence? How many of us, stressed out with a pounding headache after a long day, would feel badly if we just went to sleep without an act of kindness under our belt? What was their driving force?

Abraham and Sarah understood the secret of the soul. If I want to feel alive I must give life to my soul. If I want to feel vibrant then I must bring vitality to this world. The only way I can find purpose is by infusing the world around me with goodness. If I learn to be tolerant and compassionate I will find myself a better, more openhearted individual. I will have replaced my greedy nature, always unsatisfied, with a more noble being. I will view people through a positive light. My entire world is transformed and my life takes on new meaning.

The truth is that the giver receives more than he can ever imagine. The giver has broken free of his ego and soared above his selfishness. Think about the last time you gave a gift to someone. Remember the delicious anticipation, the happiness of the recipient, your excitement as you presented your gift? The thrill of giving remains with you long past the moment. It is the joy of the soul that you are feeling.

Abraham and Sarah had uncovered the mystical power of giving. They thirsted for *chessed* because through their compassion they revived their souls.

We have not placed *chessed*, as a priority in our children's lives. Instead we seek out opportunities to provide for their comfort and desires. We try to give them the best life possible, sometimes even beyond our means. Days go by and children have not been challenged to give of themselves. Their hearts grow constricted as they become more self-consumed.

Just as you work out and exercise your body, you must also exercise your soul. Acts of kindness maintain the strength of your spiritual nature.

Without giving, the muscles of the soul atrophy. Lacking acts of *chessed,* our children have become spiritually malnourished. Never realizing the hunger of the soul, they have binged on materialism. They are in need of a spiritual workout.

A kindergarten teacher who taught in a yeshiva, a religious school, was preparing her classroom for the new school year. She realized that a mezuzah, a scroll and casement containing the Shema prayer, was needed to be placed upon the doorpost.

According to Jewish law, the mezuzah must be placed at a certain height.

"What should I do?" she inquired of the principal. "At this level it will be difficult for the little children to reach and touch the mezuzah as they enter their classroom each day. Do I lower the mezuzah for my students?"

The principal responded. "There is never a reason to lower standards . . . not even for children. Our students need to know that at times they are required to reach up and stretch a little in order to achieve their goals."

A spiritual workout means that at certain moments your children are required to stretch a little in life. Even if you're not in the mood, give a smile. Open your hands and be generous *especially* if being charitable is difficult for you. You're feeling angry and impatient? Control your temper and don't lose it with others. Is this easy or comfortable? Of course not. It is a spiritual workout and a necessary stretch.

Train Your Children Early in Life

Many parents don't realize that kindness can be taught even to little children. I have received numerous queries from parents regarding their young kindergarteners who find it difficult to share. They hit and bite others who ask to join in their play. Instead of prodding their kids to behave more generously, they indulge their selfishness. Children grow up believing that it is okay to be egocentric, it's even the norm.

I taught a class in a private home, where some of the young moms brought their toddlers along. As we found our seats the children were settled in a nearby room. One little girl clutched her Talking Elmo doll tightly in her arms. Screaming erupted as another child tried to touch Elmo's face. The mother turned to the children and said in a most serious tone, "This is Emily's special doll. No one is ever allowed to touch it because it's her very special doll."

"Really?" I wondered. No one is ever allowed to touch her doll? How can such a child ever learn to give? Why would this child even want to give?

When my children were young I would often take them to visit with my parents. As my little ones would be sucking on a pretzel, or munching on a half eaten cookie, my mother would crouch down beside him. She would open up her hand and with a smile ask, "Can you give Bubba a piece of your cookie?"

Did my mother really want a taste of that mushy pretzel or crumbled cookie? Of course not. My mother was teaching my children, even at a tender age, to share. Their *bubba* was expanding their hearts and extending their souls. To a little child, giving up a piece of that cookie is a sacrifice. As our children grow, so, too, does the magnitude of their ability to sacrifice. If they are not directed, though, they will never mature beyond their starting point. And so, we have teenagers who are as limited in their concept of giving as the little girl who refused to share her Elmo doll.

No Pain, No Gain

I know parents and even children who really do want to be giving individuals. They seek out opportunities to show kindness—as long as their comfort level is not infringed upon. There are birthday parties and events where time is set aside to create projects for other children who are ill or impoverished. Kids are brought to toy stores and told to choose holiday gifts for needy children. We dress for charity events and raise money for a cause. The concept is indeed beautiful, but there is no real sacrifice involved.

I recall reading about a group of teenagers who sought to aid the homeless in a large urban city. As they distributed warm socks and gloves in one hand, they held their lattes in the other. The event organizer wondered, Could they not even put down their Starbucks and reach out with all their hearts? Is the discomfort of going out minus a morning's coffee too great to bear?

We are giving because it's in vogue and everyone else in the group is doing it. And it certainly is fun to attend a charity walkathon, bowlathon, or concert. Besides, it looks good in front of our neighbors, as pictures in the local paper, and great on high school résumés. Our children end up feeling good about themselves and we sit back contentedly because we've taught them compassion. But, have we really? Do our children even begin to understand what "giving charity" and "extending compassion" really mean?

Our children live a life of privilege even in their capacity to give. As they evolve into adulthood, they've never genuinely experienced the emotions of bearing another's pain and thus becoming more sensitive and caring.

We are taught in *Ethics of the Fathers* (6:6) that one who aspires to be adorned with the crown of Torah must refine his inner essence. There are various character traits enumerated through which one gains purity of soul. *"Nosei beolle im chavero,* sharing his fellow's burden, is one of forty-eight spiritual virtues enumerated. Our sages expound in their teachings of this verse and guide us toward a higher standard of moral living.

"Share another's burden"—what exactly does this mean? We are taught to help others in any way we can, whether the help entails physical, financial, or emotional strain. Feel the pain of another, we are told. Have patience and sensitivity toward others even if they may be unpleasant in your eyes and this is quite difficult for you. In other words, enter another universe; the universe of *chessed.*

At some point in life, everyone is bound to feel pain. Kids, especially, go through various difficulties. The sting of being excluded, the pain of emotional turmoil at home, the shame of being made fun of, the embarrassment of public failure in front of peers—everyone eventually goes through some discomforting experience.

Instead of discarding the experience and muttering, "Who cares, anyway," allow your child to be moved by his personal feelings of anguish. Then, when he discovers others who are hurting, direct him to understand and feel their pain.

The nebby kid that no one wants to sit next to, the kid who always strikes out, the kid who makes corny jokes that everyone snorts at, the overweight kid, the kid with the extra-thick glasses and frizzy hair that's made fun of—these are real children who are experiencing real pain. If your child is fortunate enough to be one of the "in kids," yank him out of his insulated world and sensitize him to think of others who are suffering right beside him. Steady him on the path of true compassion. Create a *baal chessed*—a master of loving kindness.

CHESSED

Understanding how crucial it is to bring compassion and loving kindness into our homes is one thing, but how do we instill these character traits within our children's hearts?

Make a Good Child Great

Moses grew up in the palace of Pharaoh. He lived in the lap of luxury, a prince of Egypt. He had a choice. Either he could remain in the sheltered confines of opulence or seek out his enslaved brethren.

"The boy [Moses] grew up . . . It happened in those days that Moses grew up and went out to his brethren and observed their burdens" (Exodus 2:10–11).

At first, Moses grew up physically. The young boy matured. There is another type of development, though, that he experienced. The second growth mentioned reveals a spiritual growth. Moses grew and flourished within.

The moment he left the palace and contemplated the pain of his brethren, Moses nurtured his soul. He observed the burdens of his people and did not ignore them. This constitutes greatness.

Moses became the awesome leader of the Jewish people because at a young age he was able to extract himself from the lure of extravagance and display compassion for the downtrodden. It would have been much easier for Moses to live in denial. He could have convinced himself that the suffering he witnessed was only temporary, the people were handling it, and besides, what could he do about it anyway? He chose, however, to exit easy street and attempt to ease the distress of the people around him. Meet greatness at its zenith.

My daughter, Shaindy, was four years old when she began kindergarten. The first day of school we looked around the yard together in anxious anticipation. The bell rang. Shaindy waved good-bye and marched off with her teacher and classmates.

A few weeks into the school year, I requested a class list from Shaindy's teacher. That evening, I told Shaindy that she could invite any child she wanted for a playdate. "I'll read you the names, and you tell me whose mommy I should call," I said.

After going through twenty-something names, Shaindy made her decision. "Can you please call Devorah Leah's mommy?" she asked.

"Sure," I said delightedly. I wasn't familiar with this little girl, but I was glad that Shaindy would have a playdate.

We made the proper arrangements. Devorah Leah's mother sounded thrilled. The next afternoon, Shaindy's preschool bus pulled up. Out jumped Shaindy, all smiles. The bus monitor descended the steps, holding a little girl's hand gingerly in hers. Devorah Leah was a tiny child who walked with difficulty. After getting off the bus, she stood behind Shaindy and grabbed on to her skirt. She sucked her thumb and looked down at the ground.

"Good luck," the bus monitor called out, and went on her way. I brought the two girls inside and watched from the kitchen. Devorah Leah did not speak. She did not play. She just sucked her thumb and held on to my daughter's skirt. I was puzzled at Shaindy's choice.

After Devorah Leah left, I called Shaindy into my room.

"Shaindy, is Devorah Leah your best friend?" I asked.

"No," she replied.

"Do you play with Devorah Leah in school?" I continued.

"No. Devorah Leah doesn't really play," she responded.

I could not comprehend.

"So tell me, Shaindelah, why did you ask me to call Devorah Leah for your playdate?"

"Well, Mommy, every day at line up our teacher calls out which girls are going home together for playdates. And every day, Devorah Leah cries. No one ever picks *her*. I wanted her to feel better so I asked if she could be the one who would come over and play."

My heart filled. This child taught me a true lesson in compassion. This delicate little soul had soared and reached the greatest of spiritual heights. Not only had she felt the pain of another, but she had tried to relieve this little girl of a heavy burden. It is up to all of us parents to help guide our children on to the path of true greatness.

Do Sweat the Small Stuff

Sometimes we think that in order to teach our children character, we must come upon some awesome experience that they will never forget. We struggle to discover an encitingly different encounter and hope that the impact will be life-changing.

A group of young parents stood beside me after a parenting event and we fell into an animated discussion about compassion.

"You know what?" one father mused, "I have this great idea. How about taking our kids on a trip to Brazil to see firsthand what it means to live in poverty? I bet our kids will feel grateful after that! We can travel around with them and try to do something special to help the poor people over there."

"I have news for you," I responded. "You don't have to travel to South America . . . you don't even have to travel. There is plenty of compassion to be learned right here in our own backyards."

Tolerance. Compassion. Goodness. Generosity. All virtues that we would like to develop within our children. You don't have to travel the world or rescue an entire village to nurture your child's good-heartedness. It is really the little moments that present the greatest opportunities to teach our children loving kindness.

Karen, a young woman who attends my parenting classes, decided to make compassion the center of her family's life. She trained her kids' golden retriever to become a therapy dog and together they volunteer each week in a day school for children with disabilities. Some of these kids are unable to communicate at all; these visits have brought them a measure of happiness that until now they've never known. Imagine the impact on her children as they watch their mother's enthusiasm as she reaches out and touches so many with her kindness.

Look out for moments to accomplish small acts of kindness each day. These seemingly light actions become the building blocks of your child's character. They are hardly inconsequential, as we might mistakenly believe. Rather, each action further expands a child's nature toward greatness.

Judaism teaches us that our character is formed according to our actions. The more frequently we do something, the more it becomes part of our nature. For example, you have one hundred dollars and you would like to donate it to charity. It is preferable to give out small bills numerous times than hand out a one hundred dollar bill just once. Each time you give, you are enhancing your nature. Acting charitably becomes a part of your essence and it is not an unfamiliar, uncommon act. Slowly but surely, your entire being is transformed.

You'd be surprised to discover that there are many opportunities for your children to act more kindly that often go unrealized. Children should be taught to use their skills and possessions to develop their ability to give. Even a teenager who drives can be encouraged to help others and not just use his driving privileges selfishly.

One morning, my sister phoned and told me how aggravated she felt. She was supposed to help her daughter move, but her car broke down. My eldest son, Moshe Nosson, overheard my conversation.

He drove out to my sister's home and spent the day helping her run errands and moving boxes.

It was a simple act of kindness of which I wasn't even aware, until my sister called to say, "Thank you." These are the seemingly insignificant moments that shape our children's character. We overlook these moments and dismiss them as small and unimportant. Our thinking is flawed.

A rabbi who is a noted educator was asked to give a lecture. As the room began to fill, it became apparent that there was a shortage of available seats. One young man went out to bring in a chair. The rabbi exclaimed: "Carry in a chair for yourself and you are just a *shlepper*. But carry in two chairs, and you have become a *baal chessed*."

The Torah places great significance on actions we may consider inconsequential. Pharaoh, the king of Egypt, proclaimed an edict on Jewish male babies who would be born. He directed two Hebrew midwives, Shifra and Puah, to kill all male newborns as they would be delivered. This way, there would be no next generation of males and the females would integrate into Egypt.

These two midwives stood up to Pharaoh and defied his orders of infanticide. They saved an entire generation of Jewish children. Who were these courageous women?

The Torah records their names as Shifra and Puah. Shifra, we learn, was really Yocheved, the mother of Moses. Puah was Moses' sister, Miriam. They are given these names as a reflection of their actions (Rashi, Exodus 1:15).

In the Hebrew tongue, *shifra* means "to make beautiful." *Puah* is defined as "cooing." The Torah testifies to the loving manner with which these two women would deliver the little babies. While under great duress and at the risk of their very lives, they did not allow seemingly small acts of kindness to pass them by. One midwife would coo and gently pacify the infant while the other washed and combed him. They would then present the terrified mother with her beautiful, calm baby. Not content with just a quick delivery and rushing away because of danger, Yocheved and Miriam took the time to welcome these babies into the world with extra love. They then helped these new mothers overcome their fear.

One could imagine that the Torah would bestow names that emphasize the heroism of these two women. After all, they dared to challenge the great Pharaoh and endangered their lives. Cooing? Singing lullabies? Brushing a baby's hair? What's the big deal?

That's just the point. Greatness is apparent in the small deeds of people, the little private acts that may never make the cover of *The New York Times* or the lead story on CNN. These are the actions that define who you are, the little moments in your busy, stressed-filled day, that you take out for others. No one sees them. No one knows about them. Practiced over and over again, these moments of kindness can change your life and the lives of your children. Your *chessed* becomes life-transforming.

Children Learn What They Live

After my father passed away, countless people visited and shared their memories with us. Many were strangers whom we had never met. Acts of incredible goodness were recalled and enumerated. Hundreds of letters poured into my mother's home, testimonials to my father's boundless love and gentle nature. I was amazed. I still marvel at the power of one. Young children, single parents, elderly individuals, congregants who had long since moved away, fellow clergymen of various faiths, physicians who had cared for my father . . . how many lives can one individual touch?

One letter in particular moved me beyond words.

At age ninety my father suffered a massive stroke. He was paralyzed from the neck down, blind and deaf. Here I was, widowed and alone. Nonetheless, I wanted to care for my father in our home. I turned the house into a hospital with a round-the-clock nurse.

On Friday, the nurse became burned out and left. It was before the Sabbath sundown when the Rabbi rang my doorbell with his usual Friday gift of cakes from the Rebbetzin. He found me sobbing at the door. He asked me, "What's the trouble?" I answered, "My father is soiled and I can't lift him." The Rabbi said, "Come and I'll help."

He did help. He lifted my father. Meanwhile, I made my father comfortable. Rabbi's image will always remain in my mind.

I read and reread the letter. I was moved but not surprised. My parents have always lived and breathed goodness. Reaching out to others was a constant priority in our home. We often accompanied my parents as they visited the sick and elderly. Young as we were, we understood the importance of our smiles and warm greetings. We watched, firsthand, as our parents invited those who felt alone or in need of a spiritual boost to our Shabbos table. We learned about our obligation to be generous and kind.

The way you live your life is the greatest teaching tool you have as you educate your children and mold their character. It is simply not adequate to speak about virtue and generosity; you must live it. Your children become eyewitnesses to your goodness. If they observe an uncaring and coldhearted attitude, they will join you on your self-centered path. They will grow up to be uncompassionate and unsympathetic. You really are your child's greatest teacher.

Being cognizant of your role helps you understand how important it is to seek out opportunities of *chessed* with your children. The world around you is filled with oceans of need—spiritual, physical, financial, and emotional.

My daughter is presently living in Israel with her husband. In an excerpt of an article she wrote, she describes her visit to the Western Wall.

> I'm at the Kosel, it is dusk and my head is right by the wall. A breeze crosses through the air and a long *kvitel* [personal prayer written and placed in the wall] falls onto my lap. I pick it up and return it to its rightful place . . . a crevice in the stones. I can't help but notice what it is. It's a bill, with dollar after dollar recorded; you can see the burden of debt slowly piling up. Yet, scrawled across it in large writing are three words in Hebrew—G-d please help.

Open your eyes and see the need around you. Organizations abound, waiting for volunteers to help deliver food, collect clothing, visit the sick, or assist those with special needs, to mention just a few. Think about the many elderly people in your neighborhood who long for someone to talk to: numerous parents facing illness at home, theirs or a child's, who would welcome your time, cards of well wishes, or a homemade dinner to alleviate their constant stress.

I have a teenage niece who in her free time visits with physically and emotionally handicapped children, and brings them to her home for the weekend. As my sister prepares fresh linens and favorite foods, my niece spends time with them and gives endless patience and love.

Don't be afraid to enter the world of *chessed*. You will have bridged the gap between your world and the world of others. Allow your children to join you as you build this incredible bridge.

I spoke with a young mother who told me that as a child she never knew the extent of her parents' generosity. They were extremely charitable but kept their acts of kindness a secret. This young woman was shocked to find out how truly generous her parents were. She felt badly that all her life she was never able to experience the joy of giving together with her parents. She added that knowledge of her parents' charity would have provided her with an added legacy as she grew.

While children do not require knowledge of dollar amounts, they should take pride in their parents' concern for others. They learn that we are obligated to open our hands and give. We do not just think of ourselves and our own needs. Involve your children. Teach them to be charitable.

When I teach my monthly young-couples class, the children of the hosting family welcome us into their home with graciousness. The room is filled with people they do not know. Together with their parents they offer warm hellos and show guests to their seats. After class they invite everyone to join them for a delicious dinner and make sure that each person is comfortable. This experience has become a priceless family legacy of opening their home and heart to others. Together, parents and children walk in the footsteps of Abraham and Sarah.

This past spring, we honored a gracious couple at our annual Hineni dinner. When this young mom was a college student, she began to discover Torah's wisdom and joined her mother, who had been studying with my mother, the Rebbetzin. Twenty years later they still continue to study and refresh their souls. When she got married, this young woman and her husband offered to host the monthly couples class that I teach in their home, so that other couples may study Torah and so that they may create a *mikdash me'at* and fill their home with blessing.

As this mom stood with her husband to accept our thanks, she addressed her young children, who were seated in the audience. I would like to share her words with you so that you, too, may be touched by the emotions that she expressed that evening. You will see life through the eyes of those who have embraced Torah's teachings as a guide to parenting and to life.

As to my little lambchops—this is my big please to you, all my little *neshamahs*. Please—always remember that you have been given the most precious gift. You are on this earth not only to be polite and to be nice, but to honor G-d and to represent Him, and to teach others about His mitzvahs through your behavior.

So be kind to other people. Not just the people it's easy to be kind to. Include other people. Not just the people you feel like including. Take care of other people—even when you feel like just taking care of yourself.

Remember who you are, where you come from, and that you have grandparents in Heaven watching over you and protecting you for thousands of years. Remember that when you are unsure of what to do and how to react. And know more than anything that you can always turn to G-d and ask for help—and when you feel better, remember to thank Him, the way Daddy and I have tried to teach you. Always study His Torah, even when you think you've learned so much, even when you're busy with other things and life is full. Because studying is what will keep you connected and true to yourself. We've been so blessed with the best teachers, and if you keep studying, you will never get lost. And G-d will help you keep His commandments and your life will be filled with blessing.

And babies, finally, remember me standing here and telling you all this and close your eyes and take a picture in your brains so that when you're older, you will always remember this moment. And never forget what Mommy learned when I first began to study Torah, what my great, great teacher once taught me: that if you take one step to G-d, He will, undoubtedly, take two steps to you.

Charity Begins at Home

As we pursue "acts of loving kindness" it is important not to overlook the numerous kindnesses we may extend to one another in our own homes. Some people are compassionate to others, but their family is left wanting. As we take on added responsibilities, children and spouses may become easily overlooked. How painful it is for children to watch their parents find time for everyone else but them.

Kids hungrily await attention and love and feel as if they are the last ones on the list. Having limitless patience for others, but then losing it with your family is a sad lesson in hypocrisy.

Children, too, need to be taught about "family kindness." Many kids are kind to "the world," but terribly mean to their siblings. They use harsh words, knock them with one-liners, or are indifferent to their pain.

Judaism teaches us that "charity begins at home." The laws of charity instruct us that one is first obligated to give to family, then neighbors, friends, and so forth.

Even casual family moments are tremendous opportunities for *chessed.* My husband and I took our children out to a local pizza shop and observed the following incident.

A family was seated at the table next to us. Their five-year-old son brushed his hand along the drink bottle, accidentally. Snapple spilled all over the table and over the pizza and went into his lap.

"Now look what you did! Can't you ever just sit normally? What's the matter with you? We can't take you anywhere!"

The little boy's eyes filled with tears.

"Yeah," added his older sister. "You're always ruining everything and making a mess!"

"You're always making a mess," parroted his three-year-old sister with glee.

Not only did these parents fail their son as they publicly humiliated him, but they taught their children to follow their unkind example. Next time someone makes a mistake what do you suppose these children will say? Will they speak with compassion or sarcasm? Think about their future relationships—how will they react in marriage or as parents?

How much kinder it would have been to simply guide their son to the nearest paper towel rack and instruct him to clean up his spill. No cynicism. No shame. Accidents happen and when they do, let's act responsibly. Isn't that a much greater life lesson?

Instead, this child remains with his parents' stinging words ringing in his ears. His siblings have learned that it's okay to hurt others with words—especially family. After all, we certainly don't speak to strangers or friends in this harsh manner.

Let us try to teach our children to be sensitive and generous with both words and deeds, with an emphasis on our interactions with our families. We will create an atmosphere of tolerance in our homes that lends itself to compassion and goodness throughout life.

Teach Your Children to Feel for Others

"Please, I need to speak to your father or mother right away."

Growing up, I heard this request almost every day. A desperate knock on our door would reveal a figure overloaded with grief. Often, the shrill ring of the phone would sound in the middle of the night. A despondent voice was heard on the line. There were times a person or even an entire family would drop in, replete with a myriad of troubles.

We would usher them inside. My parents would listen and absorb their pain. Their shoulders were weighed down with worries. Slowly, they unburdened their heavy loads.

Sometimes they would choke back tears as they recounted tales of failed marriages, deep disappointment in children, or fear as financial ruin loomed near.

Other times, I would hear sobs emanate from our living room as a worrisome diagnosis was revealed. My parents would offer soothing words, advice, and heartfelt prayers. They would try to ease the heavy burden. At times there was nothing to say, nothing to do. My parents' eyes said it all. They silently shed tears for the sorrow of another.

"You don't know what you've done for me, just by opening your heart and listening," I'd hear. "Thank you for feeling my pain. I felt all alone until now."

The individual would leave but his worries remained. They accompanied my parents throughout their day. "Did you call Mr. B?" "Did you visit Mrs. S?" "Did you look into a doctor for Mrs. R's grandson?"

The child within me took it all in. I watched as my parents listened. They shared. They were concerned. They never grew hardened or showed cold indifference. And through it all we knew that we were our parents' number one priority.

It is true that most of us do not find people on our doorstep, sobbing in the middle of the night. But it is also true that in the course of our day, we are bound to come across someone who is bearing an awfully heavy load. Friends, family, neighbors, coworkers—one doesn't have to travel a distance to uncover a heavy heart. A reassuring word could mean the world.

We often ask "How are you?" not really wanting to hear a response other than "Great." "Get over it, already," we tell those in pain. "You've got to move on." "I have no patience to listen to her story anymore." "What's with him, what's his problem? Get a grip already."

Children pick up an attitude of caring if they observe their parents' concern for others. Indifference, thoughtlessness, and aloofness all breed selfishness. One generation follows in the self-centered path of the other.

A good heart, on the other hand, enables one to open himself to the pain of another. Perhaps there is not much you can really do, but at least you can provide a listening heart. You've allowed someone to unburden their soul as their tears mingle with your own. Think about their pain and what they must be experiencing. Perhaps you can feel an inkling of their distress, an iota of their anguish. A heart that feels enables you to become a better husband or wife, a more compassionate parent, a kinder friend, a greater human being. Practicing acts of kindness helps you evolve into a more giving person. Bring your child on this journey with you and you will reveal the hidden soul.

It is not just the giving of charity that we are obligated to teach our children. As parents we are also charged with having our children understand that they can offer their hearts to others. Extend a comforting word, an encouraging gesture, a reassuring smile. Call a classmate who's been absent and tell him that he was missed. Impart in your children the ability to pray for others.

Bedtime is an opportune time to teach your children to think of others. Nighttime prayers conclude a long day. As we put our children to bed, we have time to think and reflect together. Spend a few moments teaching your child to pray. Gather names of those who need healing. Ask G-d to watch over beloved family members. When I was a little child, this was our tradition. As my own children grew, this cherished legacy has continued. My nine-year-old daughter, Aliza, will go to sleep only after reciting a prayer for those who are ill. Most are strangers to her, eclectic names she has collected of people who require a blessing for good health. Help your children grow into adults who will conclude each day by thinking of others.

Do not fear a child's hurt if his prayers seem to go unanswered. Explain to him that all our prayers have an address, no prayer is for naught. When you pray for someone, your heartfelt supplications accompany that person throughout his life.

"But what happens," I'm often asked, "if the person your child prays for dies? How do we explain that to our children?"

"When the time comes for that soul to leave this world, and unfortunately we must all leave sometime," I respond, "it does not leave alone. Instead, that soul rests on the wings of your prayer. Teach your child that no prayer is ever in vain."

A moment of prayer from my childhood stands out in my mind. My siblings and I were in our home when my parents received a distressing call. A child had suffered a terrible accident. She was on the way to the hospital, her situation precarious.

My mother gathered us around and helped us pray. We were given the little girl's Hebrew name. At the time there was a guest visiting our home. She took in the events unfolding before her eyes.

"Really, Rebbetzin," exclaimed the woman, "I think this is way too much for these poor children. They're going to cry now."

My mother turned to the woman, her eyes flashing with deep conviction. "All children cry. Some children cry for toys. Others cry for chocolate. My children will cry for the pain of another."

Say No to Mean Girls (and Boys)

Obviously, the opposite of compassion is cruelty. As much as kindness should be pursued, cruelty may never be tolerated. Once it is allowed, a breach has been formed in the wall of the soul. Actions that seemed awful the first time seem "not so bad" the next.

Children who are compassionate are kind through and through. There are no acceptable circumstances that permit children to act unkindly. We cannot look away when our children are mean. No excuses. If a child perceives that his cruelty is given tacit approval, he will grow bolder in his meanness.

Words that are spoken harshly, put-downs that completely devastate another human being, laughing at other kids just because—parents who don't put a stop to this behavior when a child is young, find it much more difficult to eradicate as time goes on. Insensitivity and lacking compassion for others become a natural side of a child's character. This hardened soul tends to grow up removed from experiencing empathy. He is unaware of the pain that he has inflicted on peers, siblings, teachers, and grandparents. He lives in his own self-made universe. "Rabbi Yehoshua says hatred of other people removes a person from the world" (*Ethics of the Fathers*, 2:16). The hard-hearted child has abandoned the world of "another."

It is vital for parents to pay attention to their children's character traits. Ask yourself these questions:

- How does my child play with other kids?
- Does my child react compassionately when someone is hurt?

- Does my child pretend not to notice or find excuses if he caused pain to someone?
- Does my child use hurtful words or make fun of others easily?
- Is my child often involved in spats or conflicts?
- Is my child mean?

Some of the responses to these questions may be painful to answer honestly. But it is far better to confront the areas in which a child requires help in refining his essence than living in denial and making believe that he's a "perfect kid."

I have watched children act out with a blatant lack of character as their parents attempt to put forth all sorts of justifications.

"Sorry, but he's really into his game, you know."
"He had a really hard day."
"It's a stage. She's just a kid, what do you expect?"
"Oh, come on, what's the big deal? Everyone knows that kid is weird, no one ever talks to him, anyway."

We can demand more from our children. They are capable of great kindness. Once we "let them off the hook," they realize that *chessed* is simply not a priority in our lives. And if it's not important enough for us to pay attention to, it certainly is not important to our children.

Kindness, Even to Animals

Abraham made it his life goal to achieve perfection in his love for G-d and mankind. Abraham once asked Shem, the son of Noah, who built the ark: "Tell me, in which merit did G-d keep you alive in the ark?"

"We survived due to our charity," replied Shem.

"What does that mean? There were no poor people with you in the ark!" said Abraham.

"I am speaking about charity to the animals," explained Shem. "We stayed awake entire nights giving them food."

"If this is so," reasoned Abraham, "how important is it to sustain human beings!" (the Gemorah 1.)

Teach your children to be kind to all of G-d's creatures. Good-heartedness becomes a part of their very nature. Have you ever been in a park and seen children throw rocks at the geese? Have you watched children tease little creatures for no reason? What about losing interest in pet goldfish and allowing them to languish, slowly?

In Judaism we call this *tzaar baalei chaim,* causing pain to a living creation. It is never permitted to inflict suffering or to torment any of G-d's creations. We become kinder by acting with compassion and so the converse is true. Abraham concluded the importance of goodness toward mankind by perceiving the significance G-d placed upon charity even to *animals* in Noah's ark. "*Olam chessed yibaneh,* the world is built through kindness," wrote King David in the Book of Psalms.

We live in a society that enables us to hurt one another with ease. With a push of the button you can degrade someone all over cyberspace. All it takes is one e-mail to spread a rumor. I have spoken with children who feel totally crushed from gossip. Plain, mean gossip. They cannot face their classmates; they lower their heads in shame. They've been blogged out of the atmosphere.

Or, one kid decides another is a loser and IMs all her friends. In an instant, she has created a pariah. One nasty text message and you've destroyed someone's world. She is left alone, with no one to sit next to on the bus up to camp. The clique, with cell phones in hand, are having a blast texting each other, indifferent to the immense pain they have caused.

The movie *Mean Girls,* a popular book and television series called Gossip Girls, dolls named Bratz, extreme violence in video games and during sports events that bring excitement to our kids . . . In what kind of world are we raising our children?

I attended a hockey league game in which my son was playing. The opposing team had many of their classmates and friends in the crowd. They were vocal in their cheering, chanting loudly for their buddies.

The goalie on my son's team was suddenly slashed. He fell to the ground, writhing in pain. The kids in the galley continued their cheering. As the goalie's helmet was removed you could see that he was in real distress. His hair was mussed, sweat was pouring down his forehead.

"Yeah, he's hurt. Awesome!" they shouted.

The minutes ticked by. The goalie caught his breath and stood up.

"Boo!" they screamed out. "*Boo!*" they shouted with all their might.

That's unkind. That's mean. It is one thing to cheer your team's success but to applaud the pain of another is cruel. Shmuel HaKattan says, "When your enemy falls, be not glad, and when he stumbles let your heart not be joyous" (Ethics 4:24). Even if your child dislikes someone, or if he's on the opposition, be careful. Never allow cruelty to creep within his soul. Once there, its tenacious tentacles take root and dominate your child's very being. Take a strong stand. In the beginning. Before it is too late.

Home Plus School Equals an Alliance of Compassion

As we prioritize *chessed* in our homes, it is important to find a school that joins us on our path of raising children with compassion. Schools that emphasize academic achievement, state test scores, and extracurricular activities, yet fail to address character issues, neglect a major function of education. Your child spends many hours a day in school. He should be educated in an atmosphere of tolerance and sensitivity toward others.

The Rosh Hayeshiva, head of the religious school that my sons attend, Rabbi Yaakov Bender, is known to be a leader in the education of compassion.

He has taken disabled children into his classrooms after other schools slammed their doors shut. The boys in his school can be found leading a blind classmate down the hall, carrying books for a child who was born without an arm, or helping a challenged child navigate his way through difficult schoolwork.

I have personally been awed as I watched my high school–aged son and his friends spend their free time visiting a classmate undergoing chemo in New York City. No one asked them, no one told them. They knew within their hearts that this was the right thing to do. A fellow human being is in pain, separated from his friends and family, feeling alone. What can we do to make it better?

I interviewed Rabbi Bender and asked him to explain his formula for success.

"How do you explain it?" I asked. "Why are the kids so happy helping other kids?"

"Listen," he said with a great smile, "it's really very simple. Kids really enjoy helping other kids. Recess arrives, the bell rings. Instead of running out that minute to play ball, the boys get together and wheel their classmate on to the playground in his wheelchair. The truth is, the kids who are helping are the ones who are gaining the most here. Wow, I'm so fortunate, they realize. And they're thrilled to help a child who's in need.

Their entire outlook on life is transformed. I've watched some of the most difficult children literally transform themselves as they've taken care of other kids who need an extra hand. A child finds success in helping others."

I asked if there was any specific thing that the children do that encourages them to learn how to give.

"Sure. Before Chanukah, I tell the kids you'll be getting gifts, even Chanukah gelt. There are kids around who can't afford a baseball glove, a bike, a new suit.

"So, I have a 'pocket fund'—pocket money we collect from the kids all year. I tell the children, speak to your parents and explain that you'd like a less expensive mitt, a lesser-line bike. The extra dollars you'll donate for another child. Take a few dollars of your Chanukah gelt and think of the children who have none.

"At the conclusion of the year, a few thousand dollars have been given by these special boys. And you know what?"

Rabbi Bender paused for a moment. "Here's the most important thing. They've learned to be givers in life. Every little exchange that trains a child to become more giving teaches them to be sensitive, kinder individuals."

"Do you think," I asked "that there is a certain point when parents and schools should start teaching their children about *chessed*?"

"Look," he replied. "Loving kindness cannot just be a one-time event. It must become part of a child's nature from when he is little. From the youngest class on, we speak about awareness of other children's struggles. Some children have experienced the loss of a father or mother. If you know this, we tell the children over and over again, be sensitive! Think before you speak. Don't go on and on about the gifts that your parents bought you or the trips that your parents took you on. Imagine for a moment—what's that like, to be missing a parent? To go home and find your father's seat empty each night; your mother's space void?"

Rabbi Bender described how he introduces this concept, of feeling another child's loss, to even the youngest class: "When you give someone a slap, it hurts. But if there's a cut, then there's an open wound, and boy, do you ache. It stings. When you hurt a child who is growing up without his mother, without his father, you've inflicted pain on someone with an open wound. He aches. This really stings him! It is up to us to teach our children sensitivity toward one another."

We have a life-changing mission here. We need to work on the whole character of our children, molded by Torah values.

A parent who attends my classes e-mailed me the following conversation that she had with her seven-year-old daughter:

> "Mommy, there is a boy in my class and he's always touching his nose."
> "Okay."
> "And he has red sores under his nose."
> "Oh, poor thing."
> "And all the kids make fun of him."
> "Oh, that's terrible."
> "I don't make fun of him, but I really feel bad because some of my friends call him gross and I don't know what to do."
> "Oh. Well, sweetie, what do you think the Torah would say?"
> "Torah would say that you can never embarrass anyone."
> "That is right, so what do you think you can do?"
> "I think I would say, come on guys, stop saying that to M, because he feels really embarrassed and maybe even sad, and think how you would feel if it was someone in your family or even you?!"

Children can be taught, they must be taught, to think of others. We are here to help guide our children and bring sensitivity to their souls. Loving kindness will then become our family's personal melody along with our school's anthem.

THE ULTIMATE *CHESSED*

After contemplating the many acts of loving kindness that pulsate through our world, it is easy to become discouraged. What can I do? What have I accomplished?

Be assured that parenting is the greatest *chessed* of all. The Hebrew word for love is *ahavah*. The root of this word is *hav*, which means "to give." Giving is not a result of love. Love is a result of giving. The more you give, the greater you love.

From the moment your child was born, you have not stopped giving. Remember waking up for early morning feedings and greeting the dawn as you cradled this newborn in your arms? Your infant was unable to say thank you, not even a smile did you receive during those first days of parenthood.

Yet, you kept on giving. And the more you gave the more you loved. You invested in this child and looked away from your tired, weary self. In the process, you learned to love as you've never loved before.

Parenthood transformed your once self-absorbed selves into a committed, compassionate family. That is the miracle of love.

As your child grows, so, too, does your ability to dedicate yourself to another. Your heart, your soul, your very being. You've looked away from your own needs and placed your child first. This is our ultimate purpose of being. To reflect G-d's compassion as we live our lives.

Every step of parenting brings with it an added opportunity to give. We give of ourselves physically, though we are beyond exhaustion. We give of ourselves financially, though nature dictates the desire to hold back. We give of ourselves emotionally, though we are sometimes tested beyond our limits. We give of ourselves, unconditionally. That is the ultimate *chessed*.

The last days of my father's illness brought us much sadness. We were shell-shocked from the blinding pace with which this awful disease progressed. Our children, especially, wished to hold on to their beloved Abba Zaydah. (*Abba zaydah* means father-grandfather. My nephew coined the phrase when he was a toddler and the name reflected the children's love for their grandfather.) He was fading from us, like grains of sand disappearing through the fingers of time.

My daughter, Shaindy, was a child of nine. She had a day off from school and asked to spend it with her Abba Zaydah. "I know I'll be a little sad in the hospital, Mommy, but I don't want to be home and not spending time with Abba Zaydah. Can I come with you?"

"Of course, Shaindy," I replied. I hugged her and brought her little body close to mine.

We entered the hospital room, heavyhearted. My father's breathing was labored. His eyes were closed shut. I didn't know if he could hear us or if he even knew that we were there.

As usual, my mother was sitting beside my father's hospital bed. Though her face was etched with grief, she lit up with joy when she saw Shaindy.

"Shaindy!" she exclaimed, as she opened her arms and showered my daughter with kisses. "Abba Zaydah will be so glad that you came to spend time with him. You know how very much he's always loved you, all of you, our special *kinderlach*."

We inched closer to my father's face. The beeping of the myriad of machines pulsated in the room.

"Can I sing for Abba Zaydah?" Shaindy whispered hesitantly.

"Of course." My mother nodded enthusiastically. "Abba Zaydah would love to hear your voice. What would you like to sing?"

"HaMalach HaGoel," Shaindy replied.

She would sing Jacob's final blessing of the angels. The blessing that my father had bestowed upon us just a few weeks prior. It seemed as if it was just yesterday that we had been comforted by the sound of my father's words. And now we were unsure if he could even hear us.

Shaindy lowered her face toward my father. She began to sing with her sweet, gentle voice. At first she was unsteady. With each word, though, she gathered her courage and sang with her heart. When she was done, the room was silent.

Slowly, very slowly, with his very last ounces of strength, my father raised his hands. One palm barely touched the other. Once. Again. And again. It was the most delicate of sounds, but it was clearly my father's applause.

Fatigued, his arms dropped to his sides. Though worn down, Abba Zaydah was still able to muster the strength from deep within and give his final appreciation to his little grandchild.

A final *chessed*. The ultimate *chessed*.

SEVEN

Discipline

I t happens almost every time. A new parenting group is formed. We meet and one of the first topics that parents request to discuss is discipline.

The frustration in the room is palpable. I look around and perceive some who are experiencing real anguish. There are those parents who feel that their entire day is spent disciplining their children. Many times it is the same sort of behavior that is being reprimanded, over and over again. Other parents feel powerless as their children continue to ignore their requests. The joy of parenting is gone.

They recall dreams of happy families, peaceful dinners, and kids playfully laughing with each other. Tantrums, whining, and children who obstinately misbehave were never part of the picture.

> I always imagined my daughter to be sweet, self-assured, and calm. Never did I think that each morning, just getting her off to school would be a battle of wills. By the time it's evening, I haven't got the strength to deal with her bedtime tantrums. I'm at the end of my rope.   EXCERPT OF AN E-MAIL THAT I RECEIVED

Whether your child is a toddler of two or a teenager of fourteen, a child out of control brings a parent frustration and pain.

Like it or not, all children require discipline. Discipline is the boundary we set in our homes that encourages the raising of a child with soul.

Children who lack discipline grow without understanding the limits of acceptable behavior. They often cross the line and then can't comprehend why we get so upset.

Imagine a beautiful garden left untended, weeds growing wildly all over. That is exactly the image of a child raised without discipline. There are no limits. Once there was magnificent potential, but now the garden is overrun. Where does one even begin to restore the possibility that once was?

"*Elokai*," Almighty G-d, the soul that you have given me is pure. You have created it, You have fashioned it, You have placed it within me." Each morning, our prayers describe the soul that lies within. Parents have the tremendous responsibility of safeguarding this sacred treasure. Proper discipline helps us mold these little souls so that they maintain their great potential throughout life.

THE KEY TO EFFECTIVE DISCIPLINE

We may have the best of intentions. We know that our children's behavior is wrong. We cajole, we scold, we bribe, we give time-outs, we attempt to employ every method in the book. Yet, we remain ineffective. What's lacking in our approach?

Effective discipline requires self-control. We cannot gain control with our kids if we are losing it ourselves. Parents who are spiraling out of control as they discipline are not respected or listened to. Perhaps they are feared for their potential outbursts, but fear only produces anger within. Parents who bully their kids never win in the long run.

If our goal is the molding of good character for life, we've gone way off course. Why is it that we lose it so easily when we discipline? Understanding our lack of control will help us regain direction.

We've all been there. Waiting on line in the supermarket as our child screams for a snack we don't want to buy. In the toy store choosing a birthday party gift as our child insists she wants the same for herself. Or picking up a child from a playdate as he lies on the floor, kicking and screaming.

Teenagers may present quite different scenarios but the results are the same. Their reactions to our *no* can leave us feeling upset and unsettled. As the confrontation escalates, so too do our feelings of anger.

When faced with frustrations in a public setting, we are embarrassed in front of others. Perhaps they'll think that we're bad parents.

In private, we think, "How dare he? Who does this kid think he is? Doesn't he appreciate everything I've done for him? How dare he!"

It becomes easy to lose ourselves in anger. We say things in the height of our emotions that we realize are wrong. Sometimes we can grab a child's hand just a little too hard. We tell ourselves, "I can't take this anymore! This kid is the most . . . child I've ever seen!" Our tone reflects our rage. The time has come to discipline effectively and firmly, without anger and lack of control.

Gaining Self-Control

Wisdom Speaks Louder Than Rage

King Solomon teaches us an elementary lesson in communication. It sounds simple yet it completely eludes many of us. He explains that words spoken gently by the wise are heard and accepted.

You are your child's role model. Your wisdom speaks louder than your rage. Children need to look up to their parents. Mothers who scream and fathers who shout cannot be respected. They are resented and looked down upon. "Here goes my mom, screaming again." "Okay, my dad's going to do his thing and lose it with me." Kids tune out. They even feel resentment and disgust.

If I want my child to listen to me, I cannot lash out in anger. The first thing I must do is work on my tone and demeanor. The yelling and screaming must stop.

I have been to homes where children misbehave and their parents then react with loud frustration. The only way that I can adequately describe the scene is a "screaming house." Mom is screaming, Dad is screaming. The kids are shouting back. There is no order. Chaos rules. This type of discipline is ineffective. It can continue for years, but to no avail.

If you recognize yourself as a screamer it is not too late to regain control. Decide now that this is your most important goal. In the beginning you may find it difficult. Perhaps you are able to restrain your temper just once a day. Slowly but surely, you will find it easier to maintain your self-control. Once becomes twice and three times before you know it.

You will speak calmly more often. You will find that your entire nature is impacted. Your children will come to respect your even tone and, with time, begin to listen to your words. They, in turn, will reflect your newfound voice and not scream as often.

True, you will not see transformation in one day. This is not an instant makeover. There will still be some difficult moments, but finding control is the first step. Change is in your hands. Discipline is much more effective when given with a firm tone rather than in rage.

I have asked parents to listen to themselves, even put on a tape recorder. They've told me that the results have been frightening. They never realized how loud they'd been yelling, how awful they sounded.

Parents who are able to speak firmly, without anger, find that the quality of their family life has been tremendously uplifted. They, themselves, gain a degree of self-respect through self-control.

Remember, our ultimate goal is discipline through good communication and respect. How can children respect and listen to a parent who reacts wildly?

Enter Your Child's Mind

A great source of anger when disciplining is our rush to judgment. We criticize our children with ease. In our mind's eye we become angry at their seemingly obvious faults and shortcomings.

> "This kid is the most stubborn kid around!"
> "I can't believe what a whiner she is."
> "I never saw such a crybaby."
> "What's with him? He's such a pain in the neck!"

Again, our sages teach us a fabulous formula for living and communicating: "Hillel says: Do not judge another person until you have reached his place" (Ethics 2:5).

Take a moment and reach your child's place. How does it feel to be screamed at in public? When was the last time you were tired, hungry, and wet, then told to sit in a restaurant quietly until served? Are we treating our kids as adults or children?

It was on a day when the snow never seemed to stop falling that I learned this lesson firsthand. My children woke up excitedly, watching the storm and planning their day's adventures.

The older kids put on their boots and snow gear, running outside with shouts of anticipation. I took my one-year-old to the kitchen with me, but he began to cry and wouldn't stop. I tried to read him a book, play a game, give him a snack, all to no avail.

My father had been visiting and surveyed the scene.

"*Shayfelah,* do you have a pot that I can borrow?" my father asked.

"Sure," I replied, not knowing what my father was thinking.

He took the pot from my hands and walked outside in the storm. A few moments later he returned. He lay a towel out on the floor and sat my little one beside him. In his hands were two spoons and a bowl. The pot was filled with white, beautiful snow.

My son stopped crying immediately.

"He just wants to play like the rest of them." My father laughed. "If he can't be out in the storm, at least let's bring the snow to him."

My father taught me to connect with my child's mind. Instead of getting frustrated, take a step back. What is my child thinking? What is he feeling?

So much of our anger would be diffused if we would take a moment and try to penetrate our child's thoughts. We would realize that our child is simply asking to be included or trying to tell us how exhausted he is. He is just lacking the ability to communicate properly.

And if discipline is required, at least we would discipline out of concern that our children gain strength of character and never from rage or anger.

Stop Comparing

There are times when we become angry because, simply put, the situation we are in is just not fair. Why is my son the one who never sits nicely in a playgroup? Why is my daughter learning disabled and failing math? How did I end up with the geeky kid who can't seem to make friends?

Understand that there is no such word as *fair* in the Torah. The concept just doesn't exist. The situation may seem unfair in our human intellect, but G-d has a master plan and everything is done for our best. We are given all necessary tools to help us accomplish our life's mission.

Judaism teaches us to be "content with our portion." Acceptance is the first step toward gaining serenity. I can spend my day surveying everyone else's children and wondering why my child is so trying in comparison. Or, I can develop my faith and understand that G-d custom-made this child for me. I was given *this* child from G-d's treasure house of souls for a reason. This child and not another.

Our morning prayers include a blessing where we thank G-d for "giving me all that I need." Everything I have—the life that I live, the spouse I am married to, the children I have been given—are all a blessing. Through them I am able to complete my life work. Instead of wondering why I couldn't have that one's spouse, that neighbor's home, that person's life, or that couple's fabulous kid, know that you have been given all the tools needed to fulfill your purpose.

Obviously, G-d believes that you are your child's most competent teacher. That's why you were chosen to be his parent. You are his perfect match, his *bashert*. Instead of "losing it," contemplate the best methods possible through which you can help your child attain his goal. You will surely shed your inner anger as you gain acceptance and serenity. Your child will benefit most as you reach out with newfound love.

Amy and Steven attended a couples' class and asked for a private session. They wanted to discuss their nine-year-old daughter, Rebecca. As we sat down together, I could sense their weariness. It took but a few moments for Amy's eyes to fill with tears.

"Every day, every moment with Rebecca is a problem. Nothing is ever simple with this child. If we say yes, she says no. Of course, when we say no, she insists yes. The whole house revolves around her. I can't take it anymore. Rebecca has exhausted me."

Steven sat with his arms folded, looking fed up. As he spoke, his eyes hardened. "I'm telling you, we've got to get tougher with her. Teach her a lesson. She's the most stubborn kid you've ever met. There's no way but her way and I've had it."

"Listen," I responded, "I know that this cannot be easy for both of you. Sometimes children are born with certain character traits that can be frustratingly difficult to deal with. The easiest thing to do is to throw your hands up in defeat or to say, angrily, let's teach her a lesson she'll remember. Then what? What have you accomplished?

"This is your daughter we're talking about. You were given this child for a purpose. As her parents, you were also handed the tools with which to deal with her strong nature. She is your child.

"Now, I want you to think about something. Every child is born with a unique soul. Your job is to draw out the beauty of her soul. Our sages teach us that each person's nature can be utilized for positive or negative actions in life.

"Rebecca is stubborn. That's a fact. But that does not have to be bad. As her parents, you must find a way to channel her stubbornness for the good. If you look at this from a different perspective, you will achieve greatness with this child.

"She can grow up and use her stubbornness for the positive. Rebecca could be a leader. If disciplined and taught properly, she will stand up for what's right. She will be tenacious for justice and truth and never just follow the pack blindly. She'll never say, "Everyone is doing it, so what can I do?" Her defiance will allow her to endure courageously as others may cower. Don't allow her headstrong nature to defeat you. Instead, set goals and channel her strength toward strong values. Discipline, yes. But discipline with a purpose in mind."

We spent the rest of the evening discussing the methods through which Amy and Steven would discipline Rebecca. (See Principles for Discipline, on page 194, which include methods that worked particularly well with Rebecca.) Their newfound resoluteness allowed them to see their daughter in a more positive light. They have continued to parent with greater confidence and determination. Rebecca has learned to channel her stubbornness toward loyalty, commitment, and beliefs. She has also come to understand that although she could state her strong opinions, ultimately some decisions will be made by her parents.

Parents, too, can find themselves altered, as they relate to their children's difficulties with greater understanding.

Perhaps you are an individual who needs help with becoming more patient. G-d has given you a child who will stretch your patience until you learn to react without snapping. Perhaps you are a person who needs to learn to be more compassionate and sensitive. You were given a child who will teach you to become kinder and more tolerant with each given day. You will be transformed into a more compassionate individual through parenting with kindness.

That other child just wouldn't complete your life's mission. Stop comparing. This soul was handpicked for you. Once we comprehend each child as our personal blessing, we can accept the difficulties with greater serenity. Trust that whatever G-d decrees is for your ultimate good.

This simple trust is called faith. When you discipline through faith you perceive each child's trials differently. Rather than concentrating on how unfair life is, think about reaching specific goals with each child.

BUILT-IN DISCIPLINE

"Hear my child, take my words . . . hold fast to discipline, they will add years of life to you. Do not let it go. Guard it, for it is your life" (King Solomon, Proverbs 4:10, 13).

The young couples that I teach asked my family to spend a Shabbos together with them in New York City. One couple hosted us all and prepared a magnificent Friday night dinner. Oval tables, covered with festive cloths, were placed around their living room and dining room. The scent of fragrant flowers filled the air. As the women blessed their Shabbos candles we began to settle in our seats.

Space was tight. My children found their place cards on a small table next to ours, squeezed into a corner. There were no other kids present, which made it an even more difficult setting for our children.

As the meal progressed, one young woman called out my name from across the table.

"Slovie, I need to ask you something," she said. "I'm watching your kids and I don't get it. Why aren't they exploding? How can they be sitting in that little cramped corner and not lose it? What's the story?"

"The story is that we Torah-discipline our kids," I answered with a smile.

"What do you mean?"

"It's not that they're angels, it's not that we're so incredible, it's the way they've been learning to live as they grow up.

"You see," I explained, "the best way to discipline your children is to teach them self-discipline. The entire foundation of Torah is our mitzvahs. Living with mitzvahs teaches us self-discipline for life.

"So," I continued, "there are times that I may want something, or I may want to do something, but I can't. It's against Torah principles. My children know that they can't always have whatever they want, whenever they want. They have learned incredible self-control from an early age."

"Like how?" she asked.

"Here, let me give you an example. Keeping kosher can sometimes be really hard for kids . . . sometimes it can even be hard for adults. You want something badly, it looks delicious, but you can't have it. It's not kosher. So you learn self-discipline.

"A few years ago, we took our kids on a ski trip. We decided to meet on top of the mountain for lunch in the early afternoon. Because we're kosher, my children were only able to have bananas, kosher yogurt, and some kosher snacks that were sold in the lodge.

"'I feel really sorry for your kids,' their instructor said to me. 'Look at all this great stuff . . . tacos, chili, burgers, and fries. And look what your kids are having.'

"'You don't have to feel sorry for them,' I answered. 'My children eat kosher and live by Torah values. They know that some things are permitted and some are not. It's okay. Not everything is here for the taking. Watch them, they're happy kids who are having a great time skiing.'"

This is the Torah way of raising children. Kids who understand that there are limits learn to live with self-discipline. They gradually learn to rule over their urges as they live a committed life.

G-d, in His infinite wisdom, has provided us with the Torah that embodies built-in self-discipline. Once my child understands that he can't have everything he desires, it naturally becomes easier to discipline him. My sweet child, sometimes the answer is simply no.

I read about a woman who was standing at a checkout counter when her son began to beg loudly for a chocolate bar. She turned to him and said, "Aaron, I'm sorry, but it's not kosher." He stopped his whining and they were on their way.

Behind her stood an African American mother whose son also began to whine for chocolate. She turned to her son and said, "Robert, you can't have that."

"Why not?" he asked in surprise.

"Because, it's not kosher. You heard the lady." Everyone had a good laugh.

When we teach our children self-control at an early age, we model ourselves after the Torah's method. We can translate the Torah's teachings into our own lives.

For example:

*"Sophie, you cannot eat before you wash your hands. Yes, you're
hungry, but there are rules that need to be followed first."*

"Max, you may not throw food across the table. Sure, it's fun. But that's not the way we eat and it's disrespectful to G-d's food."
"Danielle, you are not allowed to hit your brother, even though he's getting on your nerves. I know he's bothering you but we do not hit each other. Let's find a better way to work this out."

Don't be afraid to give your child limits. This is the benefit of raising a spiritual child. We fortify our child and help him deal with his environment.

Our children have become used to an E-ZPass life. They think that you are automatically able to pass through life's tolls and roll along it's highways. There are no apparent restrictions or costs involved.

We need to teach our kids to stop for a moment and pay the toll. There are limits and boundaries that must be respected. Sometimes there is a price to be paid. Tantrums and screaming won't make a difference.

It's not about "fair." There are certain lines in life that may not be crossed. Self-discipline teaches a child self-control. A child who can achieve self-control feels better about himself and gains self-esteem. He is on the road toward independence. He is learning how to deal with life's challenges.

• • •

Ask yourself this question: If I tell my nine-year-old to put away his dinner plate and finish his homework before he can go bike riding with friends, am I punishing him or disciplining him? Am I burdening him or teaching him self-control?

Think, also, about the times your child decided that he wanted to start a collection—Beanie Babies, baseball cards, Wacky Packs stickers—it doesn't matter. So you take your child to the store and he, of course, doesn't want to start with just one. "Everyone has so much more and besides, one is so little!"

You understand his feelings. You'd love to buy him a lot, or even the whole set if you could.

Stop yourself. You'd be doing your child a huge disservice by allowing him instant gratification. Instead, help him learn patience and self-control. What a great lesson he'd gain by understanding that he can't have it all at once; he must come to earn privileges and anticipate things, and yes, there are boundaries and limits in life.

The objective is to strengthen our children through gaining control of their urges.

The same idea may be applied to children who "answer back," scream, or erupt in tantrums. My goal is to teach my child to speak respectfully even though he is angry and upset. Through proper discipline, I am guiding my child on a path for life.

I can turn to my child and say, "I know that you are furious. You obviously don't want to listen. You can speak to me, but only if you lose the rage. Express your thoughts respectfully and I am willing to hear your words. Speak with disrespect and we cannot have a conversation."

You are granting your child the ability to free himself from the yoke of anger. This is true *chinuch*—discipline through education and direction.

PRINCIPLES FOR DISCIPLINE

There is a reason that I have reserved the topic of discipline as one of the final chapters of this book. Previously, we spoke about communication and self-esteem. In order to discipline effectively, it is first necessary to communicate properly with our children.

In addition, real self-esteem is a *must* so that children come to accept our words of guidance. As our bonds with our children grow, their trust in us deepens. Though they may not always agree with our decisions, they will respect our judgment.

There are methods through which we can help ourselves discipline more potently.

Build Communication with All Ages

BABIES: Sing and cuddle with your infant. Be affectionate. Don't think that just because he is a baby, he doesn't know the difference. Studies show that babies flourish with verbal communication and physical displays of love. Begin to speak to your infant from birth. Name the activities that you are doing. Sing songs and prayers out loud. The trusting bond between parent and child develops early in life.

TODDLERS: Toddlers crave parents' attention and approval. "Watch me," "Daddy, look at me," "Why, Mommy?" Use language that expresses excitement, surprise, or worry, and so on to reflect their emotions.

Remember not to judge quickly. Put yourself in your toddler's shoes and see things from his perspective. Don't knock his fears and call him a "baby." The world is a big place for a little child.

PRETEENS AND TEENS: The more you speak to your preteen, the easier it becomes to communicate. Utilize time together, such as car rides or shopping trips, for small talk. Seek openings in conversations. It is a mistake to leave talks to times of crisis or difficult moments that require discipline. Develop a rapport with your teen and try to relate to his interests. If your kids are into sports, take a look at the newspaper's sports section. Allow them to share last night's game highlights. Don't be too busy to attend their performances and games. Show interest in school projects. Take the time to connect with your kids so that they know how much they mean to you. Enjoy a breakfast or dinner out with just the two of you. Don't discourage his dreams or sarcastically dismiss his ideas. Ask your child for his opinions and show him that you value his judgment. Be sure to share your daily happenings—so that you, too, give and you don't just ask all the questions. Peer pressure is growing so be sure to keep family bonds strong. This is not the time to allow family rituals to be ignored. We are family forever.

Above all, no matter their age, listen to your children. Hear their fears and worries without knocking them down. Listen to their point of view. It doesn't mean that you must agree, but at least they know that they have a voice.

Just as we desire that our children listen to us, we, too, must hear their voice. Listening to your children helps keep the lines of communication open. Effective discipline rests on good communication between parent and child.

When I hear kids say, "My parents are going to kill me," or "You don't know my parents. There's no way that I can talk to them," I ache for these children and their parents.

Children and parents should understand the goal of discipline. I want you, my child, to make it through dinner without giving me attitude, calling your sister gross, pinching your brother under the table, then getting yelled at and ordered to your room. My motive is *not* because I cannot stand the aggravation and headache. I am not doing this because I had a hard day and just want you to leave me alone and behave already. Rather, I want you, my child, to understand the importance of acting as a noble human being. I am here to teach you how to be a *mensch*.

Good communication allows us to get this message across. I discipline because self-control is a foundation for life. I can convey my feelings and thoughts better if my child is open to my messages.

Discipline with Love

Our sages give us the perfect formula for discipline: "Let the left hand push away while the right hand draws near" (Sotah, 47a).

One's left hand is considered the weaker one. When you discipline, "use your left hand." When showing affection, "use your right," your stronger hand. What do our sages' directives mean?

Emotions of love should always come through when you discipline your kids. Your children should never feel that you are disgusted with them, can't stand them, or feel hatred toward them—no matter how disappointing or terrible their actions.

Children who are admonished often feel ashamed of themselves. If they feel that you are embarrassed by them, or dislike them, they can easily become alienated from you. Always be sure to balance your emotions. Counteract your negative reproach with positive gestures of love. This sounds complicated, but it's not.

Sandwich Your Discipline

When you need to speak to your child about a disturbing misbehavior, you want to touch his inner core. If you only deliver words of reprimand and appear ticked off, your child will put up a defensive posture. To be effective, let's coat the "bitter medicine" with "sprinkles of sugar" so that a child will not remain with a bad taste in his mouth and reject your words. Deliver your discipline like a sandwich: begin with a positive, admonish and deliver your message, then end with a positive again.

Begin with a Positive

When G-d called out to Abraham, He said, "Abraham, Abraham." The repetition of his name expressed love. Throughout the Torah, we are told that G-d calls out one's name as a reflection of love. When you speak someone's name, you are showing fondness for the person. If you dislike someone, you find it difficult to even say their name.

It's best to begin your admonishment at eye level, while maintaining eye contact. Bend down to look at a younger child if you must. Simply say his name. (If you find this too hard it means that you are feeling too much anger at your child right now. It is better to wait and cool off for a short period of time.)

Deliver Your Message

State the behavior that disturbed you, but don't go on and on. It's important to watch your tone. Speak seriously, with sadness or disappointment about the misbehavior, not with out-of-control anger. It is okay to say that you were worried, afraid, or disappointed. (My parents and grandparents would simply say sadly, "This behavior does not befit you." Trust me, it was effective.) Children don't want to disappoint their parents. They thrive when they give us reasons to be proud of their behavior.

End with a Positive

A sentence of hope for the future is a priceless display of our belief in our child's good character. Try to give your child a signal that you still love him. A kiss on his head, a hug, a touch on his shoulder, a kind word, or a smile are all gestures of reassurance.

For example: "Ethan, you wandered off at the mall without telling us. We were scared and worried. We know that you are responsible and will ask permission from now on, before going off on your own." Your words should be delivered seriously and not lightly, together with a reassuring gesture.

"Sandwich discipline" is much more effective than finding your child and saying, "I can't believe you! What were you thinking? Do you know how long we were all looking for you? We were about to call the police. There's no way you can ever come with us to the mall if you're going to go wandering off by yourself. Do you know how many missing children there are out there? What's the matter with you? Do we need to put a leash on you or something?"

With sandwich discipline, your child will hear your message instead of building up resentment toward you. He understands your expectations and knows that you still believe in him.

When you discipline with love you reassure your child that your positive feelings for him remain. Never allow children to think that your anger has diffused your love.

Some children are told to "get out of my sight," "you're making me sick," or "I can't even look at you." These words are a tragedy waiting to happen. Never distance your child to the point of no return. Children must feel that they have a place in your heart forever.

Keep in mind that criticism is not discipline. Children can feel that they are only criticized. "Why is your room a mess? Why didn't you remember to bring home your homework sheet? Why are you eating like that? Why don't you find something better to do? How many times must I tell you to put away your plate?"

This is not discipline. With each added criticism your child finds it easier to disconnect from you. Pay attention to the amount of negative comments you transmit to your children each day. You'd be surprised to discover how few positive interactions you have with your kids as they grow older.

Try to encourage good behavior by "catching" your child doing something good. Acknowledge his or her mitzvah.

> My children love hearing that they are mitzvah boys. My younger son has much more "spirit" than my older son so I wasn't calling him a mitzvah boy as frequently if at all. I thought he just didn't care. And then one day after class you told me how everyone needs to hear that. Well, I went home and called him a mitzvah boy that night. He was so happy. "I am a mitzvah boy, too?" he asked. Well, I felt terrible and good at the same time. Terrible for not doing it sooner and happy I was now going to. After now months of telling him what a mitzvah boy he is, his demeanor has changed and now he shows me I was right!   E-MAIL I RECEIVED FROM A PARENT

Loving discipline conveys to a child that it is possible to express disappointment, yet still love. This is an important foundation not only for parents and children, but also for future relationships.

Separate Your Child from His Action

"Bad boy!"
"Bad girl!"
"I can't believe how stupid you are, what did you do?"
"You're the biggest whiner, you're always giving me a headache."
"You are the laziest kid around."

We are not prophets, yet down the road these children will behave precisely as we described. Tell children often enough that they are bad and they begin to believe that they really are bad. "And if I'm so bad, what's the point of trying to be good?"

The "stupid one" grows up doubting his abilities.

The "whiner" grows up constantly complaining.

The "laziest kid" grows up without direction.

Pay attention to the words you use while disciplining. Telling your child that he or she "didn't behave nicely" is not the same as saying "you are not nice!"

It is important for parents to pay attention and identify character traits that need help. Don't allow actions that require discipline to pass you by. As soon as a disturbing behavior occurs, nip it in the bud. But be careful not to allow your child to feel that he or she is indistinguishable from his or her behavior. A child's personal dignity should never be attacked.

Before our patriarch Jacob departed from this world, he called together his twelve sons. "Come and gather around," he said. "Listen to me, your father."

As he spoke to each child, he mentioned their individual character traits. Jacob wished to clarify each tribe's unique mission.

He turned to his sons Simeon and Levi and chastised them. He spoke about their inner rage. But even while admonishing, Jacob denunciated their intense anger but never them.

He didn't condemn them and say, "You guys are out of control." Instead, he let his sons know how upset he was with their trait of anger. He relayed his views without demolishing his children's self-image. They were still the "noble sons of Jacob," part of the twelve tribes of Israel.

It is one thing for a parent to point out a flaw in character. It is devastating, though, for a parent to tell a child that he is defined by his flaw. Jacob taught us to separate the child from the action. Distinguish between the deed and the doer.

At the conclusion of our class, one mother told me that she had come to a painful conclusion. She realized that she had been calling her son various mean names as a way to motivate him. She felt sick to her stomach. "Slowpoke," "turtlehead," "lazybones." She hadn't meant it, the words just slipped out. She had found her son always moving in slow motion. She resolved to use more positive words to get her child to get going.

A few weeks later she relayed that her son was responding well to her new way of speaking. He confided to his mother that he always thought of himself as slow and was grateful for her changed attitude.

Discipline is a parenting tool. Utilized properly, we can endow children with positive character traits. Used the wrong way, the results can be devastating.

Don't Be Afraid to Draw the Line

Discipline helps our children become responsible adults. This is where it all begins. Already at a young age, children are faced with choices of behavior that become more significant as they grow.

Shall I grab away my sister's toy because I'm jealous or control myself? Will I wake up in time for the school bus or just roll over and oversleep? Do I ignore my mom's call for dinner and play some more Game Boy? Do I give in to peer pressure or just say no?

The foundation for handling future responsibilities rests on my child's ability to make the right choices. As a parent, I am here to help my child along the way. Sometimes, I may have to take a tough stance.

Many parents are afraid to challenge their children's choices. Maybe my child won't like me anymore? She's going to get angry and make a scene. We are afraid of seeming too harsh or intrusive. How will my child react to my no? Remember, we are not our child's best friend. We are not live-in playmates or here to hang out together.

We are parents, *horim* in Hebrew, related to the word *morim* for teachers. Parents need to be seen as authority figures, deserving of respect. We are obligated to teach our children boundaries and set standards of conduct. We educate our children in the school of values.

There may be times when you feel sorry for your child as you need to discipline him or her. "I wish I could let him sleep through the morning rush. He's so tired and the bus comes early. What's the big deal if he's late for class?" "She really wants those new Uggs but we just bought her boots last week . . . still, she'll be so happy and she's begging for them."

When you draw the line and take a stand you are really showing your child how much you love him. Imagine a young boy roaming the house, not wanting to go to sleep. He has no bedtime, no one knows if he's inside or out. His parents call out, "It's okay, we'll see you in the morning. . . . As long as we get to sleep, we don't mind."

Does that child feel cared for? Do you think he feels that anyone is genuinely concerned about his well-being? When you say no, you are saying, I care about you too much to permit this behavior. I *will not* allow you to act this way, I *cannot* allow you to speak this way. You are out of control and I love you too much to allow the deterioration of your very being.

As we discipline, we are not only setting limits. We are also teaching our children how much we love them.

A friend of mine told me that now that her son is grown she realizes that she made a huge mistake. She didn't expect more from him in life. She let him get by and never drew the line. Whatever he did was fine, as long as he was happy.

"I definitely shortchanged my child," she smiled ruefully. "He has no idea how to deal with life's realities. He's always looking for a shortcut to get by."

This generation is known as the "entitled generation." They feel entitled to life's privileges. It's all coming to them. Parents have become the "enablers." We don't want our children to go through any stress or unhappiness. And so, parents hear comments like these:

"Mom, you owe me twenty dollars."
"Dad, you need to take me to hockey."
*"Who said you could touch my things? Where did you put all my
    stuff?"*
"You need to buy me new sneakers."
"There's nothing to eat in this house. You need to get more nosh."

And we accept this type of talk. We neglect to teach our children the proper way.

I owe you? I'm your mother. I'm your father. I've given you life. How can I possibly owe you anything?

"Please, Mom, can you give me twenty dollars."
"Dad, is it okay for you to drive me to hockey now?"

Don't be afraid to teach your children how to speak with respect. Don't fear discipline. Your children will come to respect your values.

They will come to appreciate your loving concern. The friendship side of your relationship will flourish once the respect and love are in place.

King David had many sons. One son, in particular, found a special place in the king's heart. Avshalom was a warrior. He is described as a most handsome prince with long locks of hair flying in the wind. Charming and witty, Avshalom possessed a most dynamic personality. He perceived himself as an aristocrat.

Whoever came to his father, David the King of Israel, for judgment would first be met by Avshalom. He would sit at the gates of Jerusalem and say, "Look, you sound as if you're making sense. The problem is that there is no one here who will understand you. If only I'd be judge, then you could come to me. I would hear your case and judge fairly."

Avshalom would then embrace the man and make him feel understood. Slowly, he stole the hearts of the people. He slyly gained their adoration. The public came to revere him. Avshalom, he's the one who really feels for the simple man on the street, they thought.

Avshalom began to plan a conspiracy against his father. He gathered together his followers and rebelled against the king. The hearts of the people throughout the land were with Avshalom.

Imagine the pain of King David. Not only was he forced to flee his palace in Jerusalem, but his own son rose up against him! How could this be?

Our sages teach us that David neglected to admonish Avshalom with a firm hand. He saw that his son needed discipline, but he felt badly. King David's great love for his son prevented him from delivering strong chastisement.

We, too, sometimes think, "Maybe my child will grow out of this behavior? Maybe it's just a bad stage and I can ignore the nastiness." One mother told me that she couldn't discipline firmly even though her daughter displayed incredible meanness, because she wanted her child to feel good about herself. She didn't want to take away her daughter's self-esteem.

Avshalom's arrogance overtook his entire persona. He would stop at nothing to attain the kingdom, even if it meant the devastation of his father.

"David was going up on the ascent of the Mount of Olives, crying as he ascended, with his head covered [in mourning], going barefoot. And all the people with him wrapped their heads and went up, crying as they ascended" (2 Samuel, 15:30).

David, the King of Israel, was cursed and pelted with stones. People threw dirt at him. He was left to hide in the desert mountain wilderness around Jerusalem. He walked along in mourning and humiliation.

"My own son, to whom I gave life, seeks to destroy me, how can I be upset from the curse words of others?" he asked sadly. Broken physically and emotionally, David was moved to recite Psalm 3: "A psalm of David, as he fled from Avshalom his son."

After a fierce battle, the followers of Avshalom were defeated by King David's loyalists. Avshalom was riding a mule and his long hair became entangled in the branches of a thick elm tree. The mule ran off, leaving Avshalom suspended between heaven and earth. Avshalom was then killed by sword.

King David, immersed in prayer, was awaiting news from the front. He had left orders that Avshalom not be harmed. As he saw a young man running toward him, he asked: "Is all well with my son, Avshalom?"

Despite all the pain, a parent's love never dies.

When the king heard about the death of his son, he trembled. "He wept and said as he went, 'My son, Avshalom! My son, my son, Avshalom! If only I could have died in your place! Avshalom, my son, my son!'"

David was anguished. The Talmud teaches us that while lamenting for his son over and over again, David was actually praying for his soul.

There were no victory parties or triumphant parades. The day was turned into a day of mourning. David continued to cry out for his son.

King David mourned not only the loss of his son, but the loss of potential that lay within the very existence of his beloved Avshalom.

If you journey to Jerusalem, you can visit Yad Avshalom, the memorial that stands until today to Avshalom, the son of King David.

Corrective Consequences

There are times when parents notice their children ignoring their reprimands and continuing on with the same misbehavior. It seems that despite all their efforts and good intentions, no impression has been made. Some children test limits by speaking or acting out with extreme disrespect.

If our goal is to teach children self-discipline for life and the attainment of good character, then we had better make it clear that this is unacceptable. When we allow children to persistently disregard our words, we are looking away at the exact behavior that we've been trying to correct.

By ignoring intense disrespect we are neglecting our children's character. Kids will certainly not become more respectful on their own. It is left to us parents to help our children acquire appropriate attitudes for life.

Such moments bring us to consider consequences. I am loathe to use the term *punishments,* which has a connotation to most people of harshness and suffering. *Consequences,* by contrast, are the natural aftereffects of one's behavior. If you choose to behave in a certain manner, know that you must deal with its aftermath.

For example, children who leave baseballs outside, lose them. Kids who wake up too late for breakfast, miss it. Homework that gets left around goes missing. You get the picture.

Let's say your family goes out to eat in a restaurant and your child misbehaves. You've spoken to him in the past about this, but he still disrupts the evening. His behavior has made family time unpleasant for everyone.

Speak to your child (calmly, without anger) and tell him that you've noticed his misbehavior. Be specific and don't debate or argue with him.

Clearly inform him, so that he cannot feign ignorance, that if this behavior continues, there will be a consequence. Next time he will have to stay home. Children who don't appreciate the privilege of being out with their family don't come. This is the natural consequence of ruining special family time. The choice is clearly his. He will have to decide if he would like to correct his behavior or not. Then he must deal with the consequences. No one is making the choice for him. This will help your child confront his behavior and make better, more mature decisions.

Be sure to hold him to his word. If he breaks his promise, don't look away. You are molding character for life.

The consequence should relate to the misbehavior. In Judaism, we call this *midah keneged midah,* literally measure for measure. As you act, so does G-d act toward you. We take our cue from the Torah.

A mother I know received a call from her child's teacher. Her ten-year-old son had spoken exceedingly disrespectfully. After school, this child went with his mother and chose a beautiful bouquet of flowers. As his mom waited in the car, he presented the flowers along with his apology letter to his teacher. (The teacher had given permission for the visit beforehand.)

Don't think that this was an easy consequence for this child to swallow. He thought up a million excuses of why he could not ring his teacher's doorbell. But that's the point. Think about what you've done, my child. When you hurt someone you need to deal with your actions. You feel badly now. How did your teacher feel when you treated her disrespectfully? The child who brought grief will now bring joy.

Good discipline gets your child thinking and feeling.

"According to His Way"

The wisest of men, King Solomon was known across the world for his incredible insight. His books are studied even today for their rules of ethical conduct, moral teachings, and life experiences. Writing in his Book of Proverbs, King Solomon speaks about raising children:

"Educate a child according to his way" (Proverbs 22:6). According to *his* way, writes Solomon. Not your way, not your mother-in-law's way, not your three siblings' way, not even the way of your psychotherapist. "His way." Understand your child's ways.

King Solomon was trying to teach parents to approach children according to their individual natures. Some children are supersensitive. All it takes is the slightest look and they respond immediately. Add a few words of criticism and you've lost them.

Other children just don't get it. You give them your most serious look and they still have no idea how upset you really are. They require a more authoritative approach.

These kids may be siblings in the same family, it doesn't matter. They are all uniquely different. As a parent you need to understand your individual child. Figure out what works with each child.

Once you identify your child's nature and gain insight into which parenting style will yield success, you will find greater results as you discipline.

King Solomon is guiding us toward different approaches and styles of discipline. There is not only one road on which we can all travel. There are byways and service roads, too. The point is that all roads lead to the main highway of life. Parents need to navigate and explore the best route for each child.

Once we are able to approach our children according to their nature, we come to accept each child's individuality. My daughter's high school principal told us parents so wisely: "Put a child into a mold and she becomes moldy." Not all children are the same. Some parents can't accept a child who is "out of the box." They look at their child and can't believe he's theirs. Watch carefully, because this may bring a parent to feelings of disappointment and resentment that children are quick to recognize.

"How can we be so different?" parents wonder. I love piano, how can you have no interest in music? I'm athletic and fit, how did I end up with such an overweight, klutzy kid? I'm a doctor, my dream was to go into practice with my child; what do you mean you're not going to medical school?

We need to accept each child "according to his way." Let your child know that it's "okay to be me." Live by the wisdom of King Solomon and communicate with each child on his level.

Do's and Don'ts of Discipline

- *Do* avoid angry confrontations. Try not to speak when tired, exasperated, or overstressed.
- *Do* treat children with dignity. Never shame or humiliate or make fun of your child.
- *Do* choose your battles. Your home should never be a constant war zone.
- *Do* recognize your child's successes, not just his failures.
- *Don't* lose your sense of humor. You are not a drill sergeant.
- *Don't* play favorites.
- *Don't* use sarcasm or anger to discipline.
- *Don't* exaggerate misbehavior.
- *Don't* drag in past misbehaviors and mistakes from years ago.
- *Don't* carry grudges and be unforgiving.

OBSTACLES TO GOOD DISCIPLINE

A number of parents don't realize that they unknowingly place obstacles in their path that seriously hamper their ability to discipline. Awareness brings clarity and removal of these obstructions.

Comparing Children

"Why does your sister sit so nicely at the table?"

"Look at you. How does your brother stay so clean, but you always look like a mess?"

"How come your sister always does her homework without being told?"

"Watch how your friend plays so nicely with his sister. Why can't you do that?"

How do you expect your child to respond?

"Because, Mom, I'm just a mess?"

"Uh, cuz I'm lazy and selfish?"

"Obviously, I'm never gonna be as good as my sister."

Now, how would you feel if your spouse asked you:

"How does your sister somehow always have it together, but you never do?"

"How does your brother always manage to be a great father and provider, but look at you?"

There is no way that "comparative discipline" could possibly work. No child will respond to such negative comments. Remarks such as these cause anger to grow deep inside. Worse, you are sowing seeds of resentment between brothers and sisters. Focus on your child's behavior, not that of his siblings or friends.

Empty Threats, and a Lack of Consistency

"You're never coming on vacation with us again."

"That's it. No more going to restaurants with the family. From now on, you're staying home."

"No more videos. Ever."

If your words are empty threats your discipline goes up in smoke. Why would your children take you seriously? Your discipline is reduced to meaningless words that do not carry any weight. Kids can't take this sort of discipline seriously—because it's not.

A lack of consistency is another cause of ineffective discipline. If we are inconsistent, our children grow confused. Sometimes we mean what we say, other times we don't. Discipline is taken lightly, if at all.

I have watched this scenario (as I'm sure you have, too), in a park, restaurant, or at a playdate: A child behaves in an offensive manner. He is pushing, grabbing, or running around uncontrollably.

"Stop it!"

The child continues.

"Stop it right now or we're going home!"

For a few moments, the child conforms. Once the parent returns to his or her conversation, the child returns to his annoying misbehavior.

"I said stop it. Cut it out or I'm telling you, we're going straight home."

Every few minutes an abstract warning is shouted. The afternoon is spent like this: warning, repeated warning, more warning, no consequence.

It is no different with children who are teens. Parents tell children that they expect certain standards. They say that stipulated behaviors are unacceptable. There is talk about removing privileges or incurring various consequences.

Often, the children continue doing whatever it is they want to do. They realize that their parents aren't really paying attention. Parents get distracted and forget. Discipline becomes a flippant aside. If you treat discipline casually, your children will take your words lightly. Don't expect to see real results.

Even our mood can affect consistency. There are times when parents are in a good mood. Loud noise isn't bothersome. It's okay to run around and even jump on the bed. A child is under the impression that this behavior is acceptable. Difficulties the next day may bring stress and a sour mood into the home.

"What are you doing? Why are you running and making so much noise? Who said you could jump on the bed? Cut it out!"

How confusing for a child! Can I make noise and run around or not? Why was it okay to jump on the bed yesterday but not today?

Discipline should never be confusing. Decide which behaviors are acceptable and which are not. Then, stick to your positions. Don't confound children with your yo-yo parenting.

Incorrect Phrasing

We know the behaviors we'd like to see . . . we know the good character traits we'd like to cultivate in our children. How do we effectively transmit our ideas?

Sometimes, it's just a matter of proper phrasing that can make all the difference in the world.

Be Specific

Parents say:

> *"Clean up your room."*
> *"Be good."*
> *"I wish you'd help out more."*
> *"Don't stay out late."*

What's wrong with these phrases?

None of them are specific. A child doesn't know what you mean.

"Mommy, how do I clean up my room . . . where do you want me to begin?"

"Daddy, what do you mean be good . . . I thought I was good?"

Even an older child can misunderstand your request.

"You want me to help out more? I feel as if I do help out. What do you want from me?

"What do you mean I'm home late? It's only ten thirty?"

Instead of:	**SAY:**
Clean up your room. ⟶	Put away your Legos in the box. Then, please put your laundry in the hamper.
Be good. ⟶	Please stop banging the ball on the door.
I wish you'd help out more. ⟶	Please help me bring the bags in from the car and then I need help setting the table.
Don't stay out late. ⟶	Please be home by ten o'clock.

Parents who make requests from their children should try to be clear and concise. Itemize. Enumerate. Give your children specifics. You will prevent much misunderstanding and bad feeling.

Remove "I" from Your Commands

When parents give directions, they often begin with "I." "I want you to go to bed," or "I'd like you to start homework."

When children hear "I want you—" parents create a control issue. Well, children think, if you want then I don't want. Take "I" out of the command. For example, "It's bath time" or "It's time for homework." You'll find that activities will go more smoothly with your child.

Don't End Directions with a Question

I've often heard parents give great directives to their kids, but end their sentences as a question. Remember, we are not asking our children for their agreement as we parent. For example:

> *"Let's put on your jacket, okay?"*
> *"I don't want you going out so late, okay?"*
> *"You guys are going to behave, right?"*
> *"I want you to start your homework now, all right?"*
> *"Do you want to put on pajamas?"*
> *"Are you ready take a bath now?"*

If you'd like to discuss a situation or give your child a choice, that's one thing. It is entirely different, though, to make a discipline decision and then ask your child for his permission. Why should a parent ask "Okay?" Do you want your child to respond with a no? Questions following directions do not lead to effective discipline.

Never Humiliate a Child

Children have a popular rhyme that they can often be heard chanting: "Sticks and stones may break my bones, but words can never harm me."

When we were kids my mother taught us that this children's chant is simply not true.

"Sticks and stones may break my bones, yes, my children, but you can always go to the orthopedist and get a cast. Soon, you'll be healed. But words . . . words can *forever* harm you."

I believe that one mother says it best in a note that she sent to me:

I started going to your parenting classes in December '04. I had a six-year-old, a seven-year-old, and an eleven-year-old at that time. I had always told my children, as my parents told me, "Sticks and stones may break your bones, but words will never harm you." I learned soon thereafter that I had been wrong my entire life. I learned that broken bones can heal, but hurting words can break a soul and spirit forever.

I learned this in my Torah parenting class.

I consider myself blessed to have gotten this message loud and clear at age thirty-seven. I wish it had come earlier.

A DEVOTED AND GRATEFUL MOM IN BROOKVILLE, NEW YORK

There are times when you may never heal the hurt caused by your words. And it is not only children who use their words to hurt. Adults, too, can sadly destroy through shaming and embarrassing children.

When we discipline our children our words become most potent. Used the wrong way, we can cause children to feel unloved or worthless. Judaism places the highest regard on one's words. We are actually given a commandment prohibiting the hurting of people with our words, and causing them grief (Leviticus 25:17).

Our sages teach us that this includes reminding people of past mistakes or embarrassing others. It is even considered worse to hurt someone personally than financially because money can be replaced but shame lingers on. Someone who embarrasses another in public and causes his face to turn colors actually loses his share in the World to Come (Rashi, Bava Metzia 58b).

There will be times when your children will be upset with your decisions. You will deny their requests as they ask for sleepovers, junk food, or expensive electronics.

These moments will be forgotten with time, don't worry. But there are certain moments that linger in a child's mind forever. One of the most painful childhood memories is humiliation. The damage is indescribable.

I know many adults who can still recall a painful incident caused by a parent or teacher. Years may pass by, but their cheeks still redden with shame as they recollect the stinging memory.

We need to treat our children with the same feelings of respect that we desire, ourselves. "Let the shame of your pupil be as dear to you as your own," teach our sages.

When we humiliate children, all our efforts to discipline fly away in the wind. Our words fall on deaf ears and hardened hearts. Children will put up a wall of anger and retreat from our message.

Public Discipline Causes Shame

If you must discipline your child when his friends are visiting (and you cannot wait until they leave), take him to another room without causing a great commotion. Speak to him privately and in a low tone. Even discipline in front of siblings can be embarrassing. If you shame your child as you discipline you will not gain anything but his resentment. Knowing "how to discipline" is just as crucial as "when to discipline."

A first grader I know came home from school obviously distraught. After much cajoling from his parents, his words spilled out with a flood of tears.

"Today, when recess came, I tried to reach up and get a ball from a high shelf. A lot of books came tumbling down. In front of the whole class, my teacher screamed, 'What are you, stupid or something? Even a four-year-old knows not to do that! What's the matter with you?'"

"The whole class was laughing at me. I can't go back to school. Mommy, Daddy, please don't make me go back. Everyone's making fun of me, even my teacher. She hates me."

This little boy may forget the vocabulary words or science lessons he learned that year. But, believe me, he will never forget the lesson in humiliation he experienced in that classroom.

The damage inflicted is beyond words.

THE POWER OF WORDS

We underestimate the power of our words. Both parents and educators need to take a hard look at the way they communicate discipline to their children. Sarcasm, put-downs, rage, and shaming children in public or private creates a negative environment that sabotages your efforts at discipline.

Besides working on ourselves, it is a good idea to help your children work through the harshness of other people's words. Explain to them that there are times when even adults forget how to speak with kindness and sensitivity. Allow your children to tell you how they were made to feel. Instead of concentrating solely on feelings of anger, try to bring your child to a place of understanding.

Tell your children that just because they are called a name or embarrassed, this does not change who they are. They are still your same special children. Reassure them of your love.

A parent who has attended my classes for years sent me a moving e-mail about the difficulties her daughter faced in school while being disparaged and disciplined. Her teachers spoke negatively about her in front of the entire class.

In our parenting class we had recently discussed the power of words and the importance of not humiliating others.

Whenever possible, this mom has consistently shared all that she has learned with her family. I believe that her "Torah view of life" helped shape her daughter's incredible response:

C. has been having a hard time in school. It appears that there are three adults in the room, a head teacher and two assistants. Apparently, C. was reprimanded for talking in the hallway and instead of being spoken to, there was a comment or two by each teacher openly when the class returned to the room. "C. is feeling too comfortable here, she thinks that she is home!" one assistant said. "She is nosey," her teacher commented. After a fourth comment was made, she was asked to read and replied that she didn't want to. She had previously said to her teachers that her stomach hurt. To this her teacher got very upset and things got worse. She told her in front of the children that this was disrespectful to say to a teacher. C. walked out of school that day with a defeated face. She relayed the story to me and we agreed that the *lashon harah* [negative speech] was very painful, shaming, and hurtful. I could not figure out how to handle this one and I had to give it some thought. That night I had come into her room and she had written a letter to her teacher:

Dear Mrs. Teacher,

I am very sorry if I was disrespectful to you today. When I said that I did not want to read I was stuck in my feelings that you thought that I was too comfortable and nosey. When you discuss me with the other teachers in front of the class I feel sad, embarrassed, and hurt. I will try to stay focused tomorrow. If you see or hear something you do not like, can you please whisper it to me privately?

I hope that tomorrow can be a much better day.

Love, your student, C.

Slovie, I have to tell you that tears came to my eyes. This little eight-year-old teaches me every day. She knew how to be respectful and open without shame. She understands who she is, and that G-d created a strong girl who will walk the right path and keep on walking even when she is hurt. Most of all, out of this whole classroom, she is the one that is standing for not shaming others, not speaking in a way that hurts. She is teaching her world perhaps one of the greatest lessons of Torah. Love another as yourself and do unto another as you would want for yourself. She has an understanding of the way Torah lessons work in the world. She took this as a lesson of being on the wrong side of *lashon harah,* and used it for the good. I have such joy from her, thank G-d. This has even happened with a boy that everyone picked on and a girl with a weight problem.

The power of our words is incredible.

THE THREE-WAY CONNECTION:
DISCIPLINE, HONOR, RESPECT

Some parents need instruction on how to discipline. Others need to learn how *not* to discipline.

My husband and I were invited to a dinner party in a couple's summer vacation home. As we stood speaking to the host, his ten-year-old son walked by.

"Look at him," his father said, beaming proudly. "He's wearing a suit and tie and he hates it. He came over to me this afternoon to complain. 'Mommy's making me wear this itchy suit and a stupid-looking girlie necktie. Ugh! I don't want to, Daddy.'

" 'Listen, Alex,' I told my son, 'how much will it cost me to get you to wear this stuff and make Mommy happy? Because otherwise I'll hear about it for the rest of the night.' "

This conversation just cost this dad everything. Little Alex has learned that everything in life has its price—even respect. How much does it cost to listen to your mother? What would it take to get you to listen to your father? Just buy me out, Dad.

This is discipline at one of its worst moments. We give honor and respect to our parents not because we are paid to do so, or because it's convenient and we're in the mood. Children are expected to listen to their parents, to show honor and respect, simply because it is the fifth commandment: "Honor your father and mother." Period.

During one couples' class, a young father raised his hand. "I have to ask you this and I'm sure that many other people sitting in this room have gone through the same situation.

"Honestly, my dad was an awful father. He was never around for us. He never had time for me. As a little kid, I gave up on him ever coming to watch my Little League games . . . or even knowing my teachers' names. He knew nothing about my life. I don't feel like giving my father respect. Why should I? He never did a thing for me. He wasn't like all the other dads. It's not that he was abusive, but still, he'd come home from work, say he's tired, turn on the TV, and just fall asleep on the couch. He never took us anywhere. Why should I give my father anything?"

The room was silent. It was obvious that this man had touched a painful nerve among many listeners.

"Why do we honor our parents?" I asked. "Do we honor them because they're great ballplayers or super Lego builders? If a father can't hold down a decent job, is he worthy of 'honor your father'?

"What about the mothers who are never home when their kids return from school? Or the ones who are constantly on the phone and seem as if they don't want to be there? Do they deserve respect? What about the mother who serves ready-made frozen dinners each night or the father who is always in the office and never sees his kids? Does the fifth commandment apply to them? Why do we honor our parents?"

One young woman spoke out.

"I guess what you are trying to tell us is that honoring parents is a mitzvah in the Torah for us to live by. Whether our parents received a parents of the year award or not, it just doesn't matter."

"Exactly right," I agreed. "Our sages teach us that there are three partners in the creation of a child—G-d, father, and mother. When you honor your parents it is considered as if you are honoring G-d, Himself.

"The commandment doesn't say: Honor your father unless he's a loser. Honor your mother except if she's controlling and gets on your nerves. Your parents give you life and just for that, we are given this commandment. Honoring parents helps children learn gratitude for parents even if their moms and dads weren't the greatest parents in the world.

"Look, we are not commanded to love. Some people are emotionally fragile. They love one day and reject the next. Things happen. The fifth commandment is not about love or passing judgment. It's all about our behavior."

(There are guidelines in Judaism for children who, unfortunately,

come from abusive homes. We are speaking here about ordinary up-
bringings.)

Derech Eretz, *a Spiritual Standard of Living*

Honor and respect are basic foundations of our homes. Our sages give us
guidelines as to what constitutes honor and respect. As parents, we are
responsible for setting certain standards of behavior in our homes. Some
behaviors are acceptable and some are never up for discussion.

In Judaism, we call this *derech eretz*, literally "the way of the land." It
means that there is a spiritual standard of living. It is the proper way to act
in life. We establish a fundamental quality of life by which we exist. This
spiritual standard of living guides us in our day-to-day relationships in life.

Discipline is the thread that ties it all together. Some parents may express discomfort with this thought. "I want my children to be my best
friends! We're like sisters—look, we even share clothing!" Or, fathers
want to have closer relationships with their kids than they had with their
own parents. "Discipline" sounds rigid. "Respect" and "honor" sound
old-fashioned, not for today's families.

It is important for parents to realize that our children need parents to
respect. Sure, it's wonderful that you want to get along with your kids, and
you should have a warm and loving relationship. But your role in this family is not to be "best friends 4 ever." You are responsible to guide, to lead,
and to inspire. You are here to mold character and raise a child with soul.

You are your child's greatest role model. If not you, who will your
children look to for direction? Society? The Internet? Celebrities? Peers?

Let's take a look at the world around us. Perhaps years ago, children
had an array of role models in their lives. Today, we must question and
ask who is teaching our kids values? At the same time, we are obligated
to take a closer look at ourselves.

There is a trend in today's society of parents who are not interested
in growing up. We don't want to look older, act older, or even seem older.
Bestsellers like *How Not to Look Old* reinforce the trend. Botox, Restylane,
and extra-long hours at the gym have become a natural way of life.

Though well employed, these parents dress in beat-up sneakers and
expensive yet tattered jeans, and wear matching T-shirts with their two-
year-olds. They are thrilled to walk around in Juicy and Hard Tail outfits
as if they were going to high school with their teenagers. They stay out
too late, vacation hard and long, and listen to the same music as their

kids. They are more interested in fun and "getting away from it all" than in dealing with their responsibilities.

Every neighborhood has its own variety. They are easy to spot, these "Peter Pan Parents," who often try too hard to look and act as if they're still college kids or even teens. As their children grow they become stuck in time, finding it difficult to move on.

As if that were not enough, our culture allows children to be raised by nannies, housekeepers, and babysitters, while therapists and tutors pitch in on the side.

And don't think that the kids are oblivious to all this. Too often I have heard preteens and teens voice their embarrassment if their parents acted and dressed inappropriately. They are often ashamed at parties and events as they've watched their fathers and mothers behave as if they were still immature teens, using crude language and overdoing it with liquor.

Children need parents they can respect. Moms and dads who live without dignity leave children spiritually bankrupt. And what about our kids' role models in society?

Scandals swirl around famous stars. Their names often are in the headlines of the morning's news as they attempt to defend themselves against all types of charges. Some of our greatest all-American athletes disappoint our children as they seek excuses for their domestic violence or drug, alcohol, or steroid use.

Out-of-control celebs bombard our children with their outlandish antics. Their consistently bad behavior makes it all seem so normal . . . even acceptable.

Popular television shows and music encourage kids today to laugh at parents and teachers, behave rudely, and trash basic human decency. We want our children to speak with respect, to carry themselves with dignity. Yet, we allow even our little girls to wear short cropped tops, short shorts, and "eye candy" phrases across their bodies. Why is this okay? How can we then wonder why our children seem to be lacking values?

Judaism teaches us to value both body and soul. We dress with dignity, we give thought to our words and language; our lives reflect the majesty that lies within.

Effective discipline is contingent upon the relationships we have with our kids. Discipline and respect are intertwined. Parents who live with honor and dignity give their children an image to look up to and view with respect. If I respect you, Mom, I will hear your words more clearly. If I respect you, Dad, I will want to live your values and try not to disappoint you.

Your children need to honor you. Not because you crave admiration. Respect is the cornerstone of our relationships. When children display respect they are accepting their parents as their life guides. The greater their respect, the stronger the bond.

Let's establish that discipline does not create a "lack of love" or feeling of formality as we raise our children. "Respect" and "honor" are not archaic values that bring distance between parent and child. Instead, it is the lack of values, lack of discipline, and lack of self-respect that are all related deficiencies in family life today. Kids require real role models. They need to look up to people in their lives. Who should they view with greater esteem than you?

INSTILLING RESPECT

In a culture that often invites disrespect, how can we create a home that embodies good character, ethics, and a strong sense of values? Is it possible to teach our children to speak and act with nobility of spirit?

The Torah and our sages offer tools to help us instill this sense of honor and reverence within our children. We are fortunate to be given guidelines that establish *derech eretz*—a spiritual standard of living in our homes. These guidelines help parents create an atmosphere of respect.

I will mention a few for you to ponder and mull over:

Children cannot call parents (or grandparents) by their first names. (Even when they are toddlers, and we think how adorable this is. Believe me, before you know it, you will not be amused.)

Children should ask permission before sitting in a parent's designated seat; for example, a parent's set seat in the kitchen or at the dining-room table.

Children should be taught to differ with respect. For example, instead of saying to a parent "No!" or "You've got to be kidding," a child should be instructed to say, "Is it okay if I have ten more minutes to play on the computer?" "Can I please play outside a little bit longer? I'll come in when you call me." Teach children to then accept a parent's decision graciously. Do not get into heated arguments or attempt to defend yourself. Do not fall into a pattern of constant wrangling with your child. You are a parent, not your child's opponent on the debating team.

Children should be taught not to contradict or interrupt a parent. This includes the many times that parents are having a phone conversation and can't get a word in because their child insists on interrupting. I cannot begin to count the times parents have called me from a supposedly private spot, only to be interrupted as children push their limits.

"Why are you taking so long? I need my macaroni now."

"You're talking too much. When are you done already?"

This is not respectful or acceptable.

Other times, children blatantly contradict their parents.

Zoe: "When are we going to get to the mall?"

Mom: "We just left ten minutes ago. We've got another half hour till we get there."

Zoe: "That's not true. We left at least twenty minutes ago. You don't know what you're talking about."

How should we deal with this disrespect? At this point, redirect your child's way of speaking and help your child think of a more respectful manner of expressing herself. In the beginning, you may need to give some coaching, but don't get discouraged.

Mom: "Zoe, that's really not a nice way of speaking. Can you think of a more respectful way of talking to me?" (Or, "Zoe, can you say that in a better way?")

Zoe: "Okay, sorry, Mom. Do you think it's possible that we left twenty minutes ago? That's how it feels to me."

Our sages give us further guidance to help us instill an atmosphere of respect in our homes.

What is honor? they ask. Honor refers to deeds, thoughts, or words through which a parent is uplifted. Providing comfort, taking care of physical needs, or displaying a caring attitude and thoughtfulness are all considered part of the commandment (Rashi, Sifra, Leviticus 19:3).

It is not sufficient just to give to or help one's parents, even our attitude is important. Kids who help out by slamming down plates or muttering resentments and banging drawers are not displaying honorable behavior. Parents need to teach their children to act respectfully, with proper demeanor. A positive attitude is just as crucial as the action displayed. How can we teach our children to behave with honor and reverence?

Encourage your children to do things for you. (Of course, do not go overboard or take unfair advantage of your children.)

How often do parents walk into a room, and ask, "Ari, are you thirsty? Can I get you a nice, cold drink?" "Eliza, would you like a snack? What can I give you?" Children hardly ever think about their parents' needs.

Teach your children to be sensitive to their parents and grandparents, to think and act with honor and respect. When your children get a snack for themselves, they should ask if you'd like one also. When you prepare a cold drink, have children bring one for your spouse, too.

Involve your kids. Give them opportunities to develop an attitude of respect. Children should not be sitting on the couch playing video games when Mom or Dad returns home from the supermarket. As you walk into the house with grocery bags weighing you down on each arm, they should be encouraged to come and help. Instill in your children the ability to be sensitive and considerate toward parents. "Dad, I'm warming up a slice of pizza. Would you like one, too? Mom, I hear your cell phone ringing. Do you want me to run and get it for you? Dad, do you need a fork? Mom, can I take your plate?"

When children go away to camp, a summer shouldn't go by without them calling or writing home—and not just when "things" are needed. Grandparents, too, deserve thoughtful calls that don't just coincide with birthdays and thank-yous for gifts. Little acts that establish an atmosphere of graciousness slowly add up to build a home imbued with respect.

It is not about your worthiness, or whether you believe that you are at an age that demands respect. It's not about you. It is about the molding of your child's character as you create a most noble being.

Some of you may be wondering if today's kids can really be taught to behave with respect. Let me reassure you, this is not living in *Mister Rogers' Neighborhood*. This is for real, if you sincerely desire it.

A parent who attends my parenting classes met the principal of her children's public school in the hallway one day, while picking up her kids.

"Mrs. M," he called out, "can I speak with you a minute?"

"Sure," she replied.

"I heard about the parenting classes taking place in your home. If I am correct, these classes are based on the wisdom of the Torah," he said.

"Yes, that's true," she replied, not knowing exactly what to expect next.

"Well, I must tell you something that I've noticed and so have many of the teachers. All of the children whose parents attend these classes act and speak with tremendous respect. Whatever you're all doing, keep on doing it. I see a huge difference in these kids."

Parents need to take a step back and look at what their lives have become. Many homes seem to be sorry sitcoms.

When did it become okay for children to scream at parents, engage in sarcastic back talk, or become abusive?

You must decide what kind of home you'd like to create. A home where kids slam doors, surf the Web for hours, ignore their parents, and destroy their siblings? Or a home where parents are role models for respect, live genuine values, set standards for discipline, and embody commitment and faith. It is up to you.

LOOKING IN THE MIRROR

We are parents to our children and children to our parents. More important than any discussion about respect that we may have with our kids is the example we set for them as they observe us with our own parents and in-laws.

We are forced, sometimes uncomfortably, to look at ourselves in the mirror. Often we squirm and dislike the image that we find. The reflection is most troubling.

Julia, a soft-spoken mom with two preteens at home, approached me hesitantly at the conclusion of a parenting workshop.

"This is really difficult for me to express in words, but I'm going to give it a try. Last class we spoke about honor and respect. You gave an example of a father returning home after a long day's work and being ignored.

"You described the kids on the computer or their cell phones, the mom preoccupied with her stuff, and no one even bothering to get up or say hello.

"My husband is this dad. He comes home each day, calls out some greeting, and he's lucky if we acknowledge his presence with a distracted nod. I admit, I am also to blame and I never realized the harm that I was causing. I know he must feel badly, but I guess we just fell into this pattern.

"The thing is, I also realized that my husband does the same thing to my parents when they come to visit. My mom and dad walk through the door and my husband won't move from his spot on the couch. He's either watching a game or on his BlackBerry and he just sits there. He barely grunts hello, or he'll scream across the room and say there's milk and juice in the fridge.

"I spoke to my husband and I have to say, it's been a painful realization for us both. He understands that until he puts down the remote and greets my parents, our kids will follow his example. I know, too, that I need to start doing my part and teach my children to acknowledge my husband's presence when he comes home at night. It's not just about my parents anymore, now it's about us."

If we want to see our children act with *derech eretz*, we had better examine our own behavior. Our children mirror our actions and reflect our mannerisms. Our kids define "proper" and "acceptable" by watching us.

Parents who glance at caller ID and whisper, "I can't believe Grandma's calling again . . . tell her I'm not here," shouldn't be surprised when their children ignore their calls to their cell phones.

Parents who roll their eyes at their parents' words or speak condescendingly should not be shocked when their own kids speak abusively to them. I have heard parents wonder at their children's gall, not realizing the amount of times their children heard their grandparents' sanity questioned.

Children are sponges. They absorb everything—our conversations, our gestures, our attitudes, even the look in our eyes. Our actions become embedded in their minds.

THE *SHALOM BAYIS* CONNECTION

One of the greatest ways to foster respect is through *shalom bayis*—peace within our home. Husbands who put down wives, wives who make hurtful jokes about their husbands, spouses who name-call, are all sowing seeds for their children's disrespect. Don't kid yourself. A lack of respect between husband and wife causes incredible harm.

These same words that you think are so clever will be flung right back at you by your children. When a spirit of disrespect is allowed to seep into your home, the language and demeaning attitude become permissible to your children. Kids make no distinction between you and your spouse.

Even if you really didn't mean what you said, it doesn't matter. There is no going back. You have lowered the standard of acceptable behavior in your home. Trashing your spouse's self-image permits children to be disrespectful. "If you don't respect Mom, why should I? If you think Dad's no good, why would I want to be with him?" You are destroying the very fabric of your home. By negating each other you are defacing yourself in your child's mind and heart.

Pay attention, also, to the manner in which you speak about authority figures. When you put down those whom your children are expected to respect, you are ultimately sabotaging yourself. (Chapter 4 on communication also addresses this issue.)

"That teacher doesn't know what he's talking about."

"I can't believe how stupid your principal is."

"That sermon was the most boring thing ever."

You have just undermined your own authority. You don't always have to agree with all your kid's teachers and authority figures, but mocking them allows children to view authority as a joke. Jewish ethics guides us to treat each other with respect, even while disagreeing— especially our elders and those we learn from.

Chutzpah

An important aspect of establishing an atmosphere of respect in our homes is not permitting an environment of chutzpah to prevail. Just as you would be careful about the physical pollution that enters your home, you must be vigilant about the "spiritual pollution" that chutzpah brings.

Chutzpah is defined by *Webster's* as "cheek, gall, or nerve." Simply put, chutzpah is plain, utter disrespect. Children are *chutzpahdik* not only with their nervy words, but also through their cheeky attitude. Rolling their eyes, purposely ignoring you, sarcastic back talk, mocking motions behind you, are all examples of chutzpah.

If your child asks you for something with disrespect or speaks in a nasty tone, you have an obligation to teach your child that this is unacceptable. You should say calmly to your child that as long as he or she speaks without respect, you are unable to answer him or her. Younger children may be told that they need to speak in a nice voice. Tell your child that as soon as he or she is ready to speak properly, you will be happy to respond. Don't be afraid of tantrums or whining, it is important not to give in.

If you do answer and respond, you are showing them that it is okay to speak to you with chutzpah.

Once things have calmed down, it would be a good idea to speak to your child privately. Try to be self-composed and even-tempered. Make it clear to them that as much as you do love them and would like to hear their ideas and requests, you cannot tolerate disrespect.

A child who returns home from school and walks through the door with attitude should be given the opportunity to come in and do it again. A spiritual do over. Explain to your child that chutzpah cannot be part of your family life.

"Ours is a home filled with love and respect. There is no room here for nastiness."

The more times we allow our children to engage in chutzpah, the greater the volume of insolence will grow in our home.

To me, chutzpah is like a terrible, nasty virus. Once one child in the home catches it, the chutzpah easily spreads. It is hard to get rid of and saps us of our energy. Parents need to be alert for the first signs of chutzpah and eradicate this destructive attitude from their homes. Continuous chutzpah should not be ignored—even if consequences must be given. Don't belittle the harm caused to your home by a child's insolence and disrespect. Just because physical harm is not apparent to you, it does not mean that damage is not being done. Chutzpah cannot be tolerated.

I was speaking to a teenage girl and her parents. They laughingly relayed an incident that occurred with their daughter and a substitute teacher. I must admit, her sharp tongue did display acerbic wit. It also reduced her teachers to tears.

There isn't anything amusing about chutzpah. These parents emboldened their child's nerve. Unfortunately for them, they will be experiencing her razor-edged tongue sooner than they think.

Two Parents, One Voice

Discipline is an art. Husbands and wives need to paint their canvases together. I have met parents who were crushed as a result of their children's disrespect and demeaning attitude, never realizing the hand they had in this sorry situation. Successful discipline and receiving a respectful attitude from children requires a united parenting front. Children who "smell weakness" learn to play one parent against the other.

The Torah speaks about the "rebellious child."

"If a man has a wayward and rebellious son who does not listen to the voice of his father and the voice of his mother . . ." (Deuteronomy 21:18).

How did this situation evolve? What caused this child to become alienated and estranged from his parents?

Our sages teach us that the rebellious child was raised in a home where parents spoke with two opposing voices: "the voice of his father and the voice of his mother."

He heard his father's words and his mother's words and they were not in agreement. Confused, this child ends up rebelling and opposing his parents' contrary guidance.

Mom: "No more videos, it's time to go to sleep."

Dad: "Oh, come on, let her just watch another half hour. What's the big deal?"

Or:

Dad: "I see that you can't sit nicely at the table, you're going to have to go up to your room."

Mom: "Honey, I really don't think that's a good idea. He had a really long week and he'll try to be good. Let him stay here."

I've had parents tell me: "My husband thinks our daughter is too cute . . . he's mush when it comes to her," or "My wife leaves all the disciplining to me. It's always, Wait till your father gets home. The kids never listen to her."

Parents need to convey to their children a united front. Belittling one parent's discipline or debating consequences in front of children brings children to insolence. The result is that you've undermined your spouse.

Don't put the burden of discipline on one parent and appear inadequate. You are a competent adult with a role to fill.

Two voices produce one rebellious child and a world of pain. Mothers and fathers who decide to parent in unison create a world of harmony in their home.

WHEN VISION AND REALITY DON'T MEET

Remember the first moment you found out that you were expecting? Images of pink and blue floated in your mind. You studied that fuzzy sonogram picture from every angle. Will she have her mother's sparkling blue eyes? Will he have his father's cute dimple? Will she be a graceful dancer? Will he love adventure?

Wherever you walked it seemed as if, suddenly, everyone had a baby. Stroller colors caught your eye. You noticed soft little curls glistening in the sun. Cute giggles and toothless smiles made your heart sing. Dreamy scenes with your child brought beautiful visions to your mind. The days ahead held so much promise. You had great hopes and dreams for this little soul.

Time has passed. Reality has set in. Disenchanted, you have packed away your dreams like favorite clothing from your youth. They don't fit. What was I thinking?

Visions of glorious children have given way to deep disappointment. You thought it would all be so different. You do not recognize the image before you. You are not the only one.

Sensing that his death was drawing near, our patriarch Jacob sent for his son, Joseph. When Joseph was informed of his father's illness, he brought his two sons, Menashe and Ephraim, to Jacob's bedside for a final blessing.

Jacob looked at the two boys and then asked an astonishing question, "Who are these?"

Jacob had been living in Egypt and teaching these boys Torah for seventeen years. He's their beloved grandfather. Now, he asks, who are these two young men? Doesn't he know his own grandchildren?

Our sages provide us with deeper understanding. Don't think that Jacob is disoriented and doesn't recognize Joseph's sons. Instead, he is questioning their spiritual identity.

These two boys grew up in the Egyptian court of Pharaoh. Unlike the other sons and grandsons, Menashe and Ephraim were born and bred in a foreign land. Jacob was worried.

Will these two be loyal to their people? Will they live a life of faith, even after I'm gone? Do they view themselves as descendants of Abraham, Isaac, and Jacob or as the new, improved version with ties to Egyptian nobility?

Jacob wanted to bless the children, but suddenly the feeling of G-d's presence departed from him. He saw, prophetically, that these two boys would have evil kings as their descendants.

Jacob was shocked. "Who are these?" Where did these sons, who in the future would beget such immoral offspring, come from? How can this possibly be? Are they worthy of my blessing?

Jacob's mind filled with questions. Are these boys really mine? What will be with them? What are their beliefs? How will they behave down the road?

How many parents stay awake at night, wondering these very same questions: What will happen with my son? What will become of my daughter?

The difficult child, the angry child, the failing child, the rebellious child, the child who never seems to find himself . . . what will be? We cry out in anguish, what will be?

We toss and turn, hoping and praying for the best. In this mixed-up world of ours that can seem so frightening, how will my child grow? What direction will he or she take?

Who is this child of mine? I don't recognize him. I can't understand his ways.

Joseph turned to his father and responded: "*Banai,* they are my sons whom G-d has given me here.

"Please, Abba, my father," Joseph pleaded. '*Banai*'—these are mine. They are my children and they are your children. We are the sons of Jacob and we shall always walk in your ways. G-d has given me these sons. They are not accidental. These children are Divine gifts from Above."

What did Jacob do?

He placed his hands on top of his grandsons' heads and he blessed them. He drew Menashe and Ephraim close, he kissed them and hugged them. Because no matter what, these children were his gifts from G-d.

The Torah describes Jacob's eyes as "heavy with age so that he could not see."

There will be times in life when like Jacob "we cannot see." We cannot bear to look. Our vision is dimmed and we can't comprehend.

"Who are these?" we ask.

We worry. We try to scan the horizon, but dark clouds hang low and the vista ahead is hazy. We never imagined this difficult road. An uneasiness settles deep within. What should we do?

Follow in the footsteps of Jacob. Bless your children. Pierce the heavens with your tears. Bring them close . . . kiss them . . . embrace them . . . accept them for who they are . . . and love them.

• • •

A father complained to the great Chassidic Master, the Baal Shem Tov, that his son had forsaken his ways.

"Rebbe, what shall I do?"

"Love him more than ever" was the reply.

EIGHT

Sibling Rivalry

This one you won't believe."

Lisa, a vivacious young woman who regularly attends my parenting classes, was on the line. She had just returned from a family trip and had called to say hello.

"We were invited to a party that my friends threw in honor of their daughter's sixteenth birthday. They really wanted to do something special . . . anyway, since we were visiting from out of town, we were one of the first guests to arrive.

"I couldn't believe what I saw. I want to know what you think and if parents just need to accept this type of behavior as normal between siblings."

"Accept what?" I asked. "What happened?"

"Well, this birthday girl has a sister who is eighteen months older than her. When she came down the stairs to check out the room she threw a fit.

" 'I can't believe this!' she screamed. 'I thought my party would be over the top. You always do everything better for her, even her party is so much more than mine.' She had a huge tantrum, ran to her room, and slammed the door. It took an hour for her parents to get her out. I don't know what they said, but they obviously promised her something.

"It scared me for my own daughters. They're close in age and I'd never want to see such jealousy between them. Do you think it's possible for siblings to act kindly toward each other, for kids to grow up loving each other?"

"Of course I do," I replied. "When people think about siblings they automatically bring up the story of Cain and Abel. They say that from the beginning of time rivalry has been a fact of life. But Torah is filled with great examples of siblings displaying real love for each other."

Lisa asked about day-to-day living.

"Is there a way to help our children love each other better? I don't think that I could handle my kids behaving the way my nieces and nephews do, or even my friends' kids. They are always at one another's throats. What can I do differently in my home?"

Lisa's question is one that many parents ask. One of the greatest joys of parenting is watching our children get along and relating kindly toward each other. King David describes it so beautifully in Psalms: "How good and pleasant it is for children to dwell together as one."

Parents worry when their children fight. They ask themselves: Will my kids ever be able to spend time together without knocking one another down? Mealtimes, car trips, family vacations, and weekends off from school can all be ruined in an instant by their conflicts. Brothers and sisters who mock each other, quarrel, and even fight physically destroy peace within the home.

Is sibling rivalry inevitable?

There is a major difference between sibling rivalry and common children's disagreements. Kids who get along well work out their conflicts together. At times they may need some guidance and intervention, but they usually resolve their disputes easily and without venom. This is a normal part of children learning to live together and becoming a family.

Sibling rivalry, on the other hand, is a whole other story. *Rivalry* is defined as a contest, competition, conflict, or emulation, according to *Webster's*. We are talking about brothers and sisters who perceive each other as competitors. They see life with siblings as a constant tug-of-war.

These children are constantly measuring and comparing. Happiness is defined as always having more than their siblings.

"Hey! Why did she get a bigger piece of cake than me?"

"How come he got three meatballs and I only got two?"

"You never let me take a day off when I was her age, why does she get to stay home?"

The problem with sibling rivalry is that it doesn't dissipate with time. If anything, it only increases and becomes a person's nature. Children who are constantly sizing up their life by what others have can never be happy. They are forever comparing and don't know how to feel content with what they have. In their mind's eye, they are constantly being treated unfairly. Somehow, everyone else always has it better. Even as a grown adult, these old feelings resurface.

"I should have gotten that raise."

"Why does my sister have such a great life?"

"How did my brother ever get that job? I'm so much smarter than him!"

Can such an individual ever feel at peace? Can he or she ever be satisfied with what he or she has? If we could teach our children to find contentment within their own lives they would not feel the need to be competitive with their brothers and sisters.

How do children come to sibling rivalry?

The bottom line is *jealousy*. Children who are jealous of each other become rivals. They cannot bear that their sibling has something and they do not. They may not need or even like what their brother has, but the fact that he has it is distressing. Jealousy eats away at their very core.

When children come home from school viewing life through their "big eyes," they cannot understand why "Zack got to go to Disneyland and we just stayed home." Or now need something because "Sarah's mother bought her an iPod, so now, I need one, too." Envy becomes a way of life

Children who are jealous display a deficiency in character and need parents to help them refine their inner essence.

Parents, though, mistakenly feed the jealousy as they attempt to even out their children's lives. Instead of taming and controlling the green-eyed monster, they empower it and help it grow.

Children need to learn how to deal with their jealousy. Thinking that we are helping them, we give in to children's rants and raves. We feel guilty that one child has more than the other.

So, we measure the juice we pour, carefully portion out the desserts, and always buy toys simultaneously for both children. This is a huge parenting blunder. The contest between siblings only grows uglier.

CAIN AND ABEL

The first case of sibling rivalry in the world was the famous incident between Cain and Abel. Their story is a tale of jealousy. Both Cain and Abel desired to give an offering to G-d. Displaying a cavalier attitude, Cain didn't give his inferior offering much thought. G-d chose to accept only the offering of Abel, who displayed a purity of heart.

Cain grew angry. He was consumed with jealousy.

G-d wished to teach Cain the art of sincere repentance: He asked Cain, why are you annoyed? Why the dark face? You could improve yourself and find forgiveness. But if you choose not to conquer this bad character trait, know that evil will always be lurking at the door.

G-d gave Cain incredible advice. Look at yourself. Angry, upset, overcome with jealousy—what's the point? What have you gained? Instead of seeing the world through begrudging eyes, uplift yourself. Work on your character. You will become a much happier person. But if you do choose to remain in this cocoon of jealousy, know that sin crouches in the doorway. You will be haunted throughout your life; a constant dark shadow will be cast over you. You will never feel content. Envy will consume you and ultimately destroy you.

Cain refused to heed G-d's words. Jealousy simmered within. One day, an argument broke out between the two brothers.

"Let's divide the world," Cain suggested. "Abel, you take everything mobile and I will get the earth, itself."

Abel agreed. At that moment, Cain exclaimed, "Go away! You are standing on my property!" Abel ran away, but Cain pursued him, calling, "Get away, the ground is mine!"

Frightened, Abel ran up to high mountaintops in the hope that Cain would abandon pursuit. Cain followed him there, too, overtook him, and arose to slay him.

But Abel was stronger. He won the upper hand and had Cain beneath him.

"We are only two sons," wailed Cain. "What will you tell our father if you kill me?"

When Abel heard this, he had mercy, and released Cain. Cain arose, lifted up a stone, and killed his brother, Abel (the Medrash says).

What was Cain's problem? Didn't G-d tell him that he, too, could have his sacrifice accepted?

Rejection is not what troubled Cain. He wouldn't have minded if both he and Abel would have been rejected. It was the fact that his brother came out first that did not allow Cain peace of mind. Envy burned within.

Did you ever take two siblings to the beach and find that there isn't enough sand in the universe to allow them both happiness? They are always eyeing each other. What's he doing? Where's she digging? That spot looks better than mine. I want his shovel, it digs deeper holes than mine.

What I have doesn't matter, just don't let her have better or more.

Abel had a pet sheepdog. G-d told Cain that he would be required to watch over that dog for the rest of his life. He could never abandon it.

Dogs, G-d explained, are loyal creatures. You, on the other hand, have been greedy, arrogant, and disloyal to your brother. Cain, you will learn allegiance from this dog. You, a human being, will gain insight from an animal.

Just as G-d desired to teach Cain, we too, must teach our children. Of course, G-d could have accepted both offerings and looked away at Cain's poor character. But G-d is teaching us how to parent. Jealousy needs to be rooted out from one's heart. Ignore it, and it only grows and destroys relationships. You cannot live your life through envious eyes, for "your brother's blood cries out from the ground."

You are responsible for your actions and achievements, independent of your sibling's success in life. If you find your happiness only by measuring yourself against your brother or sister, you will become an angry, bitter human being.

A mom described pulling into her driveway with her teenage daughter. They were laughing together, sharing a joke and good times. Her teenage son was sitting on the lawn, brooding. As she stepped out of the car, he stood up. "Hey, why does she get to have all the happiness?" Even your sibling's happiness becomes a sore point, as if personal contentment is out of your control.

Siblings Conquer Rivalry

The Torah describes the loving relationship between Moses and his brother, Aaron. After instructing Moses to return to the Jewish people in Egypt, G-d asked Aaron to meet his brother in the wilderness. As the two meet, Moses relays to Aaron all that has happened to him.

He tells Aaron about his mission and the Divine message that he would be communicating to both Pharaoh and the Jewish nation.

There was every reason for these two brothers to display ugly rivalry toward each other.

Moses had to run for his life and flee Egypt. If we were there, we could have thought, Here I am, forced to begin anew in a country where I know not a soul. I've missed my family and my people. At least you, Aaron, have been living at home with those you love, residing in familiar surroundings. What did you do to deserve a role in this mission? Besides, I'm the one G-d spoke with and chose.

Aaron, too, could have easily displayed great resentment toward his brother, Moses.

If we were in his shoes, we could have said, I can't believe this. Here I've been struggling in Egypt, suffering with our people, while you've been living the good life in the land of Midian. I've stuck it out and now you come flying in like a superhero? Why did G-d choose you? I'm the older brother, I'm more eloquent, how dare you?

But there was none of that. Moses and Aaron followed G-d's directives without a trace of resentment or jealousy. How did the brothers achieve such total harmony?

Our sages teach us that there are times in the Torah that Moses is first mentioned and there are other times that the name of Aaron takes precedent. This is so that we may understand that both brothers were equally great.

Some may ask how this could be. Moses is known universally as the greatest prophet who ever lived. Could Aaron ever be considered his equal?

Herein lies the key to understanding and promoting love between siblings. Both Moses and Aaron were given their own separate roles, allowing them a personal, unique identity. Each brother put his heart and soul into every thought and action pertaining to his specific mission. Feeling essential and vital, there was no need for jealousy between the brothers.

Aaron never felt as if he were the lesser brother. His self-esteem remained intact because he had the knowledge that his role was just as integral as that of Moses. Each brother was given distinct and unique responsibilities. Both Moses and Aaron achieved their absolute potential and spent each day trying to reach their personal goals.

Each child needs to feel vital through his or her personal contributions to the family. A child who feels that he or she is crucial and belongs feels beloved. He or she doesn't experience resentment because his or her place in the family is secure.

If parents want children to live together peacefully they need to help children achieve harmony. Imagine for a moment, that each child is a different musical instrument.

One child is the drum, the other is the violin, another may be the trumpet. Just as there is no orchestra made up solely of drums so, too, we can't have a family where everyone is identical.

Each child needs to be perceived as a unique individual, voicing his or her own particular sound, carrying out his or her own exceptional mission. Our goal is to help our children recognize their significant potential by fulfilling their particular calling.

Children who are able to blend their singular voices together achieve magnificent harmony.

Give Each Child an Opportunity to Shine

The child who enthralls the family with her vivid imagination, the child who brings beautiful music into his home, the child who has a natural way of caring for siblings, the child who brings laughter with his joyous spirit, each of these children should feel vital to the makeup of his or her family.

A sense of achievement is determined by how well one fulfills his or her lifework. Children who perform individual roles with enthusiasm and receive familial recognition feel successful.

Kids should know that every child in the family is appreciated for his or her specific offering. Siblings who feel valued grow up confident and are secure in their position and fight less.

No parent wants to raise children with the tensions that sibling rivalry brings into their children's relationships. Thinking that they are taking preventive measures, parents become vigilant when tending to their children's physical needs. They try to assure equality, but the focus is often misplaced. Somehow, the individual emotional requirements of each child become neglected as material needs are met.

There are times when rivalry grows as parents connect with one particular child at the expense of the others. They even speak in constant glowing terms about this son or daughter, while failing to relate well to the other children.

> "Olivia is the good one. She never gives us a moment of trouble."
> "David's amazing, his teachers love him and his report cards are
>   always perfect."

Know that all children (and even adults) have a need to be acknowledged and feel loved. As difficult as it may be, your task as a parent is to
develop a strong relationship with all your children. When one child is
consistently recognized and seemingly favored, insecurity and resentment grows between siblings.

Help each of your children fulfill his potential. Give each child in the
family an opportunity to shine. Sons and daughters should feel valued
and cherished. Brothers and sisters then gain a sense of individual auton-
omy, security, and an understanding of "what makes me be me."

Self-Esteem Is the Key

Instead of encouraging children to constantly compare and measure, explore each child's unique self. (Now would be a good time to refer to
chapter 5 on self-esteem.)

Children who feel successful in their particular mission are content
with themselves. They are happy human beings. These self-sufficient
souls find no need to push others down because they never feel threatened by the prosperity and achievement of others.

Kids who feel content are not constantly looking at what they don't
have; rather, they are concentrating on what they do have. These are the
children who provide our world with sweet harmony.

Overcoming Jealousy

Help your children deal with and overcome emotions of jealousy. Teach
them that there is no one in this universe exactly like them. Just as we
each have our own unique set of fingerprints, so do we each have our
own particular mission. Children who feel inferior should be taught to
appreciate their individuality. We want our children to feel happy with
what they have, gratified with who they are.

Long ago, my mother taught me that being jealous is like desiring
someone else's attractive luggage. You lug it home excitedly, and once
opened, realize that there's nothing inside that could possibly fit. Besides,
it's not even your taste.

Parents shouldn't help children eye the lives of others. They also
should not encourage discontent by striving to equalize every situation.

Imagine for a moment a mother's excitement as she awaits her two
little girls' arrival home from school. It is the younger child's birthday
and Mom's really gone all-out. There on the kitchen table lies her little

girls' favorite American Girl doll. This doll has been the topic of conversation for months. The pages of the catalogue have been turned again and again. Fervent wishes have been expressed. Finally, Mom decides to purchase the doll along with some stylish accessories.

The two girls walk through the door together.

"Happy Birthday, Sarah!" exclaims Mom with a smile. "Come and open your beautiful present. It's been waiting for you all day."

Sarah and her older sister, Rachel, run into the kitchen excitedly. Sarah tears open her gift and jumps all over the room, shrieking in delight. Rachel bursts into tears.

"I can't believe it!" she screams. "I'm the one who chose this doll. She was my favorite first! How could you buy this doll for her? She's such a baby! I should be the one to get her first because I'm older."

Rachel then crumples on to the floor, melting into a terrible tantrum.

Mom feels awful. Here she was, excited all day, just trying to do her best. She thought that Sarah would be thrilled and Rachel would join in her excitement. Instead, Mom's miserable as she hears Rachel's cries. Crushed, she thinks that she lacks parenting skills and feels like a failure. She wonders whether she should just buy Rachel her own doll so that both girls will be happy. What should Mom do?

When children are younger it is easy to fall into the trap of thinking that buying the same toy will fix everything.

But that's not true. You are feeding your child's jealousy. Instead of buying more toys, provide your child with a great lesson for life.

Bend down and take your child's hands in yours. Look into her eyes and simply say, "I know this is hard. You feel disappointed. You wanted this doll first, but now it is your sister's turn. Your turn will come. I know that you can take a deep breath and learn to feel happy for your sister, as you would want her to feel happy for you. If you ask nicely, you may even get a turn to play with the doll."

Children also need to understand that different circumstances bring different needs. This isn't your suitcase . . . there's nothing inside that's suitable for you.

For example, your daughter, Chloe, outgrew her shoes. Your other daughter starts complaining. "Why does Chloe get to go shopping for shoes? It's not fair. I also want new shoes. You always get her all the good stuff."

You may sigh deeply and say, "Okay, we'll just get you something at the same shoe store, too."

Big mistake. You are helping one child eye the suitcase of another.

Help your children focus on their *needs* rather than their *wants*. "Chloe's shoes were worn-out. When you are ready for new shoes, I'll be happy to go shopping and buy a pair for you, also."

Here's one more example: Your children are sitting at the dinner table. You give your son, Michael, an additional serving as he finishes his first portion.

"Hey, why did Michael get more chicken nuggets? I also want more," your other child exclaims, as his plate overflows with food.

"Michael finished his dinner and asked for some more. When you are done, and if you still feel hungry, I'll be happy to give you more chicken nuggets," you answer.

Don't give in to tantrums or try to justify yourself as a fair parent. Reassure your children that you are always there for them and whenever they need something, you will do your best to help them. But do not indulge their begrudging eyes. They will find it difficult to overcome their jealous nature as their envy of others only grows. They will be unable to distinguish between "needs" and "wants." (Many adults have this problem and find themselves in heavy credit card debt as a result.)

My Sibling, My Self

Children also observe the way their parents relate to their own siblings. Many family gatherings are packed with tension-filled moments as siblings allow simmering jealousies to explode. Years of sibling rivalry reduce adults to immature, childlike behavior.

Parents who keep in close touch with their siblings teach their children to communicate with their brothers and sisters as they grow. Sharing contentedly in your brother's successfulness and reacting happily to your sister's joy helps your own children develop a "kind eye."

Many times children join their parents and visit aunts, uncles, and cousins. The entire ride home is spent listening to their parents' disparaging comments. They compare homes, spouses, kitchens, jobs . . . and anything else they can possibly think of. Siblings and spouses are sarcastically mocked. Children wonder why they must be kind to their siblings if parents hardly tolerate their own.

Parents who grumble about their lives as they eye their siblings' good fortune should not be surprised to hear their children mimic their jealous words.

I know a young child who said to his aunt, "Why does my mommy hate you so much?"

Taken aback, the aunt asked, "What do you mean?"

"Well," said the boy, "my mommy always says that you have nicer things than her and that she can't stand you. Doesn't that mean that she hates you?"

In Yiddish we call such a begrudging person a *nishtfarginer*—one who can't stand the good fortune of another. He or she sees the world through jealous eyes. If you don't want to raise a child who is a *nishtfarginer*, be sure to watch your eyes. Look kindly at your siblings and cultivate emotions of joy as you partake in their happy moments.

PRACTICAL PARENTING: BRINGING HOME BABY

There are times in our lives when we stand at a crossroads with our children. Actions taken at this time make deep impressions as we decide on the path best taken. Welcoming the birth of a new baby is such a moment.

Beth and Andrew were expecting their second child. Excited yet apprehensive, they were receiving a lot of "helpful advice" from friends and family. As their due date approached, they called to sort through all the confusion.

"This is what we don't understand," began Beth. "Over and over, everyone's telling us to brace ourselves. Samuel is three now, and he's a delightful child. Will he really turn into this monster everyone says he'll become?

"A lot of my friends see it as if a husband was bringing home another wife. How would you feel, they ask me, if your husband did such a thing to you? It seems that they've spoken to professionals who all give this scenario. . . . The jealous wife who feels betrayed. I'm told that the only way to get around the situation is to give loads of extra attention, take the older sibling out on his own quite often, and buy lots of gifts. What do you think?" Beth asked.

"First of all," I responded, "this whole idea that bringing home a baby is like a man bringing home another wife is ridiculous. Parents are supposed to have more children. Men are not supposed to have multiple wives. You should never feel guilty for bringing home your baby. On the contrary, this is a wonderful opportunity to teach your child how to love. Too many parents fear their children's reaction to the new sibling.

"Instead of helping our children expand their hearts we shower them with toys and expand their closets. We concoct the idea that every time the baby receives a gift, his sibling, too, must receive something. This becomes a lifetime pattern—you get, so I get. If someone even admires the baby we make sure to quickly compliment the older child. How could this baby not be seen as the competition?"

"I never thought of it like that," mused Beth. "This makes so much sense."

"The truth is that you and Andrew are at a really crucial juncture in your lives," I continued. "Samuel will take his cues from you. If you teach him to view his new sibling as a threat you will be planting seeds of mistrust and jealousy between your children. If you treat your children as competitors, they will perceive each other as rivals for life."

There was silence for a moment as Beth considered the arrival of her second child.

"So, what should we do?" asked Beth.

"I always like to find Torah solutions," I responded.

I proceeded to describe to Beth the creation of Adam, the first man. As G-d is about to create Adam, He turns to the angels and says, "Let us make man."

G-d certainly did not need help with creation. Our sages teach us that this is actually a lesson to contemplate as we live our lives. When you bring home your newest addition, or whenever you embark upon a new situation, include those in your life who may feel affected and misplaced. Involve them so that they don't feel excluded.

"Instead of separating Samuel and causing him to feel that the baby is his opponent, include him. Help him embrace his new sibling. Allow him to choose that day's stretchie, let him help you give a bath, even singing to the baby is a way to get Samuel to connect with his sibling. Remember that once he starts giving of himself, Samuel will invest his energy in his baby and come to feel genuine love." He will come to view this baby as his special sibling, not just belonging to his parents. This is what makes a family strong.

When we were small children my grandmother would have us color posters to welcome our newest addition home. We would help prepare the room, pile up diapers, and set a beautiful table for our parents. Then we would wait with bated breath for our baby to be carried through the door.

Who needed presents, the baby was our greatest gift!

Your attitude establishes the tone from day one. Don't set the stage for a lifetime of resentment between brothers and sisters.

Teach your child that this is his or her sibling forever. This baby is your child's as well, someone to care for and love. Don't expect anything less than love and good-heartedness between your children. This is your moment to teach your child the beauty of family.

As Children Grow

It is not enough to concentrate on preventing rivalry. Just as crucial is seeking out ways through which our children feel united. We want to build a solid, devoted family.

Children who perceive themselves as unloved or unaccepted will look elsewhere for a sense of belonging. Kids who enjoy spending time with siblings take pride in their family. Parents can help foster an environment of unity and love that will help children to form an everlasting bond together.

Create Family Time

You don't need to take an expensive vacation to create family time. All that is really required is commitment. Parents need to turn off their cell phones, reschedule appointments, and set aside time for family.

Children should see that you take "family time" seriously. Some parents design wonderful plans, have great intentions, yet somehow, the day goes by and they end up doing nothing. Or, they take the time to be together, but are continuously on their cells and BlackBerrys. Kids end up feeling disappointed and rejected.

Ask yourself, when was the last time that we had fun as a family? Do we laugh together, share jokes among us, and feel a sense of camaraderie growing?

Encourage kids to forge their relationships with outings to the park, family games, or even bike rides together. (Leaving these activities to your children and their nannies is not considered family time.) The point is, we hardly spend time together anymore so we've forgotten how to interact and develop love for one another.

Researchers have found that kids with families who have regular meals together tend to have higher self-esteem. They are also less likely to smoke, physically fight, drink, use illegal drugs, or experiment with immoral behavior.

Time spent together promotes a strong sense of family and belonging.

Give Children Tasks to Accomplish Together

By working together, brothers and sisters learn that they are all on the same team. That's what family is all about.

For example, have children set the table together, bake a cake, or collectively decorate a birthday card.

By cooperating and working jointly they will find creative solutions as they negotiate their differences. They will also share laughter, an important ingredient needed for family life to thrive.

Teach Children to Feel for Each Other

A student of mine sent me the following e-mail:

> Last week, I was traveling with our two sons. Our flight was delayed and the boys began to "horse around" with each other.
>
> My younger son fell and began to cry. His brother began to snicker and laugh out loud.
>
> After calming my son and wiping away his tears, I called his brother to the side.
>
> In the past, I would've screamed at him or just ignored his behavior. Now I realize how important it is to work on my children's character. I explained to my son that we don't laugh as others fall and certainly not at our brothers. It is never funny to watch someone get hurt. I told him that if his brother ever falls again it is his job to see to it that he is okay. I kissed both boys and we calmly went on our way.
>
> Thank you for allowing me to teach my children the art of living together as brothers. Our family life has been transformed in so many ways.

Character, Character, Character

I cannot stress it enough. Raising children with soul doesn't just happen. Parents are given the ultimate responsibility of developing their child's character.

I have watched genuinely nice kids grow into spoiled tyrants when character flaws were allowed to flourish. Parents who neglect to address their children's offensive behavior turn a blind eye to future character issues. Contentious attacks and aggressive combativeness between children signal trouble within.

Physical and emotional aggression promotes fighting and bitter rivalry between siblings. The situation often turns ugly as children inflict pain and cross the line of decency.

Just as you would never allow your children to engage in certain activities, malicious behavior should not be acceptable between siblings.

A mother at a parenting workshop I gave spoke with bitter emotion as she described dinnertime in her home. Her star athlete son, both good-looking and popular, couldn't handle even looking at his heavily overweight sister.

He expressed his deep distaste for his sibling by shouting at her, "You're a big fat pig! You're gross! I can't stand you!"

"What can I do?" his mother asked, raising her hands in despair. "He doesn't listen to me."

My heart aches for this family and all families like them. I honestly have no words to describe the immense sadness I feel when I hear such stories. We cannot allow our children to reach this point of enmity. Parents need to step in when it comes to character issues and teach children to behave with an ethical code of conduct, *derech eretz,* from the time their kids are young.

Besides inflicting pain on others, children who speak or act viciously cause incredible harm to their own souls. The hatred they spew forth leaves blistering wounds as animosity burns inside these children's hearts.

Cynics may claim that it's no big deal, this is how today's kids speak. I am telling you that our homes cannot endure if we do not value the souls within. This is one battle that parents cannot afford to lose. The future of your family is at stake.

Physical Fighting Is Never Allowed

The Torah describes an incident where Moses wanders out of Pharaoh's palace and finds two men fighting. "He said to the wicked one, 'Why would you strike your friend?'" (Exodus 2:13)

Our sages teach us that just the fact that one would pick up his hand to hit another allows the Torah to call him "wicked."

Here's a fact of life to teach your children: We do not hit, bite, strike, kick, push, or use any other means of force against one another.

It doesn't matter if the other child started first. It is inconsequential if your brother or sister called you a spoiled brat, imitated you, or made weird faces at you. We will deal with that behavior.

You, though, are never permitted to react with physical aggression. Never are you allowed to raise your hand against another. This is not the manner in which children created in the image of G-d behave. And that's the bottom line.

Children with soul must value the preciousness of life. We don't strike one another. We take the higher road knowing that there is G-dliness that lies within. Parents should always elevate children and never encourage behavior that brings them down. Physical fighting reduces man to act like an animal and not utilize the G-d-given gift of speech and understanding.

Many women tell me that their husbands have difficulty enforcing this rule. They are afraid that their sons will be perceived as weaklings or losers. The men think that not striking back trains children to let others walk all over them.

Let us be clear. By teaching our children not to respond physically we aren't allowing them to become doormats. We *are* guiding our children to seek out better solutions than punching someone in the nose. We want to communicate to our children that they can handle disagreements without lifting their hands in anger.

Physical fighting can never be the answer. Moses taught us that even the raising of one's hand is wrong. He understood the peril toward one's character development brought about by physical aggression. Once a child is allowed to strike another human being and believes this reaction to be acceptable, his soul is affected. This is clearly not behavior that encourages a child's spiritual nature to flourish.

Fighting does not allow children to explore and build their problem-solving skills based on their wisdom and ability to compromise.

Clearly, it is impossible to go through life without meeting up with those who are bothersome, annoying, or downright obnoxious. Let's say your child grows up thinking that it's okay to scuffle and hit when someone bothers you.

One day, his boss or coworker says something extremely insulting. What would your child do? Punch him out? And what about his teachers or the other kids in school? Spouses and future children?

No, we can never communicate to our children that raising our hands against another is a proper response. We want our children to act with dignity and honor. Hitting back brings our children to the same low-level behavior as the original aggressor. Remember, we are here to "raise" children and elevate them to greater heights.

Believe it or not, moments of conflict are the perfect opportunity to help direct your children toward the road best taken. We can actually use the difficult situation to better our kids' understanding of how relationships work.

Children who learn to negotiate through strength of character display self-reliance and inner qualities that speak way louder than raising hands and lashing out.

How can we teach our children good alternatives to fighting?

- Develop self-esteem so that mean comments and actions bounce off and aren't taken so seriously. Just because you call me a loser doesn't mean I am one and who cares anyway? We can then avoid "instant hot reactions."
- Children who raise their hands and fight receive automatic consequences. No matter what. (Remember the lesson of Moses.)
- Children who verbally instigate fighting should be spoken to privately, in a serious manner. Parents need to emphasize to children the impact of their painful words. We cannot allow meanness to become a habit and maliciousness a way of life. If this type of behavior continues, consequences and loss of privileges are in order.
- Give your children alternatives to fighting as you help them discover creative solutions. For example, humorous responses; ignoring someone's taunts; walking into another room; or simply telling a sibling that if you speak to me like this, I cannot play with you. These are all viable solutions.
- Two children caught physically fighting *both* receive consequences. Who began with the first blow doesn't matter.

Some parents tell me that they cannot seem to find a consequence for their child. That's impossible. Everyone has something that is important to them, we just need to think a little.

There are kids who love going out and spending time with friends, others enjoy their PlayStations, Nintendos, or computer games at home. These are just two examples of children's different natures and types of activities they enjoy. The point is, you need to know your child, and then your consequences will be more meaningful.

There are parents who mistakenly provide their children with every accessory imaginable. Thinking that all the other kids have them, these "must-haves" are easily taken for granted. Computers, cell phones, Nintendo Wiis, iPods, the latest toys, Broadway shows . . . remember that none of these items are a "right." They are "privileges" to be appreciated and earned.

A mother told me about her teenage daughter who was a source of tremendous aggravation and pain. She was exceptionally disrespectful, used incredibly foul language, and was nasty toward her siblings. The mom couldn't think of a meaningful consequence.

Describing her daughter's behavior, she spoke about the many times the teen stormed out of the house refusing to answer her cell phone.

"Who pays for her cell phone?" I asked.

"We do, of course" was the answer.

"Here's your consequence," I replied.

Privileges are earned and can be withdrawn if necessary. Children should know that bad behavior brings consequences.

Growing up with brothers and sisters is a blessing that should not be taken for granted.

Parents often express surprise to hear that they are reinforcing their children's bad behavior. How often do kids grab a toy, hit or push another child, only to receive a little slap themselves as they hear "Bad boy!" or "Bad girl!" Sometimes parents watch their kids fight and in frustration, they yell, "Cut it out! Do you guys want a slap?"

Children become recipients of the exact behavior their parents are trying to eliminate. Does this make any sense?

Recognize Positive Behavior

When children do get along, show them that you've noticed. All children crave attention, even adults appreciate a good word. Of course, positive attention is the ultimate, but to kids, negative attention is better than none. No one likes being ignored and feeling unappreciated.

When you observe your children cooperating, display your joy. It is important for children to believe that we appreciate their efforts at good behavior. Ultimately, our children wish to make us proud.

I once asked my youngest son, Eli, who was ten at the time, for his opinion as to the most serious consequence a child could receive.

"Well, Mommy," he replied, "it's when you're disappointed in me. What could be worse than that?"

Apologies and Forgiveness

Part of getting along is being able to find resolution. Children who can find the fortitude to sincerely apologize elevate themselves spiritually. Forgiveness, too, requires one to dig deep within the heart. Both words of apology and forgiveness restore peace within our families. Neither one is easy but when given they impact children's character for life.

Encouraging our children to apologize and to forgive helps kids learn about love and reconciliation. Brothers and sisters are taught to look each other in the eye and smile again, leaving hard feelings behind.

As our children build relationships we can give them tools to deal with future hurts and painful moments that they will encounter. Parents can help children unload the burdens of conflict that weigh many of us down.

Most people recognize that it takes a humble spirit to apologize. We seldom realize that granting forgiveness also requires a lack of pride. One is asked to look away from hurtful slights and extend a hand in friendship.

In Judaism, an individual who displays this strength of character is called a *mevater,* one who looks away from self-honor. This does not mean that apologizing or granting forgiveness makes you a doormat. Instead, you have risen above the conflict and found inner dignity which enables you to "make peace."

Shalom, peace, is related to the word *shalem,* complete. One who is able to communicate peace finds completion. Individuals who harbor resentments never experience true tranquility, for there are emotions of conflict churning within.

Children who are capable of offering reconciliation choose to live with courage. Parents who walk around sulking and carrying grudges discourage their children's generous spirit. We cannot expect more from our children than we ourselves are able to give.

The story of Joseph and his brothers is often used to point out conflict between brothers. On the contrary, Joseph and his brothers is a tale of forgiveness and brotherly love.

After being sold into slavery by his brothers, Joseph is finally freed from a prison dungeon and appointed viceroy of Egypt by Pharaoh himself.

Searching for food amid heavy famine, Joseph's brothers encounter him in Egypt. They fail to recognize the noble royal as their long-lost brother. Unbeknownst to them, Joseph tests his brothers familial commitment through different trials and tribulations. He observes their selfless love for one another as irrefutable proof of his brothers' changed attitude and regret for their past mistakes. Joseph sees the transformation and is ready to bring about reconciliation.

Finally, the moment of revelation arrives. Joseph cannot restrain himself any longer. He asks that everyone be removed from the room so that he remains alone with his unsuspecting brothers. He could not bear to humiliate them in front of his royal court.

Joseph cries out and begins weeping uncontrollably.

"I am Joseph. Is my father still alive?" he calls out.

The brothers are stunned. Not one dares to speak . . . they shrink away from Joseph in shame as they recall their deeds.

Joseph now reaches out to his brothers, lovingly.

"Come close to me," he whispers. "It's true, I am Joseph, your brother. You sold me as a slave, but please don't be afraid. This was to be my destiny. It was not you who sent me here, but G-d, so that I could help ensure survival amid this famine. Please hurry, and bring our elderly father to me. And don't be fearful, your children and grandchildren shall live close to me. I will always be here to help you. We are brothers."

Joseph then fell upon the neck of his youngest brother, Benjamin, and began to weep. He kissed all his brothers and wept upon them as well.

Joseph cried tears of sadness as he foresaw the pain of exile and destruction that their children would suffer. There was no bitterness; no acrimonious feelings of revenge. Only tears of forgiveness. Genuine purity of soul.

Think about it for a moment. Joseph had every reason to be enraged. No one could blame him if he acted with malice or sought out revenge. How many brothers and sisters today refuse to speak to one another over lesser, nonsensical slights? How many brothers and sisters could learn from the courage of Joseph?

After their beloved father, Jacob, passed away, the brothers returned to Joseph. They could not imagine that Joseph did not harbor deep anger against them, even after all these years. They were certain that once their father passed on, Joseph would attempt to punish them severely. The brothers flung themselves before him, asked for forgiveness, and said, "We are ready to be your slaves."

Joseph wept as his brothers spoke. "Please," he begged, "do not be afraid of me. I know that there was a Divine plan." Once and for all Joseph wanted his brothers to know that he harbored no hatred in his heart. He assured his brothers, "I will sustain you . . . I will take care of your children." He spoke from his heart and comforted them.

Joseph's story teaches us that true love among brothers is attained through apologies and forgiveness. Encourage your children's dialogue of resolution. Don't allow hatred to simmer inside the hearts of your family. Revenge and animosity have no place within the walls of our homes. Help your children grow together, not apart. Siblings are forever.

NINE

Priorities

As we near the conclusion of this book, I know that many parents may be feeling discouraged. At the end of parenting workshops I often receive heart-wrenching phone calls and e-mails that speak of deep regrets.

> *"If only I would've opened my eyes."*
> *"I wish I knew this ten years ago when I started my family."*
> *"Could've, would've, should've, what can I say?"*

A mother once sobbed on my shoulders. "I did it all wrong," she cried, "all wrong."

Please don't feel dejected. Know that it is never too late to build a bridge and reconnect with your child.

Allow me to share one of my father's favorite tales about Rabbi Yisroel Salanter, a great leader of the Jewish people who lived around 150 years ago:

> Late one evening, Rabbi Yisroel Salanter brought his shoes in for repair. The shoemaker was working by the final flickers of a candle that was beginning to burn out.
>
> "It's a pity," said Rabbi Yisroel. "You won't have time to complete the repair."
>
> "Don't worry, Rebbe," the shoemaker answered. "As long as the candle burns there is still time for repairs."

"What an incredible thought!" Rabbi Yisroel exclaimed.

Rocking back and forth he began to sing in the melody he used to study ethical works. "As long as the candle of the soul burns there is still time to mend our ways."

Don't despair. It is never too late. Tomorrow brings us a new day with new opportunities to parent with greater love and understanding.

So now, we are left with a burning question: Where does one begin?

It's true that I want to change. I know in my heart that I've made mistakes. I really do wish to start again. I want so much to make a difference in my child's life and touch his or her inner core; but at this point of my life is this even possible?

Realizing that I must take hold of this incredible gift called parenting, how do I translate my deep desire to raise a child with soul into a reality?

Begin with a fresh understanding of your priorities. Ask yourself about the purpose of your days, the meaning of your life. What moves you, what do you drop everything for, what is your legacy?

Your book remains to be written.

Honestly. Rethink it all and find the courage within to make a change.

Begin with time.

TIME

An educator shared the following incident with me:

A little boy of nine met his father at the door one evening, as he returned from work.

"Daddy, how much money do you make an hour?"

"What?"

"How much? How much do you make an hour?"

Mom and Dad caught each other's eyes unbelievingly.

"What kind of crazy question is that?"

"I just want to know, Daddy."

"I'm not even going to attempt a response. Don't ever think about asking me something like that. It's rude and none of your business."

"But, Dad—"

"I said no!"

The child persisted with his questions and was sent to his room.

Allowing some time to pass, Mom and Dad knocked on their son's door.

They found their child sobbing silently into his pillow, his little body heaving up and down with each cry. As his mother stroked his sweaty forehead, the boy's father sat beside him on the bed.

"Okay," began the dad, using a softer tone. "Do you want to tell us what this is all about?"

The child took a deep breath.

"Daddy, I never really get to talk to you or see you anymore . . . and I thought that if . . . maybe . . . you could tell me how much you get an hour . . ."

The boy pointed to his open piggy bank resting on the night table beside him, and started to sob again.

"I just thought I'd give you the same amount of money and maybe you'd find an hour of your time for me."

Mom and Dad looked at each other and then turned away in shame.

Priorities. We need to get in touch with what matters most, to ask ourselves what has lasting value in our lives.

9/11 brought us closer, but the moment came and went. For a while we decided to hug our children tighter, spend more time together as a family, and love one another more.

Mesmerized, we listened to intimate, heart-wrenching good-byes as loved ones bid their final farewells. No one called the office to check on a deal just one last time. No one expressed regret for not having played one more game of tennis or golf. Final conversations never revealed people's differences, rehashed all over again.

It was, tragically, good-bye, I love you so very much, I wish I could watch our children grow; I'm sorry I can't spend the rest of my life with you; forgive me if I've ever hurt you.

Why must we wait for such awful moments to get it straight? When will it finally dawn upon us that it is our children and families that count in life?

We are living in an incredibly materialistic society. Our obsession with having it all has removed us from devoting ourselves to the ones who need us most—our families. We check off our to-do list and then check out, outsourcing our responsibilities to convenient stand-ins.

Families today have more luxuries than any past generation, yet with all our new-and-improved living, we spend less time together. We excitedly discover the latest phones and gadgets that help keep us in greater touch, but somehow, we find ourselves farther apart. Kids run away into cyberspace as they sit in their rooms chatting with strangers while their parents remain completely clueless.

It is only when our children have grown that we realize how much time we've wasted and the awful distance that has come between us. Regret is a most painful emotion and I have witnessed its aching aftereffects, time and time again.

The Maggid of Kelm was a rabbi known for his fiery orations. "What would happen," he once asked his congregation, "if those who were buried in the Kelm cemetery could somehow return to our world for half an hour? What do you think they would do?"

Imagine. Some souls would seek out loved ones for just one more conversation, one more embrace. Others would try to accomplish an additional good deed so that they may leave a final imprint in this world. They would rush around with a burning fervor as the clocks kept ticking on.

The Maggid concluded with some final questions for people to contemplate. "And if we have more than half an hour, is that so terrible? Must we then stop appreciating our moments? And let me ask you . . . who here is certain that he even has more than half an hour?"

What a powerful thought to keep in mind as we raise our precious children!

When I was sitting *shiva* for my father, a friend of mine came to pay her respects. She sat, enraptured, listening to the many young grandchildren express their sadness and sense of loss.

> *"Who will now take us across the street to feed the ducks at the lake?"*
> *"Who will color with us the way Abba Zaydah did and help make our sun shine bright yellow again?"*
> *"Who will carry all the babies and sing them to sleep?"*
> *"Who could ever study Torah with us like our Abba Zaydah did?"*
> *"How will we go to bed without hearing our Zaydah's beautiful Shema?"*

My friend brought her chair close to mine and whispered to me. "You know," she said, "I spend so much time doing things for my kids. I take them to gymnastics, ballet, sports, and swim classes, but I realized something while sitting here and taking this all in. I never, really, spend time with my kids. I drop them off, pick them up, try to keep it all together, but their memories will never sound like this. And my husband is either away at the office or so exhausted that he barely sees our children. You are all so lucky to have been blessed with such parents."

The time has come for us to rededicate ourselves to our families. Let's stop running and start enjoying. Let's laugh together, share an ice-cream cone, or walk in the rain. More than any possession that we could ever buy our kids are the invaluable memories we create that remain with them forever.

I was in a shop and overheard a mother say to her children: "Listen, now it's my time. I bought all the stuff you guys wanted, that's it, I'm going out with Daddy. I've had it. You do your thing and I'll do mine. We're going home and I'll see you all later."

What does that mean? Of course there are times when parents need to unwind, but how can we equate buying "all the stuff you guys wanted" with providing love? There are moments when we are obligated to put our desires on hold as we take on our role as loving fathers and mothers. We have forgotten how to give of ourselves as we've become obsessed with the pursuit of pleasure.

Fathers, especially, need to wake up and recognize that their role is not limited to providing financial security.

Torah speaks to us about a father's role: "Ask your father and he shall tell you, your elders and they shall relate to you." Children are told to tap into their father's wisdom so that they may gain direction and strength of character for life.

A true father is a lasting role model who stands for way more than his annual income. He should be valued for his insights, his wisdom, and his ethical way of life. Moving beyond the "guy who pays the AmEx bill," a father should be cherished as he contributes to the emotional and spiritual security of the family.

After picking up some children from school while driving carpool, an eleven-year-old boy asked me to turn on the radio.

"Can you turn to the station that has 'all the news all the time'?" he asked. "I need to hear how the stock market did. If it went down my father will be in a bad mood and I'd better be prepared before I get home."

How terribly sad. This child will only find joy at home when his dad has had a good day on the market. The feeling this child has of his father's love is conditional upon the rise and fall of some stocks.

Our children should never think that our love for them is contingent upon external forces. Conditional parenting is not an option. Our sages teach us that any love that is not dependent on anything is a love that will never cease. It is everlasting.

In other words, love that is unconditional. Children should never feel as if they are playing a game of "hot and cold" with their parents. Is it safe to approach today or should I back away?

We must put an end to such pathetic parenting and rediscover the beauty of being genuine fathers and mothers to our children.

MARRIAGE

As we strengthen our commitment to our children we must also recommit to each other as husbands and wives. Too many parents reside in their own individual shells, living side by side, but occupying completely different worlds.

When Jacob descended into Egypt with his children, we are told that "each man and his house came." Each son brought with him his house, his *bayis,* or his *shalom bayis.*

Jacob understood that *shalom bayis* was a top priority to teach his children. If his sons and their families were to survive the heartbreaking difficulties that awaited them in Egypt, it would be only through strong, intact homes.

Mothers and fathers who parent in unity, husbands and wives who live together as one, create the foundations upon which future generations stand. (Throughout this book I have stressed the connection between a peaceful home and children's happiness, self-esteem, and our ability to communicate love and respect.)

We cannot expect families to survive life's crises unmarred if our homes are filled with the ugliness of marital strife. The style of the conflict really doesn't matter—loud arguments or silent treatments both speak of deafening pain.

A teacher at a workshop I gave shared a discussion that she had with a kindergartener she taught. The five-year-old had spoken and acted so meanly that he had brought a classmate to tears. "When you speak and behave like that," she told him, "you make the other person feel so sad, it's as if you've broken his heart."

The next day, the boy's mother dropped off her son. She smiled to the teacher and said, "Thank you." "For what?" asked the teacher, surprised.

"Well, yesterday my husband was really angry at me. He was shouting and screaming. My son came over and said, 'Daddy, don't you know that you're breaking Mommy's heart?'"

We should not anticipate our kids appreciating the blessing of family if we take each other for granted. We cannot hope that our children be committed to family life if we ourselves disconnect.

SPIRITUALITY

Priorities also mean that we value our spiritual side. Along with bestowing faith comes the gift of giving hope and trust in tomorrow. Take a grand leap and be confident as you speak to your children about G-d.

Teaching G-dliness doesn't mean that we must have all the answers or that if we don't live life perfectly, we are hypocrites. It does mean that we believe with all our hearts that life is a blessing from G-d and that it is up to us to make each day count.

Prayer is the missing link that provides an avenue to express our faith. Sharing with our children the ability to pray teaches them that one can connect with G-d anytime, anywhere.

A prominent surgeon told me that when he suffered a massive heart attack the only things his adult children were able to do in the hospital's waiting room was either pace anxiously or attempt *The New York Times* crossword puzzle. Neither brought solace.

It was only after he survived his crisis that his kids confided their feelings of void to him.

"Why didn't you ever teach us how to pray?" they asked. "We felt so helpless. . . . We had no idea where to begin."

We are here to form a path for our children. Begin to create footsteps for the next generation so that they can find their way despite the turmoil that may come to overwhelm them. Faith is our legacy, prayer our lifeline. It remains for each of us, as parents, to make a clear decision: Will I pass the torch on to the next generation?

"The beginning of all wisdom is fear of G-d." Each day we express this thought in our morning prayers. Understand this to mean a constant awareness of G-d. Providing children with cultural experiences, the best education, and proper manners just won't cut it. My parents and grandparents witnessed a most incredibly cultured people use their vast knowledge for the most unspeakable evil purposes. Even today, there are educated people who commit barbaric acts of terrorism or turn to a life of crime as we shake our heads in disbelief.

High intelligence and Ivy League schooling will not guarantee a moral life. *True* awareness of G-d brings with it a conscious decision to better our world as we fulfill our life's mission. (I emphasize *true*, because some people claim to live a life of faith yet act in ways that contradict the spiritual and moral beliefs that they speak of.)

Cognizant of our limited time here, we cherish each precious moment as an opportunity to live life to its spiritual zenith. It is awareness of G-d that propels our children to become bright starry lights in a universe gone dark.

DIRECTION

Finally, it is important that we maintain a clear direction for ourselves as parents. Where are we going? What are we trying to teach our children? How do we go about becoming our children's "life guide"? How do we suppose our children will come to live a life of values? What do we stand for? What do our children perceive when they consider our lives?

When Joseph was sold as a slave he found himself in the home of Potiphar, an Egyptian nobleman. Joseph was just a youth of seventeen, known for his astonishingly good looks.

The wife of Potiphar desired Joseph yet Joseph would not bend. One day, while Potiphar the slave master was out of the house, Joseph found himself alone with Potiphar's wife.

She wouldn't relent and tried to entice him in every way possible. There Joseph was, incredibly far away from his home and family, feeling alone and seemingly betrayed by his brothers.

As Joseph's resistance is about to break, an image enters his mind. It is *deyukno shel aviv,* the beautiful image of his father, Jacob. He runs from Potiphar's wife as his father's face remains before his eyes and reminds him of his destiny.

Deyukno shel aviv, the image of his father. Think of it as a "spiritual pop-up" that appears to your children throughout various stages of their lives, helping them discern right from wrong.

Every parent must ask themselves these questions: What is "my image" that shall remain in my children's minds? Which words of mine will resonate? Will my values accompany my children as they journey through life? And finally, what will my children remember about me?

Now you've touched upon your own *deyukno shel aviv,* your image that will remain deep within your child's heart and soul. At the end of the day, this is your legacy.

Meaningful priorities that you've lived provide your children with a "spiritual will," a moral code to live by. Priorities ring true when children are able to say, "My father, my mother, no matter how difficult the moment, they kept their faith and values intact. They showed me how to live a purposeful life. They taught me the definition of compassion and genuine happiness. They allowed me to be me yet provided a path that, one day, I hope to bequeath to my own children. I can close my eyes and envision my father's face, hear my mother's voice, and understand that I am loved forever. I see their image and know that I will always try to do what's right."

We can help our children discover a life filled with blessing if we ourselves are dedicated to living meaningful days. And once our children's eyes are opened to the sweet joy that family brings they will not be afraid to commit as they strive to build their own small sanctuary, in the future.

Priorities are: "Know three things and you will not falter in life— from where you've come, where you are going, and before Whom you will stand to provide an accounting of your life" (Ethics 3:1).

Remember, Always, from Where You've Come

Each of us has a story to tell. Each one of us comes into this world bearing unique Divine gifts that are magical. This is the blessing of the soul. Infuse your children's lives with your own personal blessing. Connect with your roots and hold on to the faith of past generations. Remember always the legacy of from whence you've come.

Know Where You Are Going

We can never lose sight of our ultimate goal. Parenting with purpose propels us toward a loftier direction. Some parents painfully look back and realize that for years they've wandered aimlessly, stood for nothing of lasting value, and spent their time chasing trivial pursuits. Take stock and chart your family's course. Live life with an internal compass and never lose direction. Redefine yourself. Remember that you are charged with a sacred mission, the raising of children with soul.

Know Before Whom You Stand to Give an Accounting

As parents, we must make each day count. Time passes quickly and we are caught by surprise as our first grader "suddenly" enters junior high.

We can easily forget that time spent with our kids is limited. Children need to witness parents living a life of meaning. We are not here forever, strong and invulnerable as we may feel. One day we will be required to answer for our lives. I, myself, came across this truth firsthand.

As the final weeks of my father's stay on this earth were coming to an apparent end, his days became more taxing and difficult. One morning, as I arrived to see him, the nurses instructed me to stand behind a screen as they dealt with my father's wounds.

I settled in and heard an agonizing sound.

"What's this?" I asked myself. I had never heard this sound before. I realized, with a jolt, that my father was crying. The sound that drew my breath away were my father's intense sobs.

The nurses had reassured me that this procedure would be painless. I couldn't comprehend my father's cries.

"Rabbi, we haven't even begun. Besides, this won't hurt. Why are you crying?"

Can you ever imagine what it was like, hearing my father's anguished cries? I sat behind the screen, frozen, not knowing what to do.

"I'm not crying because of the pain," I heard my father respond.

"So what is it, Rabbi? What can we do for you?"

"Oh," my father sobbed aloud. "I know that my time on this earth is coming to an end. Perhaps it is a week, or maybe even a day, who knows? And that is why I am crying. Soon, I will be standing before G-d, Himself, and I will have to answer for my life. And I am so scared . . ." My father's words cut deep into me, like a knife.

"But you are the kindest, gentlest human being!" the nurse exclaimed. "You are a rabbi, you've done so much good in this world, even here in the hospital you've touched so many people. Why are you afraid?"

My father did not respond. I will never forget the sound of his cries. At that moment I thought to myself: If my father, who lived a complete life of absolute kindness and faith never allowed himself a moment of arrogance as he accounted for his time in this world, what about me? How could I ever be satisfied without seeking to make my tomorrows better than today?

Isn't this a most awesome mission for us parents to internalize within our hearts? Let us commit to making our tomorrows better than today. Each morning we are given a new opportunity to love, to guide, and to inspire. Let us recognize our time with our children as most precious.

Make each day, each moment count. Find time for your family. Create memories that will endure. Live with truth, kindness, and faith. Fill your home with love and laughter. Bless your children. Parent with an understanding heart and embrace these incredible gifts from Above. Your *deyukno shel aviv* shall speak to your children and your children's children long beyond your time in this world.

Within each child lies a dormant spark, silently waiting to be ignited. Reach out and take your child's hand in yours. Illuminate a path, kindle a light. Now, watch a miracle unfold before your very eyes.

EPILOGUE

I knew. We all knew. The final week with my father was coming to a close. Every single one of us, every child and grandchild, stood together awaiting one last final blessing.

My mother was beside him, whispering the name of each child as she or he entered. She helped place his hands atop every child's head as my father, somehow, drew upon a strength I didn't know he possessed anymore.

The door opened slowly.

Mama!

My grandmother, my sweet beautiful Mama, walked slowly into the room. She leaned heavily on her cane, weary from the excruciating pain that lay before her eyes. Though Mama's tiny figure was now stooped over, her mere presence brought me quiet comfort and strength. Our Mama had endured.

I searched Mama's eyes as she surveyed the scene before her. She had survived the Holocaust, courageously began life again in a new world, and now watched as her children huddled together and tried to grasp on to life's last precious moments.

"How can this be?" Mama whispered unbelievingly. "How can your abba be going back to *shamayaim*, to heaven, and I am still here?"

My mother leaned forward so that my father might hear. "Mama is next to you," she said softly.

My father mouthed his words with difficulty. "Mama . . . always so good to me . . . thank you, Mama. . . ."

Mama covered her eyes and held her head in her hands. "*Mein kind,* you are my son for always. I always loved you."

Thinking I could offer solace, I took Mama's frail fingers into mine. Yet, it was I who felt consoled. Our silence spoke more than any words.

Carrying my one-year-old I watched with blinding tears as my father bestowed his final blessings. I was at a loss and did not want to say good-bye. Each faint word brought extreme emotion to us all. Though my father's eyes were tightly shut he was aware that we stood surrounding him. His silent tears gently fell with each labored breath.

These were our last moments together. My father parted with words of sanctity and love. I have come to understand that at the end, this is a parent's final legacy . . . a message of eternal blessing.

I remain touched by the perpetual love and Torah wisdom of my parents and grandparents. It is a love that is everlasting. A wisdom that has survived the centuries.

Time has passed. Sadly, my grandmother, Mama, left us shortly after my beloved father. The wounds of loss, though they remain, have been soothed as I behold the promise of tomorrow.

One afternoon, as I was putting the finishing touches on this manuscript, my phone rang.

My son-in-law Shlomo was on the line. His voice could hardly contain his excitement.

"Mommy, it's a girl! *Baruch Hashem,* Shaindy had a beautiful little girl."

For a moment, I could not speak. A profound sense of joy and gratitude overwhelmed me. I soon found myself on a plane to Jerusalem, longing for that delicious moment of cradling my very first grandchild.

Finally, after what seemed like an eternity, I knocked on Shaindy's apartment door.

"Mommy!" Shaindy smiled as we embraced. She held out the soft bundle nestled in her arms. "Here is our little Miriam."

Miriam. The baby had been named for Mama. I caressed this newest soul and gently traced her delicate features. Her tiny fingers latched on to mine. I was overcome with love.

The next morning brought dawn's golden hues streaming into the room. I picked up baby Miriam and kissed her silken head as I began to sing.

Once again, like so many years ago, I swaddled my precious gift from Above with the words of Modeh Ani.

An image flashed in my mind: Mama sitting at my kitchen table, as I gently placed my newborn, Shaindy, into her hands. I recalled Mama gazing intently at the baby as she hummed the words of an old Yiddish lullaby.

Mama's eyes glistened. "You know," she said, "there were moments in my life when I didn't think our family would ever see the sun shine again. Who would have believed that one day I'd be holding a great-grandchild in my arms?"

Now, years later, it was my turn to gaze intently. "Look, Mama," I whispered. "Here I am rocking my sweet grandchild to sleep in Jerusalem. Her name is Miriam. She is your namesake."

The story of *tikkun olam* begins again. The past and future merge as one. Tomorrow brings us hope as we embrace the dreams of yesterday.

My dear friends, this book has been my labor of love as I have opened up my heart to all of you. I have done so with the greatest of awe for all the precious families who try so hard to build a life together. I have shared with you the eternal truths of our Torah, and the infinite wisdom of our sages. I've opened the window to my soul with treasured memories of my past.

My story is the story of our people, of parents and children, and their love that endures. Raise your children with love, my friends. Speak to each child's soul. And may you bring children into this world who will be an everlasting source of joy and blessing.

MEDITATIONS *and* PRAYERS

"What is service of the heart?" our sages ask.

"It is prayer," they explain.

Through prayer, we come before G-d with both heart and soul. We pray for our children, health, sustenance, spiritual growth, and the wisdom and strength to endure life's challenges. We thank G-d for all the blessings in our lives. As we move closer to G-d, we become transformed through the service of our hearts.

Our sages teach us that even when the gates of ordinary prayer are sealed, the gates of tears are always open.

In this section you will find excerpts from various prayers. For the complete prayer, please refer to a *siddur,* a Jewish prayer book.

These prayers are holy. Please treat them with proper respect.

Upon waking in the morning, our first words express our gratitude for life:
Modeh Ani, I am gratefully thankful before You, G-d, for having returned my soul within me with great compassion.

A daily prayer and meditation:
May it be Your will, Hashem, my G-d, and the G-d of my forefathers, that You save me each day from audacity and arrogance, from a bad individual, a bad inclination, from a bad friend, from a bad neighbor, a bad mishap, from gossip and negative speech, dishonesty, and the

hatred of others, unnatural death, from harmful illnesses, and from bad happenings in my life. . . .

Before going to sleep at night, we recite the bedtime Shema:

Master of the universe, I hereby forgive anyone who angered or troubled me or who sinned against me—whether it was against my body, my property, my honor, or anything that belongs to me; whether he did so by accident, with desire to hurt me, carelessly, or purposely; whether through speech, action, or ideas or thoughts. . . . May no person receive a punishment because of me. . . .

May it be Your will, my G-d, and the G-d of my forefathers, that You lay me down to sleep in peace and raise me up for life that is good and for peace . . . accustom me to fulfill mitzvahs . . . Please, do not bring me to difficulties, to shame in life, and to bad illnesses. May bad dreams and bad thoughts not impede me. May my children be complete before You. . . .

Then, the Shema prayer is recited both morning and evening:

Hear, O Israel, Hashem is our G-d, Hashem is One.

Jacob's blessing before he left this world:

Hamalach Hagoel. May the angel who redeems me from all danger bless the children, and let them carry my name and the names of my forefathers Abraham and Isaac, and may they flourish and become many throughout the land.

The blessings of the angels:

Beshem Hashem. In the name of Hashem, the G-d of Israel: May Michael be at my right, Gavriel at my left, Uriel before me, and Rephael behind me; and above me the Presence of G-d.

The blessing of the children on Friday evening:

For a boy: May G-d grant that you be like Ephraim and Menashe.
For a girl: May G-d grant that you be like Sarah, Rebecca, Rachel, and Leah
Then continue for all: May G-d bless you and watch over you. May G-d illuminate His countenance for you and be gracious to you. May G-d turn His countenance to you and establish peace for you.

ACKNOWLEDGMENTS

I must express my gratitude to G-d, for granting me the love of family, the great wisdom of my parents and grandparents, and the truth of the Torah. Writing this book has been my blessing from Above.

I thank my mother, Rebbetzin Esther Jungreis, my *ema*. You have given me both life and soul. You have believed in me, inspired me, and taught me how to live. Through great sacrifice and many tears, you have forged a path for us, your children, to live by. You have kept the memory of our *zaydahs* and *bubbas* alive so that we forever remember the legacy of our roots. Though you've lived through much darkness, you have never lost your light. And it is this light that will always guide us. Your life is your greatest legacy.

Thank you, Mendy, my husband, my best friend. I know that as I was writing this book there were times when you were exhausted and tired, but still you insisted on hearing my words. You listened. You encouraged me and gave me your blessing.

You have helped me travel the distance as I teach and reach out to others. I thank G-d for bringing you across the world, into my life. Even through the most challenging of times, your commitment and faith have never wavered. Your love of life and the ability to make us smile have taught our children the meaning of genuine joy. I pray that we see continued *nachas* and joy from our *mishpachah,* our beloved family.

Thank you, my precious children. G-d has privileged me to raise children who are my everything. You have been my inspiration throughout the years. You have illuminated my life with your spirit, and I thank G-d for each one of you. You have taught me to see the world through the eyes of children; you have taught me about kindness, you have brought me laughter and love. I pray that G-d watch over you, protect you, and fill your homes with blessing.

And now I'd like to express appreciation to those who made this book a reality.

My gratitude must be expressed to Jennifer Weis and Hilary Rubin Teeman, my editors at St. Martin's Press. Your enthusiasm for this project has been exhilarating. Your words of encouragement, your insights, and your attention to details are all sincerely appreciated. Thank you for sharing my vision.

Rabbi Yaakov Reisman, our esteemed Rav, has always been a source of Torah guidance and *hashkafas hachaim* to our family. Thank you for answering my questions and calls, for looking over the Meditations and Prayers section, and for your clear insights and *daas Torah*. May Hashem bless you and your family with *arichus yamim veshanim* and good health.

Rabbi Moshe Kolodny took the time out of his busy schedule and reviewed the factual text of this manuscript. Thank you for your great wisdom and knowledge. And thank you, too, to my brother-in-law Rabbi Shlomo Gertzulin, for so graciously helping me have this done.

Fern Sidman, a woman whose patience knows no bounds. Thank you for tirelessly typing and retyping my handwritten words. No matter how often I'd fax you my corrections, no matter how late the hour, you always found the time and gave of yourself with a smile.

I have been blessed with a family of friends and friends who are family. My brothers, my sister, and their spouses are always here for me. I know how fortunate I am to have you all in my life. Our bond is forever.

The young couples whom I teach have become a special part of my life. We are the Hineni family. We've studied together for years. We've watched our children grow. We have shared moments of joy and moments of tears. I stand in awe, seeing how you've embraced the Torah's teachings, wanting to make a difference in your family's lives.

I once told you in class that children need to see your passions and loves so that they may learn what to be passionate about in life. "Don't just talk about character and Torah values," I said. "Live them, and live them with a passion."

Well, you have seized the moment. You have challenged yourselves to become better parents, better husbands and wives, better human beings. You continuously move me.

I thank G-d for granting me the honor of being your Torah teacher.